Lecture Notes in Business Information Processing   365

More information about this series at http://www.springer.com/series/7911

Małgorzata Pańkowska · Kurt Sandkuhl (Eds.)

Perspectives in Business Informatics Research

18th International Conference, BIR 2019
Katowice, Poland, September 23–25, 2019
Proceedings

 Springer

Editors
Małgorzata Pańkowska (iD)
University of Economics in Katowice
Katowice, Poland

Kurt Sandkuhl (iD)
University of Rostock
Rostock, Germany

ISSN 1865-1348   ISSN 1865-1356 (electronic)
Lecture Notes in Business Information Processing
ISBN 978-3-030-31142-1   ISBN 978-3-030-31143-8   (eBook)
https://doi.org/10.1007/978-3-030-31143-8

This Springer imprint is published by the registered company Springer Nature Switzerland AG
The registered company address is: Gewerbestrasse 11, 6330 Cham, Switzerland

Preface

The academic discipline of business informatics addresses the combination and integration of concepts, approaches, and technologies from computer science, information systems, economics, and business administration with a focus on applications in enterprises, public authorities, and other organizations. Business informatics is closely related to the area of business information systems.

The conference series on Business Informatics Research (BIR) was established in the year 2000 as the result of a collaboration of several Swedish and German universities. The goal was to create a forum for the discussion of latest research results, new research directions, and PhD topics in the business informatics community. The conference has expanded to many other countries, and usually includes workshops as well as a doctoral consortium accompanying the main conference track. The BIR conference series has a Steering Committee, to which representatives from the organizations hosting a BIR conference are invited. The 18th BIR conference was located in Katowice, Poland, during September 23–25, 2019, at the Advanced Information Technology Center of the University of Economics in Katowice.

The theme of the conference was "Responsibilities of Digitalization – Responsible designing and shaping of future technology for digital preservation, global data storage, and cost-effective management." Digitalization rapidly changes wireless, bio, and info-tech ecosystems, and enterprises must find new ways to innovate for business advantage and sustainability. Through digital transformation, the implementation of new technologies, like cloud, mobile, big data, and social networks increases intelligence and automation enterprises can capitalize on new business and optimization opportunities. Business leaders and Information Communication Technology (ICT) system developers need democratic innovation culture as well as new approaches to system design and exploitation. BIR 2019 is focused on the development of ICT systems to ensure system responsiveness, user friendliness, project agility, information availability and security, business continuity, system functionality, scalability, and efficiency. However, the ICT people are expected to develop technologies, systems, and methods while taking into account the consequences of their designs and implementations. Responsible designing of the future requires a change of ethics and learning methods to include different points of view (i.e., society, organization, individual, and information systems).

This year, the main conference track attracted 61 submissions from 22 countries. Each paper was reviewed by at least three members of the Program Committee. As a result, 17 high-quality papers were selected for publication in this volume and for presentation at the conference. They cover different aspects of the conference's main topic as well as of business informatics research in general.

The conference program also included three keynotes: "Behavioral Enterprise Architecture (management) – designing interventions based on behavioral insights" by Prof. Robert Winter from the University of St. Gallen (Switzerland); "Smart

Recommendation Systems – managerial viewpoints" by Prof. Jerzy Korczak from the International University of Logistics and Transport, Wrocław (Poland); and "In a World of Biased Search Engines" by Prof. Dirk Lewandowski from the Hamburg University of Applied Sciences (Germany).

We would like to thank everyone who contributed to the BIR 2019 conference. We thank the authors for contributing and presenting their research, we appreciate the invaluable contribution of the members of the Program Committee and the external reviewers, we thank the keynote speakers for their inspiring talks, and we thank all members of the local organization team from Katowice.

August 2019
Małgorzata Pańkowska
Kurt Sandkuhl

Organization

Program Co-chairs

Małgorzata Pańkowska   University of Economics in Katowice, Poland
Kurt Sandkuhl   University of Rostock, Germany

Program Committee

Gundars Alksnis	Riga Technical University, Latvia
Said Assar	Institut Mines-Telecom, France
Eduard Babkin	National Research University Higher School of Economics, Russia
Per Backlund	University of Skövde, Sweden
Robert Andrei Buchmann	Babeş-Bolyai University of Cluj Napoca, Romania
Witold Chmielarz	University of Warsaw, Poland
Sybren De Kinderen	University of Luxembourg, Luxembourg
Doina Danaiata	West University of Timisoara, Romania
Hans-Georg Fill	University of Fribourg, Switzerland
Peter Forbrig	University of Rostock, Germany
Jānis Grabis	Riga Technical University, Latvia
Björn Johansson	Lund University, Sweden
Christian Damsgaard Jensen	Technical University of Denmark, Denmark
Dimitris Karagiannis	University of Vienna, Austria
Marite Kirikova	Riga Technical University, Latvia
Tomas Krilavicius	Vytautas Magnus University, Lithuania
Birger Lantow	University of Rostock, Germany
Ginta Majore Vidzeme	University of Applied Sciences, Latvia
Raimundas Matulevicius	University of Tartu, Estonia
Laila Niedrite	University of Latvia, Latvia
Jacob Nørbjerg	Copenhagen Business School, Denmark
Cyril Onwubiko	Research Series, UK
Małgorzata Pańkowska	University of Economics in Katowice, Poland
Jens Myrup Pedersen	Aalborg University, Denmark
Geert Poels	Ghent University, Belgium
Vaclav Repa	University of Economics in Prague, Czech Republic
Kurt Sandkuhl	University of Rostock, Germany
Rainer Schmidt	Munich University of Applied Sciences, Germany
Ulf Seigerroth	Jönköping University, Sweden
Manuel Serrano	University of Castilla-La Mancha, Spain
Monique Snoeck	Katholieke Universiteit Leuven, Belgium
Janis Stirna	Stockholm University, Sweden
Frantisek Sudzina	Aalborg University, Denmark

Gianluigi Viscusi	EPFL-CDM-CSI, Switzerland
Anna Wingkvist	Linnaeus University, Sweden
Stanislaw Wrycza	University of Gdansk, Poland
Jelena Zdravkovic	Stockholm University, Sweden
Alfred Zimmermann	Reutlingen University, Germany

BIR Series Steering Committee

Marite Kirikova	Riga Technical University, Latvia
Kurt Sandkuhl	University of Rostock, Germany
Eduard Babkin	National Research University Higher School of Economics, Russia
Rimantas Butleris	Kaunas University of Technology, Lithuania
Sven Carlsson	Lund University, Sweden
Peter Forbrig	University of Rostock, Germany
Björn Johansson	Lund University, Sweden
Andrzej Kobyliński	Warsaw School of Economics, Poland
Raimundas Matulevicius	University of Tartu, Estonia
Lina Nemuraite	Kaunas Technical University, Lithuania
Jyrki Nummenmaa	University of Tampere, Finland
Vaclav Repa	University of Economics in Prague, Czech Republic
Benkt Wangler	University of Skovde, Sweden
Stanisław Wrycza	University of Gdansk, Poland

Additional Reviewers

Natalia Aseeva	National Research University Higher School of Economics, Russia
Dominik Bork	University of Vienna, Austria
Bartłomiej Gawin	University of Gdansk, Poland
Michal Kuciapski	University of Gdansk, Poland
Vimal Kunnummel	University of Vienna, Austria
Bartosz Marcinkowski	University of Gdansk, Poland
Christian Muck	University of Vienna, Austria
Pavel Malyzhenkov	National Research University Higher School of Economics, Russia
Anthony Simonofski	Katholieke Universiteit Leuven, Belgium
Boris Ulitin,	National Research University Higher School of Economics, Russia
Wiesław Wolny	University of Economics in Katowice, Poland

Contents

How Smart Cities Explore New Technologies

Christian Bremser[1]([⊠]), Gunther Piller[1], and Franz Rothlauf[2]

[1] University of Applied Sciences Mainz,
Lucy-Hillebrand-Str. 2, 55128 Mainz, Germany
`christian.bremser@hs-mainz.de`
[2] Johannes Gutenberg-Universität Mainz,
Jakob-Welder-Weg 9, 55128 Mainz, Germany

Abstract. The concept of smart city is considered as a new paradigm of urban development. Information and communication technologies are expected to transform cities into smart cities and improve the citizens' quality of life. However, smart city initiatives still have difficulties to leverage value from technology opportunities. How smart city initiatives examine the possibilities of new technologies is therefore a highly interesting question. Based on a multiple case study we identify two different approaches and factors that influence the choice of approach: Cities either initially focus on use cases solving urban challenges, or on a systematic build-up of a technological platform for future use cases. Innovation adoption research is used as a theoretical basis.

Keywords: Smart city · Innovation adoption · Digitalization

1 Introduction

According to the latest UN forecast, 70% of the world's population will live in cities by 2050 [1]. This means that 2.5 billion people will move to urban areas in the next 30 years. Problems such as housing scarcity, overloaded infrastructures and CO_2 pollution caused by public transport will continue to worsen as the number of city inhabitants increases. In recent years, numerous smart city initiatives have been launched to tackle these problems [2]. Their aim is to leverage developments in digitalization to create new solutions for improving the efficiency of urban services and the quality of citizens' life [3]. The politicians' conviction that technology can contribute to make the city a more liveable and sustainable place is also reflected in the figures of funding programmes. The EU is providing €718 million for smart, green and integrated transport innovations as part of the European Horizon 2020 programme [4]. Such high funding also attract the private sector. Multinational information technology (IT) companies such as IBM or Cisco have discovered the smart city market as a growth driver for their business. These companies offer a variety of integrated solutions for different smart city scenarios (e.g. IBM's Intelligent Waste Management Platform [5]). Collaborations between private and public sectors have also led to criticism of the smart city concept. Brown [6], Söderström et al. [7] and Schaffers et al. [8] criticise them as inefficient and driven by IT vendors. The inefficiency is also criticized by the European Commission [9] which stated in a working paper, that "city planners, administrators, citizens,

© Springer Nature Switzerland AG 2019
M. Pańkowska and K. Sandkuhl (Eds.): BIR 2019, LNBIP 365, pp. 1–15, 2019.
https://doi.org/10.1007/978-3-030-31143-8_1

entrepreneurs and all other stakeholders must reconsider the way they have approached urban services" to gain value from technology opportunities. Also Anttiroiko, Valkama and Bailey [10] state that the public sector has difficulty exploiting the value from new technologies. Despite these findings, there have been few attempts in science to understand how smart city initiatives leverage value of new technologies.

The introduction of new technologies is described by innovation adoption theories. The process of innovation adoption typically involves two phases [11, 12]: initiation and implementation. Within these phases, new technologies have to overcome several hurdles before being used productively, i.e. being integrated into an existing IT landscape and deployed at full-scale [12, 13]. For technology innovations, the initiation phase, where organizations search for ways to use a new technology, poses a first serious obstacle [14]. This initial step towards the exploration of technology potentials is the focus of our study. In particular we formulate the following research question: *What approaches do smart city initiatives use when they initially explore the potential of new technologies for smart services and which factors influence their choice of approach?*

To address our research questions, a multiple case study with eight smart city initiatives was conducted. The organizational adoption process [11] in combination with the Technology-Organization-Environment framework (TOE) [15] has been used as a theoretical foundation. The TOE describes the impact of technological, organizational and environmental aspects on organizational decision-making with respect to technology innovations [15].

This paper is organized as follows: The current research on technology adoption research in smart city is summarized in the next section. Section 3 presents our conceptual framework. Section 4 introduces the research design. Section 5 presents the findings from our smart city cases. A discussion of the results in Sect. 6 and a summary of the main points in Sect. 7 complete this work.

2   Current Research

The term "Smart City" has been widely used in academia, consultancies and governments. Nevertheless, there is still a lot of confusion on what it really means to be a "smart" city [16–18]. According to Anthopoulos, Janssen and Weerakkody [19] a smart city is an innovative city that uses information and communication technology to improve citizens' quality of life and the efficiency of urban services. To meet these goals, smart cities need to introduce new technologies and realize smart services that address the concerns and needs of citizens [19, 20].

Smart services are considered as core element of a smart city and understood as an outcome of innovation [19]. The term summarizes the services that a smart city delivers to its stakeholders by the use of the city's intangible resources (e.g. people, knowledge, methods) and tangible resources, in particular information systems, data, and corresponding technologies [18, 19, 21].

Previous work in the context of technology adoption in smart cities is still scarce and focuses primarily on influencing factors. These are either investigated for the general adoption of the smart city concept or for the adoption of a specific techno-logical solution. For example, Neirotti et al. [3] used in an empirical analysis a sample of 70 cities to investigate context variables that support the adoption of the smart city concept. As a result, they show that economic development and structural urban variables (e.g. demographic density, city area) drive the initiation of smart city pro-grams in urban areas. Nam and Pardo [16] and Caragliu et al. [17] argue that a successful adoption of the smart city concept depends on investments in human and social capital, investments in modern and traditional infrastructure and the participation of citizens. Batubara, Ubacht and Janssen [22] use the TOE to describe main challenges in the adoption of blockchain technologies in smart cities. As a result, it has been shown that a lack of legal and regulatory support and new governance models are considered as main barriers of blockchain adoption.

So far an investigation of the technology adoption process in smart cities has only been carried out by van Winden and van den Buuse [23]. They used a multiple case study to investigate the implementation phase of smart city projects. Based on twelve smart city initiatives they identify three types of full-scale deployments in smart city projects: roll-out, expansion, and replication. They also identify corresponding influencing factors, e.g. upscaling in the implementation stage is often hindered by an absence of knowledge transfer, a lack of funding and missing standards such as data models or IT systems.

In comparison to existing studies, our research focuses on the initial phase of innovation adoption. We investigate how cities initially explore the potential of new technologies for smart services and factors that influence their choice of approach.

3　Conceptual Model

For our study, we use the innovation adoption process [11] and the TOE framework [15]. According to Rogers [11], the process of innovation adoption is described by two major phases: initiation and implementation, with both phases being separated by an adoption decision. The initiation phase consists of the stages agenda-setting and matching. The agenda-setting is triggered by an organizational problem or by the perception of an innovation. Both force organizations to weigh up possible reactions and evaluate the potentials of an innovation. This evaluation is typically undertaken in the matching stage, where organizational members explore the capabilities of an innovation to predict its potential for specific application scenarios. If advantages are expected, the implementation phase is triggered and all activities and decisions nec-essary to put the innovation into production are carried out. The decision on how to evaluate the potentials of an innovation is determined by an agenda which results from the agenda-setting [11].

To investigate the factors that influence this decision, the TOE provides a good theoretical foundation. The TOE describes the factors influencing the adoption of innovations. These factors are clustered into three dimensions: technology, organiza-tion and environment [15]. The technology dimension encompasses the characteristics of available technologies which are relevant to an organization. The organizational dimension covers organizational attributes, such as size, formal and informal linking structures, competencies and the amount of slack resources. The organization's environment and its influence are described in the environmental dimension. It includes competitors, industry specifics and regulation. As a very generic framework, the TOE is extensively used in adoption research (for examples see e.g. [24, 25]) and can be adapted to different research contexts in a straightforward way [24]. The technological dimension reflects attributes describing existing and new technologies that are relevant for a smart city. The organization dimension covers organizational aspects of the city and its smart city initiative. The environment dimension describes the influence of the multiple stakeholders that surround a smart city.

In conclusion, the conceptual framework used in this research combines the innovation adoption process [11] with the TOE [15], as shown in Fig. 1.

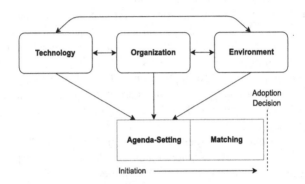

Fig. 1. Conceptual framework.

4   Research Design

This study uses a qualitative research methodology because we have little understanding of how cities explore the potential of new technologies for smart services and why they choose certain strategies. A qualitative approach allows us to obtain detailed descriptions of adoption behaviour. For our research purpose, we choose a case study method. This method is especially appropriate whenever research deals with "how" and "why" questions and facilitates analyses of contemporary phenomena in a real word context [26–29]. Our main information sources are in-depth expert interviews with key-informants (i.e. smart city representatives) and public documents from smart city initiatives.

In the sense of a strict implementation of the research design, four established quality criteria were used [26]: external validity, internal validity, construct validity and reliability. The external validity focusses on the generalizability of the results. This is ensured by replicating the case studies. Therefore we selected a multiple case study design following the "literal replication logic". The literal replication logic ensures an analytical generalization by selecting cases from a similar contextual background to predict similar results [26, 27]. In order to ensure a comparable organizational and technological context, we followed the smart city conceptualization of Angelidou [30] and selected existing major European cities with matured infrastructure. In addition, the selected cities and corresponding smart city initiatives have been validated by the smart city framework of Giffinger [31], which consists of six main components (smart economy, smart people, smart governance, smart mobility, smart environment, and smart living). Against this background, we selected only cities which are active in at least two categories. Table 1 shows the cases under study.

Table 1. Participants of case study.

#	City	Inhabitants of urban area	Role of interviewee
1	Amsterdam	>2.3 Mio.	Program ambassador
2	Barcelona	>5.3 Mio.	Catalan smart city coordinator
3	Dublin	>1.9 Mio.	Smart city coordinator
4	Cologne	>2.1 Mio.	Smart city project manager
5	Copenhagen	>1.3 Mio.	Head of IT
6	Berlin	>4.1 Mio.	Policy advisor smart city
7	Vienna	>1.7 Mio.	Expert for urban innovation
8	Zurich	>1.6 Mio.	Deputy director urban development

Following Eisenhardt [32], an a priori specification of constructs helps researchers to shape the initial design of theory-building research. In order to ensure internal validity, we followed this argumentation and developed the interview guideline on the basis of the conceptual framework described in Sect. 3 of this paper. The expert interviews were semi-structured and we kept our questions open to allow interviewees freely to speak. The first part contained general questions about the role and responsibility of the interviewee and the general goals of the smart city initiative. The remaining part of the interview guide was structured analogously to the conceptual model. The second part of our questions concentrated on activities related to agenda-setting. For example, we asked how specific needs for technology innovations are recognized, how they are prioritized and whether specific objectives for technology adoption exist. We also asked about factors that have influenced the first decisions about dealing with new technologies. Hereby we covered in particular the TOE dimension of our conceptual model. The third and most extensive set of questions was directed upon the matching stage. We focussed on "why" and "how" the initiatives explore the potentials of new technologies. These questions concerned, e.g. the methods and challenges during the identification of technology opportunities, the evaluation of technology potentials and the criteria applied therein.

Yin [26] suggests triangulation to ensure construct validity. Within the case studies, different data sources were therefore used. In addition to the key-informant interviews the rich body of public documents of smart city initiatives was analysed to validate the information retrieved from the key-informant interviews. In total 151 technology adoption related press articles, blog entries, white papers, annual reports and conference presentations were screened and 5 supplementary interviews with further smart city officials were conducted.

In order to minimize errors and biases, the reliability of the case study analysis was ensured by establishing a case study database. There, we stored all information about the data collection process, the data itself and the case study results. According to Yin [26], this helps to provide the same results in repeated trials and makes the data available for independent inspections.

The data collection started in February 2018 and stretched over a period of five months. The conversations were recorded and transcribed. Shortly after each interview, the main points and key findings were recapitulated in a contact summary sheet [33].

The analysis of the cases was carried out in a twofold way. First, we have used a within-case analysis [26] to extract all characteristic content (i.e. trigger of the process, activities in agenda-setting and matching) and influencing factors related to the agenda-setting of individual cases. For this purpose, we followed the deductive content analysis method [34] and used first-level coding [33] supported by the software f4analyse. In the second step, a cross-case analysis [26] was conducted and the cases were compared to each other. The results of these analyses are shown in Sect. 5 and discussed in Sect. 6.

5   Results from Cases

Based on the evidence from our cases, we now describe our observations about the initiation phase of technology adoption. In Sect. 5.1 we outline the different approaches cities chose, while the factors that influence this choice are presented in Sect. 5.2.

5.1   The Initiation of the Innovation Adoption Process

Agenda-setting is, according to Rogers [11], triggered by a performance gap or the perception of new possibilities. Both triggers force organizations to consider the potentials of an innovation. In the era of digitalization, cities launch smart city initiatives and examine how they would leverage new technologies for smart services. Within agenda-setting a so-called agenda is defined determining the goals for the next steps in the adoption process.

Agenda-Setting. Our analysis shows that in all smart city initiatives the combination of urban challenges (such as CO2 congestion, scarcity of housing or energy management), availability of funding and high hopes on technology innovations were decisive for the start with technology exploration for smart services. For example, this is confirmed in case 6:

> *"[..] Berlin is facing major challenges such as rapid population growth, strict climate targets and social housing. At the same time, technological innovations are playing an increasingly important role in political discussions. On the one hand, this is due to the new opportunities and its societal relevance. On the other hand, there is a multitude of new funding opportunities available [..]. Ultimately, it is the interaction of several factors." (Interview)*

Within the smart city initiatives, the exploration and assessment of new technologies was perceived as a constant and important task. A quote from case 8 emphasizes this:

> *"In order to get cities on the way to smart cities, it is necessary to focus on meaningful and economic use cases and to constantly deal with the potential of new technologies." (Interview)*

In discussions with the smart city initiatives, however, it quickly became apparent that there are different ways in which cities start to explore the potential value of new technologies.

In cases 1, 4, 7 and 8, the city administration asked the respective smart city initiative to collect possible use cases first. The focus of these use cases should be on solving urban problems. It was argued that technology creates value whenever it solves a problem. This is confirmed, for example, by a quote from case 7:

> *"In Vienna, a demand-oriented approach [for the introduction of new technologies] is chosen. If a problem requires a new solution, the appropriate means are sought to develop a suitable solution - these of course often include digital or technological components." (Interview)*

This attitude is also reflected in the goals of the first steps towards technology adoption in smart city initiatives which are summarized in Table 2.

Table 2. Goals for first steps of technology adoption in smart city initiatives.

Case	Brief description of the goal
1	Portfolio of user generated ideas for smart services based on a smart city web portal
4	Portfolio of smart services that recognize the specific needs and challenges of the city
7	Portfolio of technologically driven innovations that are linked to social innovations, and place the needs of people at the centre of this initiative
8	Web portal for smart city stakeholders to connect and foster the creation of innovative ideas for smart services

In the cases 2, 3, 5 and 6 the search for a good technological foundation was in the centre of first activities. It was considered important to deal with the technology first to facilitate a subsequent identification of use cases by a then available data and technology platform. Table 3 shows the respective goals.

Table 3. Goals for first steps of technology adoption in smart city initiatives.

Case	Brief description of the goal
2	Developed technological infrastructure and open access to city's data to accelerate innovation and digital economy
3	Digital master plan for the adoption of new technologies
5	Big data platform to enable advanced analytics in city context for future smart services
6	Link existing technologies to create new solutions and connect innovative technologies with existing infrastructures

The different goals that have been presented complete the agenda-setting stage and initiate the subsequent matching stage.

Matching. According to Rogers [11], organizational members explore the capabilities of an innovation in this stage. Therefore, cities follow two different approaches based on their agendas: A need driven and technology driven approach.

The need driven approach focusses on the development of a portfolio of potential applications solving smart city challenges. Identified use cases are evaluated on how they contribute to the superordinate smart city goals (e.g. CO_2 reduction through improvements in public mobility). If this is verifiable, corresponding technologies are implemented and the application is tested as a prototype. Typical examples for a need driven approach can be found in case 1, 4, 7 and 8.

In case 1, the initiative launched a central web portal to connect different stakeholders, receive user-initiated project proposals (e.g. ideas, how new technologies can be used to solve challenges) and attract people to launch projects as pilots. Connected stakeholders were e.g.: the city itself, private companies (e.g. Dutch telecommunication provider, Dutch post), representatives from academia and society. The smart city team assesses the project proposals. If the assessment proof successful, the project proposals are conducted as pilots in designated city areas (e.g. the Utrechtsestraat in Amsterdam city centre). The lessons learned from the pilots are then used for refinements and a further evaluation whether the goals could be achieved (e.g. people accept the technology, CO_2 pollution could be reduced). In case of a positive evaluation result, the implementation of the use case is triggered and it is rolled out to other urban areas or scaled up to the whole city.

The city in case 4 started with a similar approach. Creativity methods like design thinking were used to identify citizen's needs and corresponding smart services. The assessment of possible use cases is then conducted by a public-private partnership between the city and RheinEnergie Cologne. Criterions for the evaluation are measurable effects on the general smart city goals and a positive cost-benefit relation. If an evaluation proves to be successful, appropriate technologies were identified, pilots implemented and tested. This is confirmed by a statement from case 4:

> *"Use cases are tested and implemented locally within a limited geographical area within the city. If the applicability proves to be successful, a continuation is actively supported and the use case is rolled out to other areas of the city." (Interview)*

In the technology driven approach, cities initially invest in cyber-physical systems (i.e. combination of computational components with mechanical and electronic parts) and develop platforms that integrates different new technologies for data acquisition, integration and storage. These platform capabilities are then advertised and communicated to attract private organizations (e.g. companies, start-ups, local communities) to drive the identification and exploration of use cases, e.g. through hackathons. This approach often concentrates on certain domains of a smart city (e.g. smart transportation, smart energy). Cases 2, 3, 5 and 6 reflect this strategy.

In case 2, the city started with a massive expansion of the fibre optic infrastructure and initiated public private partnerships with private companies. These partnerships helped to deploy an internet of things (IoT) platform (i.a. installing 19,500 smart meters) and connect 90% of the households to the city's fibre optic network. Based on the public private partnerships the smart city initiative developed a central data platform, where different data sources were gathered and integrated. This data and technological platform is seen as a facilitator for the future identification and implementation of innovative use cases and the city's transformation to a smart city. This is confirmed by a quote from case 2:

"We understood that internet and new technologies were a unique and incredible opportunity to transform Barcelona [..] However, technology should not be seen as a goal in itself. Technology is simply a facilitator." (Public Documents)

The initial provisioning of data and technology was followed by the redesign of an old industrial district to shape a place, where start-ups can use the implemented technologies, analyse the generated data and identify and test potential applications.

In case 6, the connection of innovative technologies with existing infrastructure was one goal of the city's first smart services adoption efforts. Requirements for infrastructure projects were therefore utilized to anchor new technologies in the city's infrastructure. It was expected that these new technologies would open up data sources that could be of value for a later identification of smart services. A quote from case 6 emphasizes this:

"We had recently tendered new toilet houses. These are also potential carriers of new technologies. They can be equipped with a transmitter and a sensor [..] generate data of which we perhaps do not know yet what they could be used for. But that may be of great value in the future." (Interview)

5.2 Influencing Factors

Based on our analysis, different factors that influence the choice of approach could be identified. Cities following a *need driven* approach see citizens and private companies as a driver for innovations. A statement from case 1 confirms this:

"I think at the moment we see that you need leadership from the public sector, but real innovation comes from the private sector" (Public Documents)

This choice is supported by the perceived need of empowering citizens and local start-ups to raise their participation in city development. A platform where citizens can submit their ideas and vote on others' proposals for smart services should meet this need. For example, in case 1, the city is calling innovators and start-ups for ideas to solve specific challenges of the city. An online platform visualizes the progress of the proposal and stages an idea has to go through. A team of public and private smart city stakeholders decides whether an idea passes a stage.

A missing dedicated smart city budget could also be identified as an enabler of this approach. For example, in case 4 the need driven approach is seen as a way to tackle societal challenges. By addressing these challenges, the smart city initiative hopes to receive EU funds from the Horizon 2020 funding program. This is confirmed by the statement:

"Financing projects is a constant challenge as Cologne does not have a smart city budget [..] Therefore, the mediation of funds from EU projects is often necessary." (Interview)

A summary of the case specific influencing factors is presented in Table 4.

Table 4. Influencing factors for the need driven approach.

#	Case specific main influence factors	Sample statement
1	• Innovative smart services are expected as unique facilitator for sustainable economic development • Empowerment of citizens and local start-ups is perceived as important for the identification of potential smart services • Transparency in political decision on project proposals is perceived as important to increase citizen's engagement	*"Co-creating and co-developing urban solutions requires involvement and empowerment of citizens in the innovation process. This should enhance [..] accepted solutions that work and create value for all involved parties, including citizens."* *(Public Documents)*
4	• No dedicated smart city budget; dependence on third party funds • Expectation of economic returns by solving city's challenges with smart services • Coordination and communication of different projects within the city is perceived as important to identify synergies and valuable smart services	*"Smart city Cologne is at the same time a coordination and communication platform for various projects for climate protection, energy and transport change and improved energy efficiency."* *(Interview)*
7	• Empowerment of the private sector is perceived as important for identification of use cases • Single focus on smart city technologies is expected to neglect citizen participation and exacerbate the digital divide • Initial identification of lighthouse use cases is expected to attract further capital	*"Technology is only used where necessary, not wherever possible."* *(Interview)*
8	• Existing technology infrastructure is perceived as sufficient for current digitalization efforts • Synergies for new smart services are expected by the coordination of municipal companies that are already working on their own digitalization projects • Public and private companies are perceived as innovators	*"By comparison, the [technology] infrastructure in Switzerland and here in the city of Zurich is already well developed and will be further optimized."* *(Interview)*

A technology driven approach could be found, when cities see implemented technologies as the most important step, before the identification of smart services. This is confirmed by a statement from case 5:

> *"If we build a state-of-the-art digital infrastructure, we can build solutions for tomorrow."* *(Public Documents)*

Expectations of economic growth and new jobs underpin this choice. This is highlighted in case 2, for example. The city established an IoT infrastructure and made all collected data publicly available. In this way, the smart city initiative hopes to attract private companies, which in turn create new jobs and contribute to economic growth. Table 5 summarize the case specific influencing factors.

Table 5. Influencing factors for the platform driven approach.

#	Case specific main influence factors	Sample statement
2	• Welfare of citizens is expected to increase due to an open and modern technology platform • New technologies are intended to make business processes of public administration more accessible, efficient, effective and transparent • Synergies are expected by standardized information sharing within the city's companies	*"Through investment in IoT for urban systems, Barcelona [will achieve] a wide array of benefits. From reduced congestion and lower emissions, to cost savings on water and power [..]" (Public Documents)*
3	• Modern technology infrastructure is seen as a unique prerequisite for solving urban problems • New technologies are intended to increase the efficiency of the city's overall management • Job creation is expected	*"[Our technology and data] platform should lead to improved economic development by speeding up the advancement of services based on data [..]" (Public Documents)*
5	• Availability of data is perceived as a unique starting point for developing smart services • Modern technology platform is perceived as key for later smart city developments • New businesses and a highly skilled workforce are expected to be attracted by a modern technology platform	*"The City Data Exchange for Copenhagen is a solution for making public and private data accessible so that the data can help power innovation [..]If we combine data from the private sector and data from the city then [..] we can make new solutions and new products out of it." (Interview)*
6	• Data and information are perceived as essential resources of an information society • Technology innovations are perceived as complex but perceived as unique opportunity for the future development of the city • Coordination of digitalization activities in public companies within the city is perceived as important in order to guide the development of city wide technology and data platform	*"We have a supervisory board function in the federal state companies. This means that we can actively discuss and shape guidelines for project contracting."(Interview)*

6   Discussion

Based on the evidence from our cases, this study shows how smart city initiatives proceed in the initiation phase of the adoption of new technologies. During agenda-setting the city's management defines the goals of the first activities in the adoption process. As a result, we found agendas describing two different approaches smart cities initiatives use to exploit the value of new technologies: A need driven and a technology driven approach. The need driven approach focuses initially on the identification of valuable use cases for new technologies to solve urban challenges. After that, appropriate technologies were used for prototyping and testing. This is in contrast to the technology driven approach. There, the systematic implementation of new technologies is of primary interest. These technologies are considered as the basis for a subsequent identification and implementation of use cases.

Agenda-setting is the key stage in the innovation adoption process, as it determines all following steps in the initiation phase. In order to understand the decision-making in this stage, we followed the TOE framework and collected the influencing factors from the investigated cases (Tables 4 and 5). We then abstracted and assigned them to the appropriate TOE dimensions. Table 6 shows the result.

Table 6. Abstracted influencing factors assigned to TOE dimensions.

Technology	Organization	Environment
• Perceived complexity (the use of new technologies is perceived as complex [+] or not [−]) • Technology landscape (existing technology landscape is perceived as sufficient [+] or not [−]) • Information exchange (standardized information exchange is perceived as essential [+] or not [−]) • Unique benefits (it is expected that the use of new technologies supersedes other measures for solving urban problems [+] or not [−])	• Financial readiness (dedicated smart city budget is substantial [+] or limited [−]) • Perceived role of private sector (it is expected that innovative use cases come from private sector [+] or not [−]) • Perceived role of initiative (smart city initiative is primarily seen as coordination platform [+] or not [−]) • Economic returns (direct economic (e.g. job creation) returns are expected [+] or not [−])	• Information systems (IS) fashion (the use of new technologies is perceived as important [+] or not [−]) • Citizen's involvement (raise citizen's involvement is a primarily goal [+] or not [−])

Table 7 visualize the factors which had influence on a city's choice of approach. We found that cities with a need driven approach typically expect that innovative application scenarios come from private sector. Against this background, the initiatives aim to empower citizens and encourage them to participate more actively. This is also reflected by their governance model. It considers the smart city initiative primarily as a central organisation for the coordination of projects between public and private sector.

Initiatives that follow a technology driven approach perceive a standardized information exchange as a driver for innovations from public and private companies. Implemented modern technologies are seen as unique opportunity to increase efficiency of urban services and attract private companies as well as start-ups. The initiatives hope that these companies will in turn create new local jobs and identify and provide smart services.

Additionally, we found IS fashion as a general trigger of the adoption process in all observed initiatives as it reflects the hype that surrounds technology innovations such as blockchain or big data. At the same time, these new technologies are perceived as complex. A frequent argument for the perceived complexity was a lack of IT know-how in public institutions and limited financial resources that impedes the acquisition of external knowledge. Furthermore, most of the interviewed initiatives perceived their financial readiness as low and reported that they are highly dependent on regional, national or international funding schemes. The existing technology landscape was also perceived as insufficient for future requirements in the majority of cases.

Table 7. Approaches and corresponding influencing factors.

	Need driven				Technology driven			
	1	4	7	8	2	3	5	6
Perceived complexity	+	+	+	+	+	+	+	+
Technology landscape	−	−	+	+	−	−	−	−
Information exchange	−	−	−	−	+	+	+	+
Unique benefits	+	−	−	+	+	+	+	+
Financial readiness	+	−	−	−	+	−	+	−
Perceived role of private sector	+	+	+	+	+	−	−	+
Perceived role of initiative	+	+	+	+	+	−	−	+
Economic returns	−	+	+	−	+	+	+	+
IS fashion	+	+	+	+	+	+	+	+
Citizen's involvement	+	+	+	+	−	−	−	−

7 Summary

In this paper we have investigated through an analysis of eight cases how smart city initiatives start exploiting potentials of new technologies.

We could identify two different approaches for the initiation phase of technology innovation adoption: a need and technology driven approach. In the agenda-setting phase of the innovation adoption process, the city administration decides which approach to take. This choice is influenced by external and internal factors, which could be assigned to the technology, organization and environment dimensions of the TOE. In particular we found that the perceived importance of standardized information exchange, expected unique benefits of new technologies and citizen's involvement are most relevant during decision-making in the agenda-setting.

The theoretical and practical contributions of this research are as follows: Our study shows that the innovation adoption process and TOE can successfully be used to describe and understand the exploration of new technologies in smart cities. The study further contributes new factors to the existing IS adoption literature and provides a starting point for further quantitative and qualitative adoption research. From a practical point of view, cities initiating a smart city program can compare their planned activities with the different approaches and drivers identified in this paper, to possibly re-consider their way of action. Providing a method for the identification of use cases for smart services is planned as a next step in our research agenda. The corresponding design-oriented approach will benefit from the insights gained in this study.

We are sensible that our study faces limitations which should be addressed in future research: A possible restriction may result from the point in time of observation. We investigated how smart city initiatives start to adopt new technologies. During our research we have observed that the approaches of cities change over time and can coexist as the initiative progresses. A longitudinal study could help to describe and understand these changes.

Our identified approaches also open the door for further research: On the one hand, a detailed analysis of the processes within the different approaches could help to provide smart cities a suitable method for the successful identification, evaluation and adoption of smart services. On the other hand, the choice of approach and the impact on the success of smart service implementation could be investigated in order to provide recommendations for practitioners on what approach they should take.

References

1. United Nations: World Urbanization Prospects: The 2018 Revision (2018)
2. Zelt, T.: Think Act: Smart City. Smart Strategy. Roland Berger GmbH, München (2017)
3. Neirotti, P., De Marco, A., Cagliano, A.C., Mangano, G., Scorrano, F.: Current trends in smart city initiatives: some stylised facts. Cities **38**, 25–36 (2014)
4. European Commission: Horizon 2020 Work Programme 2018–2020 (2018)
5. IBM: IBM Intelligent Waste Management Platform. IBM Corporation, Armonk, New York (2015)
6. Brown, L.A.: The city in 2050: a kaleidoscopic perspective. Appl. Geogr. **49**, 4–11 (2014)
7. Söderström, O., Paasche, T., Klauser, F.: Smart cities as corporate storytelling. City **18**, 307–320 (2014)
8. Schaffers, H., Komninos, N., Pallot, M., Trousse, B., Nilsson, M., Oliveira, A.: Smart cities and the future internet: towards cooperation frameworks for open innovation. In: Domingue, J., et al. (eds.) FIA 2011. LNCS, vol. 6656, pp. 431–446. Springer, Heidelberg (2011). https://doi.org/10.1007/978-3-642-20898-0_31
9. European Commission: Analysing the Potential for Wide Scale Roll Out of Integrated Smart Cities and Communities Solutions (2016)
10. Anttiroiko, A.V., Valkama, P., Bailey, S.J.: Smart cities in the new service economy: building platforms for smart services. AI Soc. **29**, 323–334 (2014)
11. Rogers, E.M.: Diffusion of Innovations. Free Press, New York (2003)
12. Fichman, R.G.: The diffusion and assimilation of information technology innovations. In: Zmud, R.W. (ed.) Framing the Domains of IT Management: Projecting the Future Through the Past, pp. 105–127. Pinnaflex Publishing, Cincinnati (2000)

13. Bremser, C.: Starting points for big data adoption. In: Proceedings of the 25th European Conference on Information Systems, pp. 1–14 (2018)
14. Curry, E., Dustdar, S., Sheng, Q.Z., Sheth, A.: Smart cities - enabling services and applications. J. Internet Serv. Appl. **7**, 6 (2016)
15. Tornatzky, L.G., Fleischer, M., Chakrabarti, A.K.: Technological innovation as a process. In: Tornatzky, L.G., Fleischer, M. (eds.) Processes of Technological Innovation, pp. 27–50. Lexington Books, Lexington (1990)
16. Nam, T., Pardo, T.: Smart city as urban innovation: focusing on management, policy, and context. In: Proceedings of the 5th International Conference on Theory and Practice of Electronic Governance, pp. 185–194 (2011)
17. Caragliu, A., Bo, C. Del, Nijkamp, P.: Smart cities in Europe. In: Proceedings of the 3rd Central European Conference in Regional Science, pp. 45–59 (2009)
18. Angelidou, M.: The role of smart city characteristics in the plans of fifteen cities. J. Urban Technol. **24**, 3–28 (2017)
19. Anthopoulos, L., Janssen, M., Weerakkody, V.: Smart service portfolios: do the cities follow standards? In: Proceedings of the 25th International Conference Companion on World Wide Web, pp. 357–362 (2016)
20. Pourzolfaghar, Z., Helfert, M.: Taxonomy of smart elements for designing effective services. In: Proceedings of the 23rd American Conference on Information Systems, pp. 1–10 (2017)
21. ITU-T Focus Group on Smart Sustainable Cities: Technical Report on Smart Sustainable Cities: An Analysis of Definitions (2014)
22. Batubara, F.R., Ubacht, J., Janssen, M.: Challenges of blockchain technology adoption for e-government: a systematic literature review. In: Proceedings of the 19th Annual International Conference on Digital Government Research: Governance in the Data Age, p. 76:1–76:9 (2018)
23. van Winden, W., van den Buuse, D.: Smart city pilot projects: exploring the dimensions and conditions of scaling up. J. Urban Technol. **24**, 51–72 (2017)
24. Baker, J.: The technology-organization-environment framework. In: Dwivedi, Y., Wade, M., Schneberger, S. (eds.) Information Systems Theory: Explaining and Predicting Our Digital Society, pp. 231–245. Springer, New York (2012). https://doi.org/10.1007/978-1-4419-6108-2_12
25. Oliveira, T., Martins, M.F.: Literature review of information technology adoption models at firm level. Electron. J. Inf. Syst. Eval. **14**, 110–121 (2011)
26. Yin, R.K.: Case Study Research: Design and Methods. SAGE Publications, New York (2003)
27. Dubé, L., Paré, G.: Rigor in information systems positivist case research: current practices, trends, and recommendations. MIS Q. **27**, 597–636 (2003)
28. Benbasat, I., Goldstein, D.K., Mead, M.: The case research strategy in studies of information systems. MIS Q. **11**, 369–386 (1987)
29. Darke, P., Shanks, G., Broadbent, M.: Successfully completing case study research: combining rigour, relevance and pragmatism. Inf. Syst. J. **8**, 273–289 (1998)
30. Angelidou, M.: Smart city policies: a spatial approach. Cities **41**, 3–11 (2014)
31. Giffinger, R., Fertner, C., Kramar, H., Kalasek, R., Pichler-Milanovi, N., Meijers, E.: Smart Cities: Ranking of European Medium-Sized Cities (2007)
32. Eisenhardt, K.M.: Building theories from case study research. Acad. Manag. Rev. **14**, 532–550 (1989)
33. Miles, M.B., Huberman, A.M., Saldana, J.: Qualitative Data Analysis: A Methods Sourcebook. SAGE Publications, Los Angeles (2013)
34. Mayring, P.: Qualitative Inhaltsanalyse: Grundlagen und Techniken. Beltz, Weinheim und Basel (2008)

Comparison of Different Requirements for Digital Workplace Health Promotion

Fujan Nuryan Dehkordi[1]([⊠]), Michael Fellmann[1],
and Rüdiger Breitschwerdt[2]

[1] Institute of Computer Science, University of Rostock,
Albert-Einstein-Straße 22, 18059 Rostock, Germany
{fujan.dehkordi,michael.fellmann}@uni-rostock.de
[2] Business Informatics, Wilhelm Büchner Hochschule – Mobile University
of Technology, Hilpertstr. 31, 64295 Darmstadt, Germany
ruediger.breitschwerdt@wb-fernstudium.de

Abstract. Nowadays, workload is constantly growing and competition brings pressure on employers and employees. In addition, more and more people have mental challenges. Meanwhile digital health apps become more and more a trend. However, it is a complex task to set up an application for described problems. The purpose of this paper is to analyze various perspectives for requirements in digital Workplace Health Promotion (dWHP). We analyze findings that consider requirements of dWHP based on expert interviews and a literature review. This contribution summarizes categories of requirements. Moreover, these categories are compared with two existing dWHP apps and their feature areas. The comparison of requirements regarding reviews, interviews and functions of existing dWHP apps show similarities but also differences. Finally, these aspects are considered intensely and investigated for dWHP from three perspectives. The results imply a need for future research on sustainable use of dWHP and provide guidance for important content-related components.

Keywords: digital Workplace Health Promotion (dWHP) · mHealth · Expert interviews · Comparison · Literature review · Requirements

1 Motivation and Relevance

High workload and stress are gaining importance in daily life. In Germany, physical illness has risen from 2% to 16.6% over the past 40 years [1]. Also, the cost of mental illnesses is € 44.4 bn. per year in 2017 [2].

Mental illnesses are also the most common cause of early retirement. The retirement age is rising, however the average age for early retirement is 48.3 years [1].

Moreover, due to the global competition employees' and employers' requirements increase and force them to protect and promote health [3]. Governments are also obliged to develop laws that protect and promote the health of employees. Volume V of the German Social Insurance Code (SGB V) § 20 requires health insurers to commit themselves to health issues and prevention [4].

© Springer Nature Switzerland AG 2019
M. Pańkowska and K. Sandkuhl (Eds.): BIR 2019, LNBIP 365, pp. 16–29, 2019.
https://doi.org/10.1007/978-3-030-31143-8_2

In addition, the future of work is characterized by an aging workforce. Fraunhofer IAO have been researching socio-demographic change for more than 15 years. They identified health promotion as a challenge for especially medium-sized companies remote from attractive metropolitan regions. Those have also difficulties recruiting qualified young employees. In Germany, the number of people within the working age will drop from currently 50 million to about 44 million in 2030. Flexible working models and mobile use of digital technologies, on one hand, and higher health orientation among managers and organizations on the other hand, will be two key factors for keeping up the competition and employee satisfaction.

An increase in flexible forms of work and employment, with positive health benefits is fundamentally associated with digitization. However, the latter produces also new burdens for stakeholders and social insurances by affecting mental and social working conditions. Moreover, new workload and resource constellations arise. The demands on individual self-responsibility and self-control increase significantly [5].

Meanwhile using smartphones and digitization is an integral part of the organization's workflow and processes. German TK, health insuring appr. 10 million Germans reports over 400.000 Health apps already existing on the market. Over 60% of the respondents are willing to use one [6].

The goal of this contribution is to support Workplace Health Promotion (WHP) with digital aspects. WHP follows a holistic approach that includes not only typical health promotion actions, but also aims at improving

- the management and corporate culture,
- the working environment,
- the compatibility of private life and work, and
- age-appropriate work [7].

Moreover, the conscious control and integration of all operational processes targeting maintenance and promotion of employees' health and wellbeing. Applications on desktops and notebooks not only allow the retrieval of data and information but also the acquisition of new data, evaluation of data and further processing. While offline solutions dominated in the past, the trend is towards mobile applications and use of storage options via the Internet. In addition, an interaction with other users gains value [8]. The combination and fulfillment of all those criteria is a big challenge for the creation of an application. Therefore, it is essential to know requirements for a sustainable and stable WHP application.

This article is structured as follows. In a first step, we describe related works partially focusing this topic (Sect. 2). After the methodological part (Sect. 3) we then systematically construct a data model based on requirements. After presenting the content and results from an empirical investigation, we point out important requirements in a discussion (Sect. 5) and conclude with areas for future research (Sect. 6).

2 Related Works

The review of Dehkordi et al. [9] represents a large literature research on the subject dWHP. The evaluation of this review will be considered in this contribution. However, this search has been expanded with terms of requirement and requirement engineering in important database such as Google Scholar. The detailed description can be find in (Sect. 4.2).

- CHM = Corporate health management
- CHP = Corporate health promotion
- COHP = Company health promotion
- OHP = Occupational health promotion
- WHM = Workplace health management
- WHP = Workplace health promotion

Most reviews related to this topic highlight extending work requirements into employees' private lives [10] and how to. "However, the "reasonable design" requirement is not a strict one" and no testing cases exist for these requirements [10]. There are reviews pointing out the organizational requirements and communication difficulties [11]. A lack of resources, no fit between intervention and or lack of managerial support [11, 12]. Moreover, there are researches for requirements describing only the aspects of data security [13].

Other meta-analyses emphasize the studies on creating technical sensors and based on a framework to derive requirement for a case study [14]. A review designed to convey a particular message and objective to promote a healthy environment for certain challenges in motivation category.

TK insurance also investigate the aspects and the trend of dWHP. In this review called #whatsnext trend study 9 of 10 interviewed identify leadership as a key for dWHP [15].

However, no review could be found addressing the combination of the aforementioned topics of interest.

3 Methodological Considerations

We have developed the model in a systematic, stepwise approach using established requirements. These requirements were elicited from literature (RS = Requirement State of the art), from survey among practitioners (RI = Requirement Interview), and by investigating two prototypical systems (RA = Requirement existing app) already on the market. Requirements elicitation for RS was part of our previous work [9]. First, requirements are extracted from the three sources (RS, RI, RA). Subsequently, these requirements are merged into categories representing the intersection of needs for digital Workplace Health Promotion. Figure 1 provides an overview of each step of the research process. In the next stage we are going to describe this in more detail.

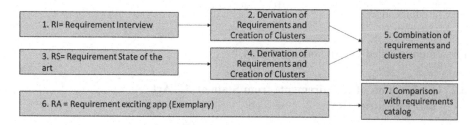

Fig. 1. Overview of the research process

3.1 Elaboration of Requirements from Interview with Experts (RI)

The requirements have been derived based on experts' interviews. Overall, the questionnaire has been answered by 12 people. Seven of the participants are experts specialized on WHP topic in their companies. Five of the participants are general experts in WHP organizations or statutory health insurers (Fig. 2).

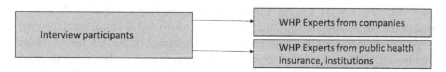

Fig. 2. Overview experts

The questionnaires were compiled from the literature and iterative review of the questions. An empirical research is developing with the help of qualitative research. For the evaluation of the questionnaire, we followed a qualitative content analysis: as theoretical foundation, basic procedures were used according to Mayring [16].

In the results section, the experts are labeled (from A–M) and their statements are numbered (for example 1–100). This type of representation gives a clear and comprehensible overview of results. This method, the standardized questionnaires and the obtained results are described closer in Gebhardt et al. [17]. For developing the categories, most answered questions' responses were taken. The expert lists the questions as important. The statements were grouped and prioritized according to the amount and repetition of experts' replies. The questionnaire provides the basis for the creation of the categories. Two questionnaires were defined. On the one hand the focus was on experts from the companies. On the other hand, the general experts from public health, WHP institutions and insurance were questioned. Both questionnaires contain questions about communication, information, motivation and app features [17]. However, the questions alone are not enough, the answers of the experts confirmed our selection and helped to limit the number of categories. Four of five categories were established from requirements from interviewed experts:

- Memory,
- Information,

- Communication,
- Motivation.

For a more detailed description see Sect. 4.1.

3.2 Elaboration of Requirements from State of the Art and Literature (RS)

Requirements from literature have been elicited by reviewing related works found in the databases Scopus, Aisel, Googlescolar, SpringerLink, Ebscohost (incl. Information Systems Journal, Information Systems Research, Journal of the Association for Information Systems, Journal of Information Technology, Journal of Management Information Systems, MIS Quarterly). Here "it is necessary to consider the relevant literature by combining the aforementioned keywords with IT terms such as application, app, or smartphone" and the topic requirement. The described keywords were also used in Dehkordi et al. [9]. New is the fact of combination with the term requirement (Sect. 2).

In addition, more databases have to be explored: Pubmed, IEEE Xplore, ISI Web of Science, Medline, ACM Digital Library (Association for Computing Machinery), Journal of the Association for Information Systems (AIS) and ScienceDirect (Journal of Strategic Information Systems) thus ensuring also coverage of the AIS senior scholar's journal basket. The result of this review and its method is described more detailed in IT-Support in Workplace Health Promotion: Mobile Apps on the Rise [9].

We examined our findings for comparison reasons. Further we created categories [18] and within them categories to identify similarities [9]. Furthermore there is an overview of the category names after reviewing all finding of the state of art [9] a new category called *notification* was added to the category list. The Category *memory* represents different kinds of reminders and user control of those reminder functions. The category *information provision* describes how the information can excess and delivered to users. The category *special features* is about the content of the app functions and provides all messages the users and the experts see as a feature for an application. The category *notification* might be similar to the "memory" categories at first view, but this section is considered more as warning and reinforcement of reminder. These reminders have an alarm function and are used for example for following situation: The course has already begun, and the participant is not absent, but has also not canceled this session. He is going to notify with a loud tone, in case he forgot to come to the course. In the category *communication* we investigate what role communication tools will play in companies if the networking of employees proves important. The category *motivation* describes which functions could motivate the employees and if a motivation feature is essential for an application.

- Category names Overview:
    - Memory
    - Information provision
    - Special features
    - Notification
    - Communication
    - Motivation

3.3   Elaboration of Requirements from Existing Apps (RA)

In the next step, after creation of the categories, we search for examples from practice: Digital WHP examples already used on the market. The first providers could be found in the corporate Health Convention fair in Stuttgart on 9th–10th of April in 2019 [19]. Moreover a sample selection resulted from a search in Googleplay and Apple's Appstore. With the term WHP we revealed 20 corresponding providers. In order to find out which of these apps should be taken into consideration as an example, the number of downloads and the rating in each store were considered. This method helps to have a precise selection process and to pick out an established app. Some of these apps have already been featured in the press (newspapers, journals, etc.). They were partly nominated for various awards such as i-award or startup awards. A request for cooperation has been sent out to these companies. There were six participants ready to collaborate with us. A part of those wants to remain anonymous for privacy reasons. For the evaluation, questions were shaped to expose the categories. In section below there are examples for examining app features by means of designing questions for category information. These questions help to investigate all apps equally.

- Is the information flexible available to the participants?
- Can the participant retrieve information about relaxation techniques?

4   Content and Results from Empirical Investigation

In this section we present all requirements identified: Those are first considered individually, subsequently there is an overall rating across all requirements. Here we answer the question which features for a dWHP can be significant.

4.1   Requirements Form the Expert Interviews (RI)

In this section, there is a listing that more accurately categorizes requirements of the expert. One of the most mentioned requirements is the sending of the reminders. Experts would like to turn the notifications on or off themselves. Being informed too often leads to ignore the reminder and get annoyed of it. They want to have control over the messages themselves. Moreover, a reminder should exist which announces the courses. For instance: "your back fit- Course starts in 15 min." Other experts have the requirement to use this application from everywhere, such as home office, car or other corporate locations (Table 1).

In category *information*, for experts it is central to get the information as concisely and precisely as possible, too. This information should be brief but correct and well documented. Another recommendation is to offer alternatives in different prevention fields such as body exercises, nutrition, stress management, addiction. It should provide recommendations for the user which field of prevention they should consider more. An example: The user would like to eat a chocolate croissant, here the app should offer a healthy alternative.

Table 1. Requirements form the expert interviews (RI)

Category name: memory	Expert statement
The app should provide adjustable reminders	B84, A101, D100, D112, I47, L30, L41, M48
The app should announce the actions	D102
Category name: information provision	
The information should be accessible from everywhere	B83
The app should be flexible in working hours and the information could combine working space and the app	C41, A35, M33
The information should also be provided via desktop connection	B98
The information should be well prepared	E101, E54, I44, L32, L60
The app should provide courses should be offered digitally in different languages.	G29
Category name: special features	
The app must provide features such as active break, methods for stress management	E95, G44, M46
The app should provide exercises for Progressive muscle relaxation, eye relaxation	H60, J42
The app must provide a drinking control app	H68, L47, M51
The app could provide general E- Learning functions	L37
The app could provide setting up a workplace ergonomically	L33
The app could provide filter offers by location	G39
Category name: notification (alert)	
The app could provide a pay-attention function Example: a ringing function for a course start	L52
Category name: communication	
The communication should be multichannel (Omni)	A67
The app should offer alternatives for the healthy handling in the prevention fields	A113
The app should support healthy leadership	B11, C44, D85-D87
The app should provide more communication about existing courses and a help feature to choose the right course	B72, E82
The app could create a networking process for employees in a company	B74, C54
Category name: motivation	
The app should provide feedback function	D110, D123-D124, H62, K31
The app should provide push notifications	C61
The app should provide collection of credit points for specific course and functions	A110
The app must provide gamification aspects	C54, H64
The app should provide monetary/non-monetary reward	E115
The app must provide anonymized Challenges	A110, C68, D127, E115, J42
The app should provide anonymized Challenges with fitness trackers	E88, K31, L52
The app should strengthen of group dynamics	B75, M53
The app should provide collecting points	E115

Some experts do not only see the benefit for the user moreover provide a tool for successful leadership. Overall, this is a profit for both the employer and the employee. The leadership is supported in strategic question und healthy management of the employees.

The experts point to the motivation category and contribute this area also a high priority for requirement in an application. Many experts are of the opinion that building a network also increases the motivation. For network processes it is interesting to know which individual performs what task in the company or in which region. Moreover, Expert C sees the potential in an app in networking between the employees. For example: Which courses are offered online and who is participating. This fact strengthens the group's dynamics.

4.2 Requirements from State of Art (RS)

In this part, we will evaluate the already existing state of art paper [9] and find out requirements in this review. Furthermore, the most important requirements are summarized and explained in the following section (Table 2).

Table 2. Requirements from State of Art (RS)

Category name: information	Which paper
The information should be well prepared	Paper [20]
Category name: special features	
The app must provide features for stress level	Paper [21]
The app must provide additional Emails for information spreading	Paper [22]
Category name: notification	
The app must provide e-mail as an alert function	Paper [22]
Category name: communication	Which paper
The app could create a networking process for employees in a company	Paper [22]
Category name: motivation	
The app should provide feedback function	Paper [23, 24]
The app must provide anonymized Challenges	Paper [21]
The app should provide anonymized Challenges with fitness trackers	Paper [21]
The app should provide motivational notifications	Paper [22]

The results of the review confirm that the focus of the applications is on category information and motivation. The review of Aneni et al. [22] is about 29 different studies about physical activity's outcome and therefore plays an important role in our evaluation. The applications are using "email support for [...] motivational messages, and social networking" [22]. Some application offers dietary logs with 7 individualized emails with feedback sheets. Moreover, an application IG is an interventions plus self-monitoring with e-diary and has an online access to therapists. For the information part, there are weekly emails with weight loss lessons.

Furthermore, in an application for smoking cessation with personalized assessments, an e-mail support with motivational information is existing. This application has the ability to send out emails to the mailing list as a notification and in case of alert.

In Guertler et al.'s review is investigated "how the use of a smartphone app may be helpful in increasing engagement with the intervention and in decreasing nonusage attrition" [21]. For a challenge, a software has been implemented on a web-based version, an application on smartphones and a fitness device for the execution of 10,000 steps. This survey shows that the motivation of the users grown.

Dunkl et al. investigate the behavior of the leadership and the results show that young professional were the most users consuming the feedback functions in dWHP [24].

4.3 Requirements from Existing Apps (RA)

In this part, the categories were compared to existing apps. The requirements were found based on the company's information on the website. We search for the word WHP on internet, GooglePlay and app store. The providers are still working on a test version for our research. Therefore, we evaluated the available information. Table 3 lists companies and their corresponding apps.

Table 3. Requirements from existing apps (RA)

Company's name	Name of the dWHP
SMOVER	SMOVER
BeLabs UG	BEVIGO
Windhund GmbH	Windhund Workplace
eTherapists GmbH	HUMANOO
Profession Fit BGF GmbH	PROFESSION FIT
Blacksquared GmbH	Changers CO2 Fit
Vitaliberty GmbH	Digital Health Guide
go4 health GmbH	go4h-framework
Motio GmbH – Management personeller Ressourcen	Digi-Care
Team Gesundheit Gesellschaft für Gesundheitsmanagement GmbH	Team Gesundheit
Machtfit GmbH	machtfit
Healthclapp	Healthclapp
IKK gesund plus	IKK impuls Werkstatt
MediExpert	The Cube
Epripay GmbH	Vitalticket Aktivticket
Fit im job AG	myChange
SHENTI SPORTS Group GmbH	FITMIT5
Monsenso ApS	Monsenso
Mindance GmbH	Mindance

Two well-reputed apps are Windhund Workplace [25] and Changers CO2 Fit [26]. The Changers CO2 Fit is an application for creating challenges for participating in health actions. The company starts with their own teams. "Award bonus points for kilometers traveled on foot and by bike and for participating in health activities." It offers also social commitment by connecting the employees' participation with individual donation projects or tree planting. In the app store, this app had an average rating of (4.1/5) with 168 reviews and over 10.000 downloads in google play. Changers CO2 Fit is a great example for the category of motivation for anonymized challenges also with fitness tracker and category information for topic networking.

The Windhund Workplace app has over 500 downloads in google play. The Health topics are explained to the employee by means of modules which take from a few days up to 2 weeks. The end user receives "content snacks" on the corresponding topics such as interaction about 5 min per day, modules are gradually released, each employee receives a black roll massage ball to perform the various exercises.

In Windhund Workplace, messages can be switched off. According to the provider, individual push messages can be created. Also, Changer CO2 fit app reminders can be turned off, just as examples from category *memory*.

Both apps do not need any certain OS. The apps are available for smartphone and tablet, as well as via the web platform. Both apps provide features for breathing techniques. Changers's CO2 Fit exists in 10 different languages which helps an international company to use this app in different corporate locations.

4.4   Combination of the Requirements

In this section, the sources are merged to create a complete picture of requirements. In the Table 4 we summarized the most important categories and requirements form experts (RI) and state of the art (RA). One of the similarities is in the category information provision. Five experts have the opinion, that the information should be well prepared. The information should be short, compact and clearly visible writes also Umanodan et al. in his research.

Observing all the research process, the *motivation* category is already seen as a necessary category by these three elaborated requirement fields. Furthermore, this category is also well used in Changers CO2 Fit, in Guertler et al.'s review and also by the experts D, H and K. Additionally, providing a feedback function and use an anonymized challenge for motivate the employees are mentioned by eight different experts and three different apps which were investigated in state of art.

Moreover, both investigating apps provide gamification aspects, for example, challenges or reaching certain milestones. Moreover, Changer CO2 fit describes the reward in the form of planting real trees.

The integration of management in a dWHP was considered as important by three experts. First, the leaders have a role model function so their motivation is automatically a motivation for the employees and make dWHP more attractive. Second, a feature of the dWHP should train leaders to be result-oriented, inspiring and healthy. This requirement could not be found in RA and RS.

Table 4. Merge of the Requirements form experts (RI) and state of the art (RA)

Category name: information provision	Combination of RI and RA
The information should be well prepared	E101, E54, I44, L32, L60, Paper [20]
Category name: special features	
The app must provide features such as active break, methods for stress management	E95, G44, M46, Paper [21]
Category name: communication	
The app could create a networking process for employees in a company	B74, C54, Paper [22]
Category name: motivation	
The app should provide feedback function	D110, D123-D124, H62, K31, Paper [23, 24]
The app must provide anonymized challenges	Paper [21]
The app should provide anonymized challenges with fitness trackers	A110, C68, D127, E115, J42, Paper [21]

In conclusion, expert L assumes the category notification helps the users with repetitive reminder and alert for attentiveness functions. For RA and RS in comparison, there is no clear demarcation between category *memory* and category *notification*.

5 Discussion

As mentioned above, all three resources focus on category motivation. Although the experts consider this topic as very important, the reminders should be adjustable and individual for every users and shouldn't be excessive. The users are not allowed to be stressed or annoyed by the reminders of the application.

Furthermore, certain requirements which are needed by the management. One of characteristics of this app could be a number of sick days of all the employees and the value of this app to decrease these sick days. However, in a dWHP the leadership needs a consolidation of all important information which have a sustained effect. The management level needs compact statistics for prediction a trend. Moreover, it also needs a view to anticipating negative developments in the company and suggestions to counteracting them. However, the topic data privacy should be considered strongly for the employees. Additionally, information flow helps to identify which actions are currently being offered and for what actions a high demand is expected.

Generally speaking, the information should be well prepared not only by provision the information but also by content of the information. The content should be well investigated and scientifically proven. This aspect was also seen as important requirement by one expert.

Nevertheless, it exists a lack of requirements in these categories. In the category information experts expect actions for the employees working in home office, on the road or at certain flexible workplaces. Both the state of the art and existing apps evaluations represent no special features for employees working in home office. Furthermore, it is not clear what offers and actions they can use specifically in this work period. Moreover, a critical aspect is the availability of an application. For employees with flexible workspace the information should be existing from anyplace. In category communication, experts propose a "finding alternative" feature. The app should also be able to respond to spontaneous requests - a requirement example from Interview partner A: "He's in a hurry in the lunch break and has to eat at Mc Donald. The user should be offered alternatives where he can eat fast but still healthier. Moreover, a low calorie alternative should be suggested."

6   Conclusion and Fields for Future Research

Meanwhile, dWHP provides a great potential for the companies. Nevertheless, the phenomenon in companies is not trivial compared to health apps of end users. A health app is for the end user easy to install on your smartphone or tablet. A health app in a company certainly has complex conditions. Although requirements are deeply investigating form different perspectives, however, we should also consider a certain semantic bias because of the limitations in searching the literature in terms of filters, more experts could be interviewed by the research team. A limitation for this work is also the unavailable and less complete information from the existing apps. A demo or a test version could help us to analyze the app not only based on screenshot and the information on the internet. Moreover, the apps modify the features rapidly. Therefore, it is possible, that the apps may have changed and also the mentioned results. Moreover, there are recommendations for future research: As next steps we will investigate if the elaboration of the requirements is applicable internationally and feasible for all involved participants. We will also clarify if the requirements match for employees of all ages and company sizes.

Regarding to the cluster information provision and the futures research it is essential to have a stable system and guarantee reachability of information from everywhere. All the apps let the users having access from different system type such as app or web-based system. Only two apps don't offer the information form different channels. In this case, a correct mix for distribution of information on fitness tracker, app, web-based system should be considered.

In this contribution we investigate dWHP requirements from different perspectives. We discover gaps and similarities of these three perspectives (RI, RS and RA). On the one hand, this paper helps developers to understand the needs of the dWHP better. On the other hand, this research should help the experts to see which apps already exits and which dWHP were investigate by the literature. We have to explore if the aforementioned components are sufficient and whether the existing apps and the described components are accepted by users. Moreover, in the conclusion the focus is on German dWHP apps in the future also international apps will be considered.

Finally, information provision and exploring the requirements regarding to dWHP in different branches will also be subject of future research. According to statistics, there are 16 work branches exists [27]. After overviewing, the requirements can be transferred to all this branches. However, for certain actions and special features such as eLearning programs or setting up a workplace ergonomically, it is necessary to create requirements for each branch and answer the question how far these requirements are sufficient for a dWHP system.

References

1. BKK Dachverband e.V.: PsyGa- Daten und Fakten. PsyGa. https://www.psyga.info/psychische-gesundheit/daten-fakten. Accessed 07 May 2019
2. Peter, R.: Berufliche Gratifikationskrisen und Gesundheit, pp. 386–398 (2002)
3. Pundt, J.S.V.: Erfolgsfaktor Gesundheit in Unternehmen-Zwischen Kulturwandel und Profitkultur (2006). Pollon-hochschulverlag.de
4. BGM: rechtliche Rahmenbedingungen - hkk Firmenservice. hkk Krankenkasse. https://www.hkk.de/firmenservice/gesund-im-unternehmen/gesundheit-im-unternehmen/bgm-rechtliche-rahmenbedingungen. Accessed 09 May 2019
5. Bertelsmann Stiftung: Arbeit und Gesundheit in Zeiten der digitalen Transformation (2018)
6. Krankenkasse, T.K.: Wie smart ist Deutschland?
7. Betriebliche Gesundheitsförderung. AOK - Service für Unternehmen. AOK– Gesundheitskasse, CW Haarfeld GmbH. https://www.aok-business.de/gesundheit/was-ist-bgf/betriebliche-gesundheitsfoerderung/. Accessed 10 May 2019
8. Walle, O.: Digitales BGM, Arbeitsschutz Office, Arbeitsschutz, Haufe, in Arbeitsschutz Office, Haufe
9. Dehkordi, F.N., Breitschwerdt, R., Fellmann, M.: IT-Support in Workplace Health Promotion : Mobile Apps on the Rise, vol. 1, pp. 38–50
10. Ibrahim, A., Steinberg, S.R.:1 Toward a critical theory of youth. In: Critical Youth Studies Reader, pp. 1–40 (2016)
11. Lier, L.M., Breuer, C., Dallmeyer, S.: Organizational-level determinants of participation in workplace health promotion programs: a cross-company study. BMC Public Health 19(1), 1–8 (2019)
12. Wierenga, D., et al.: What is actually measured in process evaluations for worksite health promotion programs: a systematic review. BMC Public Health 13, 1190 (2013)
13. Carolan, S., Harris, P.R., Cavanagh, K.: Improving employee well-being and effectiveness: Systematic review and meta-analysis of web-based psychological interventions delivered in the workplace. J. Med. Internet Res. 19(7), 1–18 (2017)
14. Koldijk, S., Kraaij, W., Neerincx, M.A.: Deriving requirements for pervasive well-being technology from work stress and intervention theory: framework and case study. JMIR mHealth uHealth 4(3), e79 (2016)
15. Gesundheitsberichte, D., et al.: Vorstellung der Studie # whatsnext - Gesund arbeiten in der digitalen Arbeitswelt, pp. 1–6 (2017)
16. Mayring, P.: Qualitative content analysis. FQS Forum Qual. Soc. Res. 1(2), 10 (2000)
17. Gebhardt, S., Dehkordi, F., Breitschwerdt, R.: Bachelorthesis: Empirische Analyse des Bedarfs von Apps im Betrieblichen Gesundheitsmanagement, Flensburg (2018)
18. Orwat, C., Graefe, A., Faulwasser, T.: Towards pervasive computing in health care - a literature review. BMC Med. Inform. Decis. Making 8, 26 (2008)
19. Corporate Health Convention - Corporate Health Convention (2019). https://www.corporate-health-convention.de/. Accessed 11 May 2019
20. Umanodan, R., Shimazu, A., Minami, M., Kawakami, N.: Effects of Computer-based Stress management training on psychological well-being and work performance in Japanese employees: a cluster randomized controlled trial. Ind. Health 52(6), 480–491 (2014)

21. Guertler, D., Vandelanotte, C., Kirwan, M., Duncan, M.J.: Engagement and nonusage attrition with a free physical activity promotion program: the case of 10,000 steps Australia. J. Med. Internet Res. **17**[1](7) (2015)
22. Aneni, E.C., et al.: A systematic review of internet-based worksite wellness approaches for cardiovascular disease risk management: outcomes, challenges & opportunities. PLoS ONE **9**(1), e83594 (2014)
23. Coulter, C.H.: The employer's case for health management. Benefits Q. **22**(1), 23–33 (2006)
24. Dunkl, A., Jimenez, P.: Using smartphone-based applications (apps) in workplace health promotion: the opinion of German and Austrian leaders. Health Inform. J. (2016). https://doi.org/10.1177/1460458215623077
25. Windhund Workplace App - Digitale Lösung für das Betriebliche Gesundheitsmanagement. https://www.windhund.com/de/windhund-workplace-app/#. Accessed 11 May 2019
26. Changers.com: Occupational Health and Motivation Platform. https://changers.com/. Accessed 11 May 2019
27. Statista Branchenübersicht. https://de.statista.com/statistik/kategorien/. Accessed 11 May 2019

Blockchain Awareness Among Computer Science Students: A Preliminary Study

Dariusz Dymek[1(✉)] ⓘ, Mariusz Grabowski[1] ⓘ,
and Grażyna Paliwoda-Pękosz[2] ⓘ

[1] Department of Computational Systems, Cracow University of Economics,
Rakowicka 27, 31-510 Kraków, Poland
{dariusz.dymek,mariusz.grabowski}@uek.krakow.pl
[2] Department of Computer Science, Cracow University of Economics,
Rakowicka 27, 31-510 Kraków, Poland
paliwodg@uek.krakow.pl

Abstract. The main goal of research was to investigate to what extent computer science students are familiar with blockchain technology (BC). The survey was conducted among the students of Cracow universities. In order to analyze deeply the results of the survey, indicators of the knowledge factor and the usage factor were developed to assess knowledge and usage of BC respectively. The main findings point out to the popular internet portals and conversations with other people as the main sources of information on BC for students. Students are less likely to obtain their information from university classes and lectures, television, radio, and other media. The percentage of active BC users almost doubles the percentage of respondents having specialized knowledge, therefore the relationship between knowledge and usage of BC is rather weak. Traditional banking and trade are the most frequently indicated areas of BC applications by the respondents. The conducted research also shows that BC may be perceived as a tool for social/technology evolution and revolution. The survey results have important implications for universities as they confirm that university curricula are not updated sufficiently quickly to keep up with the emerging technologies.

Keywords: Blockchain · Emerging technology · Education

1 Introduction

In 2008 Nakamoto [13] presented the concept of digital blocks connected into chains that might facilitate on-line payments in peer-to-peer networks, currently known as blockchain technology (BC). Blockchain is most commonly associated with digital cryptocurrencies. However, this technology has limitless possibilities of applications, as Casino et al. [3] described in their recent systematic literature review, that apart from financial applications include governance, education, privacy and security, business and industry, data management, integrity verification, and the Internet of Things. Despite the still growing interest of researchers that investigate the perspective applications of BC, the factual uptake of this technology is still low. According to Gartner report [7] only 1% of companies have adopted BC and 8% of companies are planning

M. Pańkowska and K. Sandkuhl (Eds.): BIR 2019, LNBIP 365, pp. 30–43, 2019.
https://doi.org/10.1007/978-3-030-31143-8_3

to implement some kind of blockchain based solutions in the immediate future. Besides, about one fifth of companies noticed that BC implementation requires new skills that are currently scarce among IT professionals. In view of the growing research interest in BC, a still low level of the uptake of this technology, and the arising need of IT specialists with the new type of skills, we became interested in the way information about emerging technologies is spreading among future IT professionals and how they absorb these technologies.

While there is a lot of publications that tackle different aspects of BC usage [3, 8, 19] there is a research gap concerning the perception of this technology by potential users, especially by technical students who are entering the professional world and will be responsible for developing solutions based on this technology. This was the main motivation for undertaking the current study, in which the main goal is to investigate the awareness of BC among computer science students. In particular, we would like to answer the following research questions:

(1) What are the main sources of knowledge for students of the blockchain technology?
(2) Are there any relationships between knowledge and usage of the blockchain technology?
(3) What areas of blockchain technology usage (other than cryptocurrencies) are students familiar with?
(4) What are the students' expectations concerning blockchain technology?

In order to answer the research questions, we developed a pilot survey that was distributed among students of Cracow universities. The analysis of the results provides useful implications for universities on how students embrace emerging technologies, although it should be noted that the results ought to be generalized with caution taking into account the preliminary nature of the research.

The manuscript is organized as follows. The next section presents research background followed by a description of the research method. Then the results of the survey are presented together with their analysis, discussion, and implications. Summary of the research is provided in Conclusion section.

2 Research Background

Blockchain belongs to "an emerging digital technology that combines cryptography, data management, networking, and incentive mechanisms to support the checking, execution, and recording of transactions between parties" [18, p. 3]. It can be perceived as a distributed digital ledger allowing only appending new transactions. A transaction is stored in the form of a timestamp block that is linked to the previous block in the ledger. To prevent changes in the blocks already present in the ledger, a block keeps information about its predecessor in the form of cryptographic hashes [18].

It should be noted that blockchain enables conducting transactions in a peer-to peer network without the necessity of involving a third party (the validator of the transaction) [6]. The transaction validation (that manifests itself in adding new transaction blocks to the chain) is performed using so called consensus mechanisms [3], e.g.:

- Proof-of-Work (PoW) – involves performing by an entity to be verified (prover) some computational operations, results of which might be easily checked by the verification entity (verifier) [11]. This mechanism is used for mining cryptocurrencies, e.g. Bitcoin,
- Proof-of-Stake (PoS) – in the context of cryptocurrencies it is based on the concept of coin age [12] or stakeholder wealth [18]. It requires much less computational power than PoW,
- Proof of Elapsed Time (PoET) – a random number generated by a node (i.e. "any entity that connects to the blockchain" [3, p. 56]) determines when a node can add a new block [4, 10]. Similarly to PoS, it requires less computational power than PoW and is fair in terms of facilitating the concept proposed by Nakamoto "one-CPU-one-vote" [13, p. 3].

Blockchain networks might be categorised into [2, 3, 19]:

- public – decentralized, permissionless, anyone can read, send transactions, and take part in a consensus process (an open network of nodes [18]). Examples: most cryptocurrencies including Bitcoin, Ethereum, Litecoin, Ripple [5, 13],
- consortium (federated) – partially decentralised, the right to read is public or restricted to participants, "the consensus process is controlled by a pre-selected set of nodes" [2]. Examples: industry and banking sectors [14],
- private – centralised, the right to read is public or restricted, transactions restricted to one organisation. Examples: databases.

The blockchain properties that are vital for its prospective applications include [19]: decentralization, persistency, anonymity and auditability. These are the key drivers in refining/updating/facilitating the idea of smart contracts proposed by Szabo in 1997 [16], i.e. automatic execution of contracts that by using BC can greatly reduce costs and time of transactions [6].

3   Research Method

The study was based on primary data of quantitative and qualitative nature. The research-based survey was conducted with the use of G Suit Google Cloud package which provides CSAQ (Computerized Self-Administered Questionnaire) functionality. The survey contained questions which represented a mix of closed-ended (including multiple-choice) and open-ended items. The open-ended questions gave the respondents an ability to express their competency or subject knowledge in the absence of a relevant answer. The collected answers from open-ended questions where the subject of qualitative analysis, while the rest were analyzed quantitatively. The survey questions relevant to the current study are presented in Appendix A.

The process of the survey development involved inputs from three external experts, who were asked to review a draft questionnaire prior to its distribution. Their feedback was essential in constructing the final version of the questionnaire and contributed to the overall accuracy, consistency and comprehensiveness of the research tool.

The answers were collected among the students of computer science majors at Cracow universities. The respondents represented various years of studies. The choice of respondents was subject to the main goal of the research which was to diagnose the awareness of new technology among computer science students. The survey was open for ten calendar days in April and May, 2019. Since the answers were collected electronically via a web-based application, the respondents were not limited to a specific time or space to provide their answers.

The starting point for the data analysis was to define the main criteria for the distribution of respondents in relation to BC. We developed two indicators:

- knowledge factor (KF) that captures respondents' technological knowledge connected with BC,
- usage factor (UF) that captures the use of BC solutions by respondents.

The knowledge factor was based on the answers to questions 3, 4 and 5 (see Appendix A). Question 3 answers were scored from 0 to 11 points, one point for every proper answer, question 4 answers were scored from 0 to 6 points, one point for knowing the consensus method and two points for being familiar with its mechanism, and question 5 answers were scored from minus two to plus four, the lowest value assigned to the worst answer, the highest to the best answer. The weighted sum of points obtained from questions 3, 4, 5 was calculated; the weight being one with an exception to question 3 to which the weight three was assigned because it was the most complex question. Finally, the achieved result was normalized and expressed as a percentage of the maximum value (i.e. 21). Based on the value of KF, the following three levels of the technological knowledge of the respondents were distinguished:

- low (L) indicating poor knowledge of BC (KF < 30%),
- medium (M) indicating an occasional/random knowledge of BC (30% $\leq$ KF < 50%),
- high (H) level indicating good knowledge and understanding of the technological aspects of BC (KF $\geq$ 50%).

The usage factor was assessed on the basis of the first item in the questionnaire. Since the most widespread and popular use of BC are cryptocurrencies, it was assumed that knowledge of particular cryptocurrencies, and in particular their use can be the basis for determining UF. UF was calculated as a normalized value of the sum of the points achieved by respondents (one point for knowing the listed cryptocurrency, two points for its usage, and additional two points for pointing out other cryptocurrencies) and expressed as a percentage of the maximum points available to achieve, i.e. eight. Based on the value of the UF, three groups of respondents were distinguished:

- low usage (L) covering respondents who have not had contact with cryptocurrencies (UF < 30%),
- medium usage (M) comprising respondents whose contact with cryptocurrencies is sporadic or narrowed to practically one cryptocurrency (30% $\leq$ UF < 50%),
- high usage (H) which includes respondents actively using cryptocurrencies (UF $\geq$ 50%).

In order to provide deep answers to the research questions we analyzed respondents' answers to their source of BC knowledge, known areas of applications, and expectations towards BC in relation to the level of their knowledge and usage factors.

4 Results

4.1 Respondents' Characteristics

The survey was directed to approximately 600 randomly selected students of Cracow universities, the majority of which studied at the authors' home university – the Cracow University of Economics. 98 students provided answers to the questionnaire items, which resulted in a 16% response rate. Due to the online form of the survey the participation in the survey was voluntary. Table 1 presents the respondents' structure. The vast majority of respondents were male; more than half of respondents study part-time; the majority of respondents are taking part in undergraduate majors.

Table 1. Respondents' structure.

Variable	No.	%
Gender		
Female	15	15%
Male	83	85%
Form of study		
Full-time	26	27%
Part-time	72	73%
Type of studies		
Undergraduate	61	62%
Postgraduate	37	38%

Table 2 shows the distribution of respondents accordingly to knowledge and usage factors. The highest percentage of respondents has low or medium level of BC knowledge. As far as usage factor is concerned, it is worth paying attention to the high percentage of active users (H), which does not differ much from the percentage of respondents who do not use cryptocurrencies (L).

Table 2. Distribution of respondents according to knowledge and usage factors [%].

Factors	L	M	H
Knowledge factor (KF)	39	37	24
Usage factor (UF)	48	10	42

Note: L, M, H – low, medium, high
levels of factors.

4.2   Sources of Knowledge

The distribution of respondents accordingly to sources of BC knowledge is presented in Table 3. In the column 'Total', the percentage of all the respondents who marked a source of knowledge in their answers is provided (multiple choice was possible) whereas the other columns present the percentage of respondents from groups L, M, H that indicated the listed source of knowledge.

Table 3. Knowledge sources [%].

Knowledge source	Total	Knowledge factor			Usage factor		
		L	M	H	L	M	H
Popular Internet portals	66	74	72	46	64	70	68
Television, radio or other media	8	11	11	0	13	0	5
Specialized industry-specific Internet sites	47	29	56	63	38	20	63
Papers and scientific briefings	44	37	50	46	43	80	37
University classes and lectures	10	11	14	4	17	20	0
Conversations with other people	59	63	56	58	66	80	46
Other	5	0	0	21	2	0	10

Note: L, M, H – low, medium, high levels of factors.

It is worth noting that direct interpersonal contacts (conversations with other people) are an equally important source of knowledge for all groups of respondents. What is noticeable, only 10% of all students marked university classes and lectures as a source of BC knowledge. At the same time, according to the criterion of KF, people with little or medium knowledge about technological aspects of BC derive their knowledge mainly from popular internet portals, while for people with high knowledge the main source of knowledge are specialized industry websites.

Taking into account the criterion of UF, it is worth noting that students that use cryptocurrencies (UF = H) much more often use specialized websites than other students, although they use popular websites as the source of knowledge with similar frequency to other groups of respondents. In addition, respondents that belong to high usage groups are less likely than students from other groups to use scientific sources or acquire knowledge from university courses, which would indicate their lower interest in theoretical or technological aspects of BC technology.

4.3   Relationships Between Knowledge and Usage

The distribution of respondents accordingly to KF and UF is presented in Table 4. The numbers in the table represent the percentage of all respondents that belong to each category.

Table 4. Respondents' distribution according to knowledge and usage factors [%].

		Usage factor		
		L	M	H
Knowledge factor	L	21	4	13
	M	20	4	12
	H	6	2	16

The results portrayed in Table 4 indicate that the respondents having low UF have rather low or medium KF, whereas respondents with high UF are evenly distributed among KF categories. The respondents with medium UF constitute only ten percent of the examined population. As far as the KF is concerned the respondents with its low level and low UF comprise the biggest group (21%). On the contrary, the group characterized by high UF and KF represent 16% of the examined population. The respondents with medium KF include approximately one third of the respondents' population.

Treating the UF and KF indicators as measures on the nominal scale, the χ^2 test was used to assess the relationships between them. Due to the number of observations with UF belonging to the M category being less that the required number of observations (minimum 5) [1, p. 179], in the analysis we omitted these observations. The results indicate the existence of a weak relationship between knowledge of BC and the tendency to use BC based solutions (for significance $\alpha = 0.05$ and 2 degrees of freedom, the border value of the χ^2 distribution is 5.99 whereas we obtained 8.06, with the Cramér's V equal to 0.3025).

4.4   Areas of Applications

Table 5 shows the distribution of students across the areas of possible BC applications (other than cryptocurrencies).

Table 5. Areas of applications pointed out by respondents accordingly to their knowledge and usage factors [%].

Area of applications	Total	Knowledge factor			Usage factor		
		L	M	H	L	M	H
Traditional banking	52	39	56	67	49	30	61
Insurance	19	3	31	29	21	10	20
Healthcare	19	3	19	46	17	10	24
Administration	34	11	31	75	32	0	44
Logistics	29	13	31	50	30	30	27
Trade	59	68	61	42	60	60	59
Education	10	11	6	17	13	0	10
Public transportation	9	11	3	17	9	0	12
Other	8	5	8	13	9	30	2

Note: L, M, H – low, medium, high levels of factors.

Almost 60% of respondents indicated Trade as an area of possible BC application. However, respondents with high technological knowledge (KF = H) indicate this area much less frequently. They also indicate other areas more frequently. This dependence cannot be seen in the respondents' distribution accordingly to UF.

4.5 Expectations Towards BC

To assess respondents' expectations towards BC we developed a questionnaire item (see Appendix A, no. 7), the goal of which was to get the respondents' view concerning possible paths of BC development. Students chose one of the three answers provided.

The first answer: "Public registers in various areas (administration, judiciary, science, medicine) where high level of confidence is desired" is connected with existing institutions implementing BC and as the result changes in society functioning. We called this path Social Evolution.

The second answer: "Creating of new values (concepts), e.g. cryptocurrencies which can have a revolutionary impact on the society" implies that BC will change social relations in a revolutionary way. We called this path Social Revolution.

Finally, the third answer: "BC used as one of many available database technologies utilized to solve specific problems in an innovative way" means that BC is reduced to just another IT tool. We called this path Technological Evolution.

Students' expectation towards BC's future applications in relations to their KF and UF are depicted in Figs. 1 and 2 respectively. Interestingly, respondents with a high knowledge of BC (KF = H) perceive it primarily as a tool for Social Evolution, whereas respondents with low knowledge (KF = L) see it as a tool of Social Revolution. The analysis based on UF does not give such unambiguous results, although also in this case, the expectations of the Social Revolution are lower in the group with high usage factor (UF = H) than in the other two groups.

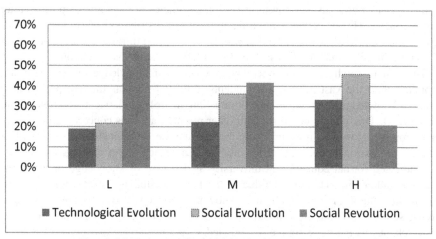

Note: L, M, H – low, medium, high levels of knowledge factor.

Fig. 1. Expectations of respondents towards BC in relation to their knowledge factor.

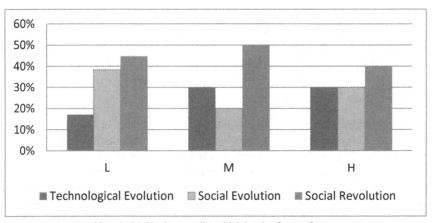

Fig. 2. Expectations of respondents towards BC in relation to their usage factor.

5 Analysis of Results and Discussion

The respondents' population was dominated by males, but it is not surprising as computer science belongs to a rather technical domain, and women's representation in this domain is still low [15, 17].

It is noticeable that the percentage of active users of BC is almost double the percentage of students with high technological knowledge, which means that ready-to-use solutions based on BC might be comparatively easy to use. The polarization is visible in respondents in relation to their BC usage; two groups dominate: non-users and those who intensively use cryptocurrencies. A relatively small percentage of respondents in the medium level of usage may result from the fact that it includes people who are either just starting to use cryptocurrencies or have given up usage after a brief contact. However, the approximately uniform distribution of students accordingly to their knowledge is noteworthy, with more than half of respondents interested in BC. These findings indicate that BC in general attracts students' attention.

The first research question concerns the sources of knowledge on BC. It is not surprising than the vast majority of students indicated popular Internet portals as a source of knowledge, at the same time diminishing the role of classic media (television, radio, press). This finding complies with other research analysis concerning the young generation [9]. However, it is surprising that despite the fact that BC has been present in the IT professional environment for more than a decade, the percentage of students who indicated formal education at university as a source of knowledge of this technology is rather low. This may be due to the fact that students of computer science, starting their studies, might already have known the concept of BC from other sources. Having some idea about BC (though not necessarily correct), they do not treat university classes as the main source of knowledge on this subject and perceive it as an auxiliary source. Interestingly, specialized web-sites and scientific publications play a very important role as a source of knowledge, especially within the group of students with high level of BC knowledge.

As far as the relationships between knowledge and usage are concerned (research question 2), the results show that within the group with high knowledge, a significant majority (2/3) are also active cryptocurrency users. Similarly, more than half of students with a low level of knowledge belong to the group of students who do not use cryptocurrencies. The results of the statistical analysis imply that there is a weak relationship between technological knowledge and the use of solutions based on a given technology. The questions about the direction of the implication remain open, i.e. whether the students with better knowledge of BC reach sooner for the solutions based on cryptocurrencies, or whether the students using cryptocurrencies deepen their knowledge about the technological aspects of the solutions used. These issues require further investigation.

Interesting results appear when analyzing data on potential areas of usage indicated by the respondents (research question 3). In the entire population, the most frequently indicated areas of application are Traditional Banking and Trade. Since BC is commonly associated with cryptocurrencies, which play a similar (but not identical) role to money, it means that this technology itself is still perceived through the prism of cryptocurrencies, which seems quite natural. It is worth paying attention to the distribution of responses in relation to the knowledge factor. Within a group with low level of knowledge factor, the two areas mentioned above have a dominant position and constitute over 60% of the areas indicated by this group of respondents. However, within the group with a high level of knowledge factor these areas account for slightly more than 30% of all indicated areas, and the most often indicated area is Administration. Besides, students with high level of BC knowledge point out a more diversified range of BC applications than others. Thus, the results indicate that knowledge of technological aspects facilitates understanding of the potential use of BC in other applications. This result is in line with the common sense knowledge that people who know more about a specific domain have broader horizons.

As far as students' expectations towards BC are concerned (research question 4), it can be noticed that the better knowledge of technological issues, the more restrained the expectations regarding the effects of implementing this technology. Such a result can be interpreted in two ways. On the one hand, one can assume that knowledge of the details of technology affects the formation of more realistic expectations towards it, but on the other hand, it can be explained that focusing on technological aspects may make it difficult to see the innovative potential of this technology. This result (duality in the educational process) should be taken into account when designing university curricula: it should be ensured that the innovative aspects are ahead of the technological aspects. In this approach, technological issues would complement students' knowledge rather than being the starting point for acquiring it.

Furthermore, it can be seen that people with greater technological knowledge tend to perceive this technology as another tool that may result in evolutionary changes in the society functioning rather than a revolutionary technology, which will change socio-economic relations in a quick and significant way. This limitation of expectations is reflected in the fact that with the increase in knowledge of technology, the knowledge of its limitations is also growing. In this context, it is worth referring to the previous analysis of sources of knowledge, which shows that people who are less familiar with technological aspects of BC are more likely to use popular internet portals that do not always present balanced positions in many areas, often focusing only on the most media-rich slogans. Hence, in this group the revolutionary changes caused by BC are expected. The situation is different in the case of the usage factor criterion. Data analysis based on this coefficient does not indicate significant differences between groups. In each group, the most common occurrence is the expectation of a social revolution, although even in the case of this coefficient, the most balanced distribution of responses occurs in the high BC usage group.

6   Implications

On the basis of the conducted research the following implications might be drawn:

- BC is still largely perceived through the prism of cryptocurrencies and universities should place more emphasis on other significant areas of BC applications that might be important for the future society,
- when designing university curricula, special attention should be paid to introducing the innovative aspects of new technology first and then moving on to technological details. This order ensures that students will get a big picture first without narrowing their perception of new technology just to technical issues,
- current university curricula do not catch up with changing technologies; they should be adjusted more quickly to provide students with up-to-date professional knowledge of emerging technologies; elaboration of methods for quick adjustment of university curricula to the changing technological environment is needed,
- taking into account the relatively low level of knowledge of BC's technological aspects, students should consider putting more emphasis on a detailed understanding of the technological basis, forcing a deeper understanding of the technology itself and perhaps a revision of their previous views on the domain,
- students should appreciate more formal university education as the one that sets a solid foundation for their further investigations of technologies.

7   Conclusion

The manuscript presents the results of a preliminary investigation into the perception of blockchain technology by computer science students. The authors developed the survey that was addressed to the students of Cracow universities. 98 students took part in the survey, mainly from the Cracow University of Economics. The basics for the data analysis were knowledge and usage factors calculated on the basis of students' answers. The main findings of the survey are summarised below.

Firstly, the students' main sources of BC knowledge are popular Internet portals, interactions with other people and specialised, professional web sites, the latter used mostly by students who represent the relatively high level of BC knowledge. Secondly, blockchain technology (especially cryptocurrencies) might be used without the technical knowledge. However, the interest in the technical issues might encourage the usage. Thirdly, despite the vast range of possible applications of blockchain technology, it is still perceived mostly in the context of cryptocurrencies and domains connected with finance. Finally, the knowledge of technical issues influences the perceptions of possible areas of applications, i.e. knowledge contributes to a more careful consideration of usage.

The main limitation of the current study is the lack of respondents' representativeness. We directed the questionnaire to the students of Cracow universities, however the vast majority of respondents who submitted their answers were from the Cracow University of Economics. Hence, the research might be perceived as local and the generalization of its results should be made with caution. However, in our opinion the research results and implications might be to some extent representative since Cracow is a huge academic and business center, with headquarters of companies that operate globally. Therefore, graduates of Cracow universities enter the global labor market and their knowledge is to some extent representative of the population of computer science graduates.

In future research we would like to extend our research to other universities, not only in Cracow but also in other cities in Poland, and to conduct a comprehensive analysis that would take into account other criteria (e.g. working/non-working students, full time/part time students) and investigate deeply the relationships between knowledge and usage of technology. Furthermore, we would like to analyze the content of the courses taken by students in relation to their knowledge and usage factors. Besides, a comparison of results with other studies concerning students' awareness of technologies might also comprise a promising path for future research.

Acknowledgments. This research has been financed by the funds granted to the Faculty of Management, Cracow University of Economics, Poland, within the subsidy for maintaining research potential.

A. Appendix: Questionnaire (Translated into English)

1. Blockchain technology (BC) is most often associated with the concept of cryptocurrency. Mark one of the following three options against each item: *I do not know; I know; I have used it.*

   Bitcoin; Ethereum; Ripple; Other (please specify)

2. Mark the main sources of information concerning blockchain technology.

   Popular Internet portals; Television, radio or other media; Specialized industry-specific Internet sites; Papers and scientific briefings; University classes and lectures; Conversations with other people; Other (please specify)

3. To what extent do the following sentences fit your perception of blockchain technology? Mark one of the following three options against each item: *Not applicable to BC; Applicable to BC but not crucial; Crucial for BC.*

It is a distributed system; It is a database; It is a register that resembles an accounting book; Used for cryptocurrency transaction processing; Thanks to cryptography the operations are anonymous; Thanks to cryptography data are persistent; Enables databases with a high level of security; Ensures complete data security; Enables data processing with a higher efficiency than that of traditional methods; Thanks to cryptography frauds are not a threat; Used for processing of banking transactions

4. In the concept of BC, saving the content requires its authorization by specific instances. This authorization is based on various algorithms of the so-called consensus. Indicate which of the approaches listed below are familiar to you and to what extent. Mark one of the following three options against each item: *Not familiar; Familiar but I have not analyzed its mechanism; Familiar with its algorithm.*

PoW (Proof of Work); PoS (Proof of Stake); PoET (Proof of Elapsed Time); Other (please specify)

5. Mark the best description of the BC application for content storage.

Can use any database (including commercially available databases, e.g. relational databases); Requires tailored, dedicated database systems customized to its specific forms of collected and stored content; Does not utilize database systems at all, because it relies on other solutions; I do not know how content is stored in BC

6. Indicate which areas of BC applications other than cryptocurrencies you have heard of. Indicate one or more options:

Traditional banking; Insurance; Healthcare; Administration (central, local); Logistics; Trade; Education; Public transportation; Other (please specify)

7. Which of the BC applications are the most promising according to you?

Public registers in various areas (administration, judiciary, science, medicine) where high level of confidence is desired; Creating of new values (concepts), e.g. cryptocurrencies which can have a revolutionary impact on the society; BC used as one of many available database technologies utilized to solve specific problems in an innovative way; Other (please specify)

8. Characteristics of the respondent

Gender (male/female); Form of study (full-time/part-time); Type of studies (undergraduate, postgraduate)

References

1. Balcerowicz-Szkutnik, M., Sojka, E., Szkutnik, W.: Wnioskowanie statystyczne w przykładach i zadaniach. Wydawnictwo Uniwersytetu Ekonomicznego w Katowicach, Katowice (2016)
2. Buterin, V.: On Public and Private Blockchains (2015). https://blog.ethereum.org/2015/08/07/on-public-and-private-blockchains/. Accessed 30 Apr 2019
3. Casino, F., Dasaklis, T.K., Patsakis, C.: A systematic literature review of blockchain-based applications: current status, classification and open issues. Telematics Inform. **36**, 55–81 (2019)
4. Chen, L., Xu, L., Shah, N., Gao, Z., Lu, Y., Shi, W.: On security analysis of proof-of-elapsed-time (PoET). In: Spirakis, P., Tsigas, P. (eds.) SSS 2017. LNCS, vol. 10616, pp. 282–297. Springer, Cham (2017). https://doi.org/10.1007/978-3-319-69084-1_19
5. Cofnas, A.: Cryptocurrencies. Planet Forex, pp. 79–89. Springer, Cham (2018). https://doi.org/10.1007/978-3-319-92913-2_7
6. Corrales, M., Fenwick, M., Haapio, H.: Digital technologies, legal design and the future of the legal profession. In: Corrales, M., Fenwick, M., Haapio, H. (eds.) Legal Tech, Smart Contracts and Blockchain. PLBI, pp. 1–15. Springer, Singapore (2019). https://doi.org/10.1007/978-981-13-6086-2_1
7. Gartner report, May 2018. https://www.gartner.com/en/newsroom/press-releases/2018-05-03-gartner-survey-reveals-the-scarcity-of-current-blockchain-developments. Accessed 30 Apr 2019
8. Girasa, R.: Technology underlying cryptocurrencies and types of cryptocurrencies. Regulation of Cryptocurrencies and Blockchain Technologies. PSFST, pp. 29–56. Springer, Cham (2018). https://doi.org/10.1007/978-3-319-78509-7_2
9. Gyan, P.Y., Rai, J.: The generation Z and their social media usage: a review and a research outline. Global J. Enterp. Inf. Syst. **9**(2), 110–116 (2017)
10. Intel: Sawtooth Lake (2017). https://intelledger.github.io/. Accessed 06 May 2019
11. Jakobsson, M., Juels, A.: Proofs of work and bread pudding protocols (extended abstract). In: Preneel, B. (ed.) Secure Information Networks. ITIFIP, vol. 23, pp. 258–272. Springer, Boston, MA (1999). https://doi.org/10.1007/978-0-387-35568-9_18
12. King, S., Nadal, S.: PPcoin: peer-to-peer crypto-currency with proof-of-stake. Self-published paper, 19 August 2012
13. Nakamoto, S.: Bitcoin: A Peer-to-Peer Electronic Cash System (2008)
14. R3, Building the new operating system for financial markets (2015). https://www.r3.com. Accessed 30 Apr 2019
15. Shein, E.: Broadening the path for women in STEM: organizations work to ad-dress 'a notable absence of women in the field. Commun. ACM **61**(8), 19–21 (2018)
16. Szabo, N.: The idea of smart contracts. Nick Szabo's Papers and Concise Tutorials, vol. 6 (1997)
17. Vardi, M.Y.: How we lost the women in computing. Commun. ACM **61**(5), 9 (2018)
18. Xu, X., Weber, I., Staples, M.: Architecture for blockchain applications. Springer, Cham (2019). https://doi.org/10.1007/978-3-030-03035-3
19. Zheng, Z., Xie, S., Dai, H.N., Chen, X., Wang, H.: Blockchain challenges and opportunities: a survey. Int. J. Web Grid Serv. **14**(4), 352–375 (2018)

Researching Participatory Modeling Sessions: An Experimental Study on the Influence of Evaluation Potential and the Opportunity to Draw Oneself

Anne Gutschmidt[(✉)], Valentina Sauer, Marvin Schönwälder, and Tom Szilagyi

Computer Science Department, University of Rostock, 18059 Rostock, Germany
`anne.gutschmidt@uni-rostock.de`

Abstract. This paper deals with the question of how participatory enterprise modeling sessions should be implemented such that participants feel that they own and identify themselves with the models. We present an experiment about the following conditions: (1) the participants were either asked to draw the model themselves or a tool operator took on that task, and (2) the participants were either introduced to a secretary keeping a protocol of their individual contributions or they were not. Our results indicate that neither participation nor the feeling that the model is "mine" is influenced by the conditions. However, participants who did not model themselves showed higher identification with the model. The study gives hint that we should not overestimate the value of stakeholders physically modeling themselves.

Keywords: Participatory enterprise modeling · Experiment · Psychological ownership · Identification with models

1 Introduction

Digitalization requires companies to constantly reconsider their business and their goals. Enterprise modeling helps companies creating an overview of their business including goals, requirements, structures and processes. Thus, it facilitates the planning of future changes [33]. Goal modeling as part of enterprise modeling requires brainstorming and discussing about a company's goals, and problems which might hinder the accomplishment of these goals. Participatory modeling seems particularly well-suited for such tasks. Its idea is to let stakeholders actively take part in modeling activities following a concept of democratic decision making. That way, stakeholders can directly contribute to the creation of models which will at best lead to higher commitment to the models and greater support of implementing the ideas and goals suggested by the models [33,36].

In the context of enterprise modeling, digital tools are getting more and more attention. In particular, the multi-touch table allows several persons to model at the same time while its use appears to be very intuitive [15,16]. However,

M. Pańkowska and K. Sandkuhl (Eds.): BIR 2019, LNBIP 365, pp. 44–58, 2019.
https://doi.org/10.1007/978-3-030-31143-8_4

existing studies of team modeling at the multi-touch table have mainly focused on the balance of the team members' contributions in terms of discussing and physical modeling [6,11,32] giving the impression that balanced contributions represent an ideal state.

This raises the question whether it is indeed necessary that members of a modeling team discuss and draw and write to the same extent in order to make the modeling process successful. The second question is how the participants' behavior could be influenced such that they contribute more when they would maybe have acted more passively? Participatory enterprise modeling is usually supported by (1) a facilitator, assisting with his or her modeling expertise in the discussion and modeling process, (2) a tool operator who helps digitizing the model, and (3) a secretary who keeps a protocol of the whole decision process [33]. These persons may have an impact on the participants' behavior and motivation. In this paper, we concentrate on the latter two roles. The tool operator may take over the burden of correctly applying a modeling notation and handling a (software) tool. Nevertheless, the tool operator may also take away the possibility to directly input ideas and to get acquainted with the model more closely. In this paper, we particularly investigate the impact of being able to model oneself on the identification with the final model and on feeling that one owns the model, following works on the extended self [7,23] and psychological ownership [3,27,29]. Both constructs have been shown to play a role in positive behaviors, such as extra-role behavior, and attitudes, such as affective commitment. Such consequences would all be desirable in the context of enterprise modeling. Furthermore, we emphasize the role of the secretary with regard to his or her being able to evaluate individual contributions. This may motivate participants to expend more effort. This reasoning is based on studies that have shown that the possibility to evaluate one's performance mitigates the effect of social loafing, a frequently observed reduction of motivation in group work [17,21].

We conducted an experiment with 25 teams of three persons where we manipulated the possibility to draw oneself and the potential of individual participation evaluation. Either a tool operator drew the model alone or the participants modeled themselves, and either a secretary was introduced who was openly taking notes of the individuals' contributions or there was no secretary. We measured participation in terms of time spent on discussing and modeling, identification with and psychological ownership of the final model.

In Sect. 2, we will present a review on group work, psychological ownership, extended self and identification leading to our hypotheses. In Sect. 3, we will describe our method, followed by our results in Sect. 4. We conclude our paper with a discussion of the results, limitations and implications of our study.

2   Theories and State of Research

2.1   Group Work

When we work in groups we usually expect to do a better job than we would do alone. Physical and/or mental power of many individuals is joined presumably resulting in better performance.

Working in groups, however, may not always result in better performance. Performance loss may be caused by difficulties regarding coordination (e.g. we have to hear somebody out before we may speak and voice our own thoughts and ideas), by cognitive restraint (others voicing their ideas and waiting to hear them out may disrupt our own train of thought), or by reduction in motivation. Social loafing is an example of reduced motivation. In contrast to similar effects such as free riding [14,20], social loafers are probably not aware that they expend less effort on a task when they work in a group than when working alone [39]. This effect usually occurs in group tasks where individual contributions are pooled in one final group result and can thus no longer be retraced to the respective originator [21]. According to a meta-analysis by [21], evaluation potential turned out to be most effective in mitigating social loafing, beside task meaningfulness and expectation of co-workers' performance. Evaluation potential comprises (1) the possibility to identify individual contributions [39] and (2) the possibility to compare a performance to a standard [17]. The standard may be objective, e.g. how many errors should have been found in a text, or social, e.g. comparing one's performance with that of other persons or groups [18]. Those who evaluate a person's performance could be the experimenter, co-workers or oneself [18,21]. In sessions of enterprise modeling, a secretary is usually present to document the decision making process and connected rationales [33]. It is our idea to use the secretary as an evaluating party who keeps track of who contributed which idea or suggestion. This must be openly communicated to participants of the modeling session indicating that contributions can be identified for each participant and compared among them. Contributions refer both to speaking and modeling activities. Consequently, we hypothesize that persons will expend more effort on modeling (H1) and discussing (H2) when they know their individual contributions can be evaluated by the secretary than without secretary.

However, when a tool operator takes on the task of modeling, the participants might have to give more explanation of what should be modeled to their teammates and the tool operator. Thus, we hypothesize that there will be more discussing activity when a tool operator is present than without tool operator (H3).

2.2 Psychological Ownership

When we think of ownership we probably think first of ownership in a legal sense; e.g. owning a car, a yacht or a house. However, ownership can also be felt by a person although he or she does not necessarily legally possess the target of ownership, like the laptop or car a company has provided for working purpose. Moreover, the target can also be intangible, such as an idea [4]. [31] define so-called psychological ownership as "the state in which individuals feel as though the target of ownership or a piece of that target is 'theirs' (i.e., 'It is mine!')" ([31], p. 86).

Many researchers such as Pierce and his colleagues were mostly interested in employees' psychological ownership towards their organization [9,24,30,31] or job [25,27] as it is assumed to cause several positive, but also negative effects.

On the one hand, psychological ownership towards an organization or the job, respectively, is reported to have a positive influence on job satisfaction and organizational affective commitment (the desire to stay in a company) [3, 25,37,38]. Some studies also showed an influence of psychological ownership on employees' behavior in terms of extra-role behavior (citizenship behavior) [3,27,37,38]. On the other hand, [30] claim that psychological ownership may be the cause of negative effects such as employees not sharing responsibilities or information and territoriality [9,10]. In the context of enterprise modeling, we assume that psychological ownership towards enterprise models might lead to commitment and higher engagement for the implementation of suggested ideas.

Addressing the question of how psychological ownership emerges, [30,31] specify three so-called "routes". First, by executing control over an object we develop a feeling of ownership. Thus, the target of ownership must be available and should be malleable and flexible enough to change it. Second, by getting to know the target very intimately we develop a feeling of ownership towards this target. The more information we have gained on the target, and the more familiar we are with it, the more will we feel attached to it [31]. Third, a feeling of ownership will emerge when we invest time and energy on a target. Part of us will flow into the target by creating, shaping or changing it [31].

In an enterprise modeling session, a tool operator modeling alone might restrict the participants' control over the model creation process. By not being able to model oneself, participants may be deprived of the possibility to expend physical effort and to actively get to know the model. They cannot autonomously create, position, nor describe model elements. The tool operator always works as an intermediate, possibly creating distance between participants and model. Thus we hypothesize that participants who do not have the possibility to draw themselves will show lower psychological ownership (H4).

With a secretary being present, participants might be more aware of their own contributions which might again lead to higher psychological ownership. That is why we hypothesize that the presence of a secretary will lead to higher psychological ownership than without secretary (H5).

2.3 Extended Self and Identification

Possession and the self of a person are often considered as connected. This is also reflected in the need of defining one's identity through possessions as a major root of psychological ownership [29,30]. [19] claimed that it was difficult for us to distinguish between what is me and what is mine. [7] referred to [19] when he introduced the construct of extended self. According to Belk, our possessions help us to define our selves. However, the self is not only extended by material possessions. Belk's list of categories belonging to the extended self comprises "body, internal processes, ideas, and experiences, and those persons, places, and things to which one feels attached" ([7], p. 141). Belk states that the more we feel a target to be part of our extended self the more care and attention we will give to it. Moreover, studies have shown that identification, with a product or a social group, leads to affective commitment [1,8]. Affective commitment refers to an emotional attachment to a target including the desire to maintain the connection to the target [26].

According to [34], there are three ways to extend the self: (1) by executing control or having power, mastering or conquering, (2) by creating, and (3) by learning to know something. [12] speak of investing psychic energy in terms of time and effort as part of our selves which makes the target of our efforts eventually become a part of us.

Identification is often referred to in social context where it means the process of identifying oneself with a certain social group. E.g. organizational identification refers to employees' overall bond to an organization [13], already giving hint on its important influence on commitment. However, the identification construct has also been applied in the area of consumer psychology where researchers have investigated whether involving customers into the design or production process raised the customers' identification with the product leading to further positive effects [1,22,23]. Identification happens in a process where we compare the self with a target concerning values [23], goals, and certain characteristics [1]. When a customer is involved in creating a product, it will become part of the extended self and should thus reflect the person's identity both to the self and to other people. A product becoming part of the extended self will, according to [1], lead to identification with the product, represented by a congruence between the customer's self-image and the product's image [1,5,22,23].

In the context of enterprise modeling, participants of a modeling session feed models with their knowledge, ideas and thoughts. So, the model should both become part of the extended self and reflect the participants' identities to some extent. There should eventually emerge a congruence between the participants' identities and the model.

If participants are, however, hindered to draw the models themselves the feeling of extending the self might not arise as they might not feel completely in control of the creation process. Therefore, we hypothesize that the presence of a tool operator will lead to lower identification with the enterprise model than without tool operator (H6). A secretary who is able to evaluate individual contributions might lead to more engagement which might then result in more identification. Moreover, facing evaluation potential, participants might reflect more on their actual input into the model. So, we hypothesize that participants that are introduced to a secretary will show higher identification with the enterprise model than those participants of sessions without secretary (H7). Figure 1 gives and overview of all hypotheses.

3   Method

3.1   Experimental Design

In the experiment, we had two independent variables, the possibility to model oneself and the potential of evaluation. Thus, we used a 2×2 design (tool operator present vs. modeling oneself $\times$ secretary was introduced vs. no secretary). If a tool operator was assigned to the team, the participants were not allowed

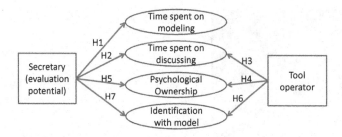

Fig. 1. Hypotheses on the expected differences caused by secretary and tool operator.

to touch the tabletop, at most they could point at interface elements. Teams without tool operator were supposed to draw the whole model on their own. If a team was presented with a secretary we explicitly pointed out that this person would document who made which suggestion in order to compare their level of participation afterwards. Each team was assigned randomly to one of the four possible treatments. The dependent variables we present in this paper comprise participation in terms of time spent discussing and modeling, psychological ownership and identification with regard to the final model.

3.2 Setting and Procedure

The study took place in a multimedia lab of the chair of Business Information Systems of the University of Rostock which was equipped with a multi-touch table the participants were meant to use for modeling. By using the multi-touch table we hoped to attract more participants. Our own studies have shown that multi-touch tables are equally suited as whiteboards for specific tasks such as creating small goal models performed in teams of three [15,16]. The multi-touch table was equipped with a software that was especially developed to be used on a tabletop. It is a model editor allowing users to create a goal model following the 4EM notation [33]. Several users can work in parallel on the same device with this software. Figure 2 shows a team interacting with the software, and a sample model in the editor.

The lab was furthermore equipped with a camera system allowing us to film the modeling session from the ceiling. In addition we used a second camera capturing the front of the team.

We arranged meetings for teams of three persons at the participants' convenience. Thus some of the team members knew each other before, some met for the first time. Each meeting started with introducing the participants to each other. To create a relaxed atmosphere, cake and drinks were offered. The participants signed a statement of a agreement which contained a description of the following procedure.

As most of the participants were not familiar with enterprise modeling, we presented them with a video tutorial about goal modeling in the 4EM method. 4EM is meant to be applied especially by non-experts of enterprise modeling.

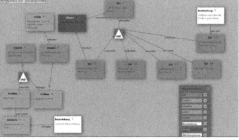

Fig. 2. A modeling team interacting with the goal modeling editor on a multi-touch table, and a sample model in the editor.

It is clearly structured and easy to learn. We chose the goal model as it is usually used as a starting point for enterprise modeling [33]. It uses colored rectangles representing goals, problems and restrictions which may hinder goals etc. These elements are connected via arrows representing relationships (see Fig. 2).

After the tutorial, the participants were each given handouts of the task and the modeling notation. The leader of the experiment was always present to assist when questions about the modeling notation arose. When a team was not allowed to model themselves, the leader of the experiment also took the role of a neutral tool operator. If only the tool operator was to draw, the participants were told to give exact instructions of what should be modeled, how model elements were to be placed etc. If no tool operator was assigned to the team, the participants were additionally given a brief introduction to the modelling software installed on the tabletop.

A second person, supervising camera and lighting, also took the role of the secretary for those teams to whom we pointed out that individual contributions would be evaluated. We told the participants that the secretary would take notes of who made which suggestion in order to compare their contributions after the session. Furthermore, at the end of the modeling, the participants were asked to mark the elements of the model to which they had contributed using differently colored snippets.

The teams had to create a goal model for a pizza delivery service. The text already gave hint on some of the fictitious company's goals and problems. The participants were furthermore encouraged to draw from their own experience and knowledge and add their own ideas. We used a time restriction as we experienced that not all participants were willing to spent several hours on the experiment. To keep comparability between the trials, we set a time limit of thirty minutes which worked out well in a previous study with a similar task [16].

After the thirty-minute session, the participants were asked to fill out a questionnaire comprising questions about demographic variables, tabletop and modeling expertise, psychological ownership, and identification with the model.

3.3 Measurement of Dependent Variables

In the experiment, individual participation with respect to discussing and modeling, respectively, were measured using the overall time spent on these activities while working on the given task. For this purpose, we used a software called ELAN [40] to mark the time segments in the video recordings of the modeling sessions where each individual had spoken or directly interacted with the tabletop software. In case participants were not allowed to model themselves, only the time spent on discussing was elicited.

Secondly, psychological ownership was measured using a scale by [37] which was translated into German and tested by [24]. As [37] investigated psychological ownership towards a company we had to substitute the term company by the word model. The scale comprises seven items such as "This is MY model" and "I feel a very high degree of personal ownership for this model." Two of the items reflected a feeling of collective ownership, e.g. "I sense that this model is OUR model." Nevertheless, [37] suggested a one-dimensional construct. Three participants did not rate the item "This is OUR model" leading to two less data records in the treatment group with only a tool operator and one less in the treatment group with only the secretary. A confirmatory factor analysis using SPSS Amos did not lead to satisfactory model fit with one factor (CMIN/df>2.5, RMSEA>0.1, GFI>0.9). Standardized regression weights indicated two factors separating items of individual (my/mine) from collective psychological ownership (our). Removing the two latter items, the confirmatory factor analysis lead to good model fit (CMIN/df = 1.111, RMSEA = 0.039, GFI = 0.974). The standardized regression weights were mostly greater than 0.6 except for two items with values slightly below 0.6 (0.55 and 0.57). Thus, we kept these items in the model. As the two removed items semantically reflect collective psychological ownership and reliability analysis lead to an acceptable Cronbach's alpha of 0.735, we consider both items forming that second construct. Collective psychological ownership could, however, not be included in a confirmatory factor analysis as the item number is too low for Amos. The scores for individual and collective psychological ownership were determined by calculating the mean value over the respective item values for each participant.

Furthermore, we assessed identification with the final model using a visual scale by [35]. It depicts two circles, one representing the self, the other one representing another target (the model). At seven distinct levels, the two circles are illustrated with different proximity, with the extremes of maximum distance and complete overlapping. The participants had to choose the level which best represented their relationship to the model. This concept of overlapping depicted in this scale is in accordance with the idea of extended self and identification as presented by [1,5,22,23]. Following the reasoning of these authors, the model should become a part of the participant's self leading to a congruence of the participant's image and that of the model. [2] used a similar scale in one of their studies.

3.4   Data Evaluation Methods

To test our hypotheses, we compared mean values in the treatment groups using two-way ANOVA with one exception: For the hypothesis concerning the modeling activity, a T-test had to be used because only the two treatment groups could be considered where the teams were in fact allowed to model. Except for modeling activity, heteroscedasticity was rejected by the Levene test for all variables. The T-test in SPSS, however, includes a correction for the case of inhomogeneous variances. Since we did not have hypotheses on interaction effects we may only explore the respective results.

3.5   Sample

On the whole, 75 persons, 36 women and 39 men, between age 19 and 54 ($\mu = 26.5, \sigma = 6.2$) took part in the study forming 25 groups of three persons. The numbers of participants in the treatment groups are shown in Table 1. 55 of the participants were students. We recruited persons from very different domains, such as biology, chemistry or philosophy while students or graduates of business information systems (13) and students of psychology (26) represented our greatest groups. In nine of the teams, all three members had not met before. In ten of the teams, the members knew each other before. In the remaining six teams, there was one unknown person working with two persons who had already met before. Experience with the 4EM notation and tabletops was measured with a five point Likert scale (1 no experience, 5 very experienced) showing average values of 1.4 ($\sigma = 0.9$) and 1.23 ($\sigma = 0.6$), respectively. Sixteen persons stated that they knew further modeling notations such as EPK, BPM, or UML.

Table 1. Treatment groups and participant numbers.

	No secretary	Secretary
No tool operator	6 groups/18 persons	7 groups/21 persons
Tool operator	6 groups/18 persons	6 groups/18 persons

4   Results

The T-test for modeling activity did not show any significant difference between the groups where a secretary was introduced and those without secretary ($T = -0.914, df = 30.406, p = 0.368$). Thus H1 is to be rejected. The results of the two-way ANOVAs are presented in Table 2. As can be seen, neither secretary nor tool operator did have a significant effect on psychological ownership (individual and collective) or discussion activity. Concerning identification with the model, we did not find a significant difference caused by the secretary. However, there was a significant effect of the tool operator on identification. Thus, only H6 was confirmed concerning a difference between the treatment groups, however, the difference was to the opposite of what we expected. Table 3 shows that identification with the model was rated more highly by those participants who were not allowed to model themselves.

Table 2. Results of the two-way ANOVA

	df	F	p
Time spent on discussing			
corrected model	3	0.553	0.648
Secretary (H2)	1	0.746	0.391
Tool Operator (H3)	1	0.543	0.464
Secretary * Tool Operator	1	0.256	0.615
Individual Psychological Ownership (my)			
corrected model	3	0.744	0.529
Secretary (H5)	1	0.833	0.365
Tool Operator (H4)	1	0.639	0.427
Secretary * Tool Operator	1	0.818	0.369
Collective Psychological Ownership (our)			
corrected model	3	0.935	0.429
Secretary (H5)	1	1.314	0.256
Tool Operator (H4)	1	1.390	0.243
Secretary * Tool Operator	1	0.083	0.774
Identification with Model			
corrected model	3	1.785	0.158
Secretary (H7)	1	0.619	0.434
Tool Operator (H6)	**1**	**4.749**	**0.033 ***
Secretary * Tool Operator	1	0.074	0.786

Table 3. Mean values and standard deviations for dependent variables separated by absence/presence of the two dependent variables.

Dependent variable	Indep. variable	No		Yes	
		μ	σ	μ	σ
Time spent on modeling (seconds)	Secretary	395.9	92.6	437.8	184.4
Time spent on discussing (seconds)	Secretary	474.8	176.8	434.7	198.3
	Tool operator	437.3	166.1	472.0	210.2
Individual psychological ownership	Secretary	2.5	0.9	2.3	0.8
(1-5 scale)	Tool operator	2.3	0.9	2.5	0.8
Collective psychological ownership	Secretary	3.9	0.8	4.2	0.7
(1-5 scale)	Tool operator	3.9	0.8	4.2	0.8
Identification	Secretary	4.3	1.3	4.5	1.0
(1-7 scale)	Tool operator	**4.1**	1.1	**4.7**	1.2

5 Discussion

5.1 Summary and Interpretation

We have presented an experiment where we tested different conditions in participatory enterprise modeling sessions. We investigated the influence of evaluation potential and the opportunity to directly model oneself on participation, psychological ownership of and identification with the final model. The two independent variables were manipulated based on the presence or absence of two actors that are usually suggested to take part in participatory modeling: a secretary documenting the participants' suggestions and ideas, and a tool operator taking on the task of manually creating the model. We hypothesized that evaluation potential represented by the secretary's observation and documentation would lead to higher level of participation in terms of modeling and discussion, and to higher psychological ownership and identification. We furthermore hypothesized that the presence of the tool operator would cause distance between participants and model resulting in lower psychological ownership and identification. Our results, however, show that most of the hypotheses have to be rejected. Only identification was significantly influenced by the presence of the tool operator. The participants who were not allowed to model themselves, identified themselves more highly with the models than those who could draw and write themselves. As interactions were not significant, we will not explore them any further.

Considering descriptive statistics, participants who were modeling themselves spent more time on actual modeling when a secretary was present. However, these participants tended to talk less. Modeling might require additional cognitive effort which might make talking at the same time more difficult for some participants. In contrast, participants with a tool operator might have talked more because they had to give exact instructions of what was to be drawn and written. On the whole, the behavior shows a high degree of variance in the participation variables such that no significant differences could be found between the treatment groups. We presume that the study setting itself, including the video recording, might already have caused the impression of evaluation potential such that the secretary did not add any motivation gain for some participants. This might also have lead to missing effects on psychological ownership and identification. It was our duty to inform the participants that they would be filmed, however, stressing the assurance of anonymity might mitigate the observation effect. We will have to do further pre-tests to find a setting that will better discriminate the effect of the secretary. In addition, task meaningfulness, another factor potentially mitigating social loafing [21], could have played a role, such that the participants generally did not find the task interesting enough, or motivational stimuli were missing, e.g. rewards or acknowledgement.

It seems that the tool operator did not cause the distance between participants and model we expected. Possibly, being able to tell somebody what to do might have increased the feeling of being in control. We also suspect that the instructions the participants had to give to the tool operator constitute a meaningful effort the participants expended substituting physical interactions.

These instructions also made their personal contributions more public. Parallel working was made impossible, all the ideas had to be processed in sequence during modeling. The team had the opportunity (or was "forced") to follow the whole creation process registering all the team members' input. Maybe this even helped in getting to know the model intimately. Presumably, as we instructed the tool operator to act strictly neutrally, the participants did not experience any loss of control over the creation process. All team members had the same chance to incorporate their ideas into the model. This might be the reason why psychological ownership was not influenced by the tool operator. Moreover, because participants were more aware of their own level of participation through public instructions to the tool operator, identification might have been higher. Their public instructions to the tool operator might have increased the feeling of control and consequently of extending the self.

Although we used a scale measuring overall psychological ownership we found the items to load on two factors. The descriptive statistics show that collective psychological ownership was generally higher than individual psychological ownership. [28] stated that psychological ownership may also occur on a collective level. It is based on the collective belief that a target or a piece of it is regarded as "ours" (not only "mine") and everybody agrees on this collective ownership. The routes to collective psychological ownership should be the same for collective psychological ownership as for individual psychological ownership, except that control, intimate knowing and investing the selves must be shared, and the members of the group must be aware of and agree on this [28]. Moreover, the target of ownership must be available, malleable and attractive to all members of the group [28,29]. [28] claim collective psychological ownership to have both positive and negative effects. They assume it "have a positive effect on several group-level outcomes such as pride in sharing, learning, effort, cooperation and productivity, and a negative effect on social loafing" ([29], p. 258). This provides us with another possible explanation of the missing effect of the secretary on participation. Maybe a generally high collective psychological ownership (see Table 3 with maximum value 5) already lead to a motivation level which could not be outdone with a secretary. In future studies, we will consider using a scale measuring collective psychological ownership in particular.

5.2 Limitations

Although we had a very heterogeneous sample comprising participants from very different domains, external validity is limited. A fictitious task was set in a laboratory environment. Nevertheless, we claim that experimental studies as ours are a prerequisite before expensively testing conditions in a real enterprise context. Our analyses have only concentrated on comparing the treatment groups. However, having the opportunity to model oneself does not necessarily mean that a person will do so. We are interested in scrutinizing correlations between, for example, extent of modeling activity and psychological ownership. Future studies may be improved by measuring perceived control, intimate knowing and investing the self to discriminate their effect on psychological ownership.

5.3   Implications

Facing the constant need for innovation in the age of digitalization, stakeholders represent valuable resources who should be involved in companies' idea creation and decision making. Our paper focuses on participatory enterprise modeling as a tool of stakeholder involvement, especially aiming at how they can be supported in the modeling process. We consider identification with an enterprise model and feelings of ownership towards models as desirable because we expect this will increase commitment to the model and the agenda connected with it. For example, assuming a model of a company's goals has been created by a team of stakeholder representatives, we expect that their identification with and their commitment to the model, and their perceived ownership will lead to higher dedication on implementing planned actions and reaching the goals contained in the model. The study presented here gives hint that we do not have to burden participants with managing a modeling notation or a software tool themselves. In fact we should probably not overestimate the value of drawing and modeling oneself. In participatory modeling sessions, facilitators and tool operators should neutrally implement the ideas of the stakeholders in the model. It seems that instructing a tool operator in front of the team has a positive effect on identification. If everybody had the opportunity to directly work on the model, this might lead to parallel working and consequently to less awareness of what others are doing and to reduced knowing of the details of the whole model. In future studies, we would like to explore more conditions of modeling sessions, e.g. the use of personal workspaces where participants may take notes of their ideas before the model as a whole is created. Moreover, we are interested in the overall effect of participatory modeling on commitment and psychological ownership towards the company, and the stakeholders' willingness to promote their ideas.

References

1. Atakan, S.S., Bagozzi, R.P., Yoon, C.: Consumer participation in the design and realization stages of production: how self-production shapes consumer evaluations and relationships to products. Int. J. Res. Mark. **31**(4), 395–408 (2014)
2. Atakan, S.S., Bagozzi, R.P., Yoon, C.: Make it your own: how process valence and self-construal affect evaluation of self-made products. Psychol. Mark. **31**(6), 451–468 (2014)
3. Avey, J.B., Avolio, B.J., Crossley, C.D., Luthans, F.: Psychological ownership: theoretical extensions, measurement and relation to work outcomes. J. Organ. Behav.: Int. J. Ind. Occup. Organ. Psychol. Behav. **30**(2), 173–191 (2009)
4. Baer, M., Brown, G.: Blind in one eye: how psychological ownership of ideas affects the types of suggestions people adopt. Organ. Behav. Hum. Decis. Process. **118**(1), 60–71 (2012)
5. Bagozzi, R.P., Dholakia, U.M.: Antecedents and purchase consequences of customer participation in small group brand communities. Int. J. Res. Mark. **23**(1), 45–61 (2006). https://doi.org/10.1016/j.ijresmar.2006.01.005. http://www.sciencedirect.com/science/article/pii/S016781160600005X

6. Basheri, M., Burd, L., Baghaei, N.: A multi-touch interface for enhancing collaborative UML diagramming. In: Proceedings of the 24th Australian Computer-Human Interaction Conference, OzCHI 2012, pp. 30–33. ACM, New York, NY, USA (2012). https://doi.org/10.1145/2414536.2414541

7. Belk, R.W.: Possessions and the extended self. J. Consum. Res. **15**(2), 139–168 (1988)

8. Bergami, M., Bagozzi, R.P.: Self-categorization, affective commitment and group self-esteem as distinct aspects of social identity in the organization. Br. J. Soc. Psychol. **39**(4), 555–577 (2000)

9. Brown, G., Pierce, J.L., Crossley, C.: Toward an understanding of the development of ownership feelings. J. Organ. Behav. **35**(3), 318–338 (2014)

10. Brown, G., Zhu, H.: my workspace, not yours: the impact of psychological ownership and territoriality in organizations. J. Environ. Psychol. **48**, 54–64 (2016)

11. Buisine, S., Besacier, G., Aoussat, A., Vernier, F.: How do interactive tabletop systems influence collaboration? Comput. Hum. Behav. **28**(1), 49–59 (2012)

12. Csikszentmihalyi, M., Halton, E.: The Meaning of Things: Domestic Symbols and the Self. Cambridge University Press, Cambridge (1981)

13. van Dick, R.: Commitment und Identifikation mit Organisationen. Hogrefe Verlag (2004)

14. Drewes, S., Schultze, T., Schulz-Hardt, S.: Sozialpsychologie - Interaktion und Gruppe, chap. Leistung in Gruppen, pp. 221–244. Hogrefe Verlag, Gttingen (2011)

15. Gutschmidt, A.: Empirical insights into the appraisal of tool support for participative enterprise modeling. In: Proceedings of the 9th International Workshop on Enterprise Modeling and Information Systems Architectures, Rostock, Germany, 24–25 May 2018, pp. 70–74 (2018). http://ceur-ws.org/Vol-2097/paper12.pdf

16. Gutschmidt, A.: On the influence of tools on collaboration in participative enterprise modeling—an experimental comparison between whiteboard and multi-touch table. In: Andersson, B., Johansson, B., Barry, C., Lang, M., Linger, H., Schneider, C. (eds.) Advances in Information Systems Development. LNISO, vol. 34, pp. 151–168. Springer, Cham (2019). https://doi.org/10.1007/978-3-030-22993-1_9

17. Harkins, S.G., Jackson, J.M.: The role of evaluation in eliminating social loafing. Pers. Soc. Psychol. Bull. **11**(4), 457–465 (1985)

18. Harkins, S.G., Szymanski, K.: Social loafing and self-evaluation with an objective standard. J. Exp. Soc. Psychol. **24**(4), 354–365 (1988)

19. James, W.: The Principles of Psychology. Read Books Limited, New York (2013). No. Bd. 1

20. Jonas, K.W.: Sozialpsychologie. Springer-Lehrbuch, Heidelberg (2014)

21. Karau, S.J., Williams, K.D.: Social loafing: a meta-analytic review and theoretical integration. J. Pers. Soc. Psychol. **65**(4), 681 (1993)

22. Kleine III, R.E., Kleine, S.S., Kernan, J.B.: Mundane consumption and the self: a social-identity perspective. J. Consum. Psychol. **2**(3), 209–235 (1993)

23. Kwon, S., Ha, S., Kowal, C.: How online self-customization creates identification: antecedents and consequences of consumer-customized product identification and the role of product involvement. Comput. Hum. Behav. **75**, 1–13 (2017)

24. Martins, E.: Psychological Ownership in Organisationen: Explorative Untersuchung der Antezedenzen und des Entstehungsprozesses. Rainer Hampp Verlag (2010)

25. Mayhew, M.G., Ashkanasy, N.M., Bramble, T., Gardner, J.: A study of the antecedents and consequences of psychological ownership in organizational settings. J. Soc. Psychol. **147**(5), 477–500 (2007)

26. Meyer, J.P., Herscovitch, L.: Commitment in the workplace: toward a general model. Hum. Resour. Manag. Rev. **11**(3), 299–326 (2001)
27. Odriscoll, M.P., Pierce, J.L., Coghlan, A.M.: The psychology of ownership: work environment structure, organizational commitment, and citizenship behaviors. Group Organ. Manag. **31**(3), 388–416 (2006)
28. Pierce, J.L., Jussila, I.: Collective psychological ownership within the work and organizational context: construct introduction and elaboration. J. Organ. Behav. **31**(6), 810–834 (2010)
29. Pierce, J.L., Jussila, I.: Psychological Ownership and the Organizational Context: Theory, Research Evidence, and Application. Edward Elgar Publishing, Cheltenham (2011)
30. Pierce, J.L., Kostova, T., Dirks, K.T.: Toward a theory of psychological ownership in organizations. Acad. Manag. Rev. **26**(2), 298–310 (2001)
31. Pierce, J.L., Kostova, T., Dirks, K.T.: The state of psychological ownership: Integrating and extending a century of research. Rev. Gen. Psychol. **7**(1), 84–107 (2003)
32. Rogers, Y., Lim, Y.K., Hazlewood, W.R., Marshall, P.: Equal opportunities: do shareable interfaces promote more group participation than single user displays? Hum. Comput. Interact. **24**(12), 79–116 (2009). https://doi.org/10.1080/07370020902739379
33. Sandkuhl, K., Wißotzki, M., Stirna, J.: Unternehmensmodellierung: Grundlagen. Methode und Praktiken. Xpert.press, Springer, Heidelberg (2013)
34. Sartre, J.: Das Sein und das Nichts: Versuch einer phänomenologischen Ontologie. Philosophische Schriften]: [Gesammelte Werke in Einzelausgaben, Rowohlt (1994)
35. Shamir, B., Kark, R.: A single-item graphic scale for the measurement of organizational identification. J. Occup. Organ. Psychol. **77**(1), 115–123 (2004). https://doi.org/10.1348/096317904322915946. https://onlinelibrary.wiley.com/doi/abs/10.1348/096317904322915946
36. Stirna, J., Persson, A., Sandkuhl, K.: Participative enterprise modeling: experiences and recommendations. In: Krogstie, J., Opdahl, A., Sindre, G. (eds.) CAiSE 2007. LNCS, vol. 4495, pp. 546–560. Springer, Heidelberg (2007). https://doi.org/10.1007/978-3-540-72988-4_38
37. Van Dyne, L., Pierce, J.L.: Psychological ownership and feelings of possession: three field studies predicting employee attitudes and organizational citizenship behavior. J. Organ. Behav. Int. J. Ind. Occup. Organ. Psychol. Behav. **25**(4), 439–459 (2004)
38. Vandewalle, D., Van Dyne, L., Kostova, T.: Psychological ownership: an empirical examination of its consequences. Group Organ. Manag. **20**(2), 210–226 (1995)
39. Williams, K., Harkins, S.G., Latané, B.: Identifiability as a deterrant to social loafing: two cheering experiments. J. Pers. Soc. Psychol. **40**(2), 303 (1981)
40. Wittenburg, P., Brugman, H., Russel, A., Klassmann, A., Sloetjes, H.: Elan: a professional framework for multimodality research. In: 5th International Conference on Language Resources and Evaluation (LREC 2006), pp. 1556–1559 (2006)

Automated Formal Verification of Model Transformations Using the Invariants Mechanism

Boris Ulitin$^{(\boxtimes)}$, Eduard Babkin , Tatiana Babkina ,
and Arsenii Vizgunov

National Research University Higher School of Economics,
Nizhny Novgorod, Russia
{bulitin, eababkin, tbabkina, anvizgunov}@hse.ru

Abstract. The article is devoted to the problem of automated formal verification of modeling artifacts during engineering of digital transformations. Automation significantly increases the quality of model transformations since many manual errors are eliminated. However, the formal checking the correctness of such automation remains an open question. One more problem is the dependence of the procedure for checking the correctness of transformations on the modeling languages of the source and target models. In the article we represent the solution, based on the formalism of invariant checking, that allows modelers to formally test the correctness of model transformation regardless of a modeling language.

Keywords: Model transformation · Graph transformation · Model checking · Formal verification · Invariants

1 Introduction

Engineering of digital transformations became a highly demanded and challenging topic both for practitioners and academy. New flexible forms of inter-organizational communication leverage design of dynamically bonded organizational bodies. Fractal organizations [1] or autonomous distributed organizations (DAO) [2] give bright examples of such new organizational forms.

Apart from economic and social benefits such new kinds of organizations draw attention to new problems of decision support [2]. In the context of fully digitalized information landscape importance of resolving the issue of semantic interoperability during decision procedures cannot be overestimated.

Typical procedures of situation analysis and decision making involve multiple kinds of models which mimic different aspects of an enterprise. For better sensemaking and comprehension of the situation multiple model-to-model (M2M) transformations are frequently applied. Resent results show that even in the context of a traditional enterprise available formal methods of model transformations still need improvements. For example, works [5, 7, 10] demonstrate the insufficient level of formal verification during model transformations.

© Springer Nature Switzerland AG 2019
M. Pańkowska and K. Sandkuhl (Eds.): BIR 2019, LNBIP 365, pp. 59–73, 2019.
https://doi.org/10.1007/978-3-030-31143-8_5

That article aims at proposing a new approach to automated formal verification of model transformations, which includes a formal model and corresponding algorithms for verification. Application of our proposals should assist dynamically composed fractal organizations in the process of semantic integration and decision support. In comparison with other known results our approach brings several new contributions. At first, that proposed approach is automated and language-independent. Since we use the graph-oriented general approach and the corresponding transformation, it is possible to apply the algorithm of model transformation verification to any modeling (in general case, domain-specific) language. The second advantage is that proposed approach implements the mechanisms of invariants in the process of verification of model transformations, thereby formalizing it. Finally, the verification procedure supports the verification of direct, as well as bidirectional model transformations.

In the scope of our research we evaluated the models and methods proposed in the context of software engineering models transformations. The results of evaluation confirmed by the application of the proposed approach to the transformation from UML Statechart into Petri net models.

This article describes our approach and presents results as follows. In Sect. 2 we give main aspects of M2M transformations and define criteria for its verification. Section 3 contains the algorithm, applied for the automated verification of model transformation correctness in terms of the approach proposed. Section 4 is devoted to the application of proposed approach to the case of Statechart and Petri net models. We conclude the article with the analysis of the proposed approach and further research steps.

2 Background

2.1 Definition and Approaches to M2M Transformations

Before the analyzing the process of M2M transformations and its validation, the definition of them should be formulated. From the formal point of view, the basic concept of transformation definition is a production rule which looks like $p : L \to R$, where p is a *rule name*, L is a *left-hand side* of the rule, also called the pattern, and R is a *right-hand side* of the rule, which is called the replacement model (or the target model). Rules are applied to the starting model named the source model. From this point of view, the model transformation is a sequenced applying to the starting source model M_0 of finite set of rules $P = (p_1, p_2 \ldots p_n) : M_0 \xrightarrow{p1} M_1 \xrightarrow{p2} \ldots \xrightarrow{pn} M_n$.

Transformations can be classified as *horizontal* or *vertical* according to the direction. The horizontal transformation is the conversion, in which the source and target models belong to the same hierarchy level, for example, a conversion of model description from one notation to another. The vertical transformation converts the models which belong to different hierarchy levels, for example, mapping objects of the metamodel to domain model objects. In what follows, the authors concentrate on the horizontal transformations, implemented between different modeling languages.

Depending on the language on which the source and the target models are described, horizontal transformations can be divided into two types: *endogenous* and *exogenous*. An endogenous transformation is the transformation of the models, which are described on the same modeling language. An exogenous transformation is the transformation of models, which are described on different modeling languages [3].

Such separation is important since there are two main approaches to M2M transformation: *operational* and *declarative*. The former is based on rules or instructions that explicitly state how and when creating the elements of the target model from elements of the source one occurs. Such a specification mainly combines metamodeling with graph transformation [4, 5], triple graph grammars [6] or term rewriting rules [7].

Instead, in declarative approaches, some kind of visual or textual patterns describing the relations between the source and the target models are provided, from which operational mechanisms are derived e.g. to perform forward and backward transformations. These declarative patterns are complemented with additional information to express relations between attributes in source and target elements, as well as to constrain when a certain relation should hold. The Object Constraint Language (OCL) is frequently used for this purpose [8].

Many of the previous approaches already tackle the problem of automating model transformations in order to provide a higher quality of transformation programs compared with manually written *ad hoc* transformation scripts.

However, automation alone cannot protect against conceptual flaws implanted into the specification of a complicated model transformation. Consequently, a formal analysis carried out on the source and the target models after an automatic model transformation might yield false results, and these errors will directly appear in the target application code. As a summary, it is crucial to realize that model transformations themselves can also be erroneous and thus may become a quality bottleneck of a transformation-based verification and validation framework (such as [9]). Therefore, prior to analyzing the target model, we have to prove that the model transformation itself is free of conceptual errors.

Unfortunately, it is hard to establish a single notion of correctness for model transformations. In what follows we analyze existing criteria of M2M transformations correctness and choose the best ones for automated M2M transformation process.

2.2 Correctness Criteria of Model Transformations

When we talk about correctness of the model transformation, the properties are introduced, addressed by the verification of the model transformation. There are several works [5, 10] which introduce the problem of verification by defining the set of properties to be addressed. However, the contents of these proposals are mostly included and generalized in [11]. Based on this work, the following categories of properties can be identified: language-related and transformation-related properties.

Language-related properties refers to the computational nature of transformations and target properties of transformation languages. As introduced in [11], a transformation specification conforms to a transformation language which can possess properties on its own. In this context there are four properties of interest.

- *Termination* property, which guarantees the existence of a target model, i.e. that the transformation execution finishes for any well-formed transformation specification;

- ***Determinism (Confluence)*** property, which ensures uniqueness of the target model for a given source model and transformation specification;
- ***Typing*** property, which ensures the well-formedness of the transformation specification in terms of the transformation language chosen;
- ***Preservation of Execution Semantics (Dynamic consistency)*** property, which states that the transformation execution must behave as expected according to the definition of the transformation language semantics.

As you can see, these properties are mostly connected with the possibility of the transformation itself. From this point of view, they form the semantic requirements for the transformation correctness. In our case, during the analysis of the correctness of automatically generated transformations, the most interesting are termination, confluence and dynamic consistency properties. These criteria allow us to check not only the correctness of the constructed models and transformations between them, but also to make the procedure for such verification independent of the specific model description languages.

Along with this, syntactic criteria can also be entered. These criteria are represented by transformation-related properties, which can be separated into two categories.

- ***Syntactic correctness***, which includes ***Conformance and Model Typing*** and ***N-Ary Transformations Properties***, to guarantee that the generated model is a syntactically well–formed instance of the target language.
- ***Syntactic completeness***, to completely cover the source language by transformation rules, i.e., to prove that for each construct in the source language there is a corresponding element in the target model.

These properties are responsible for the correctness of the structures used to describe the source and the target models, as well as the transformations between them. Syntactic correctness and completeness were tackled in [5] by planner algorithms, and in [12] by graph transformations. Recently in [4], sufficient conditions were set up that guarantee the termination and uniqueness of transformations based upon the static analysis technique of critical pair analysis.

However, no approaches exist to reason about the semantic correctness of arbitrary model transformations, when transformation specific properties are aimed to be verified. In what follows, we describe the unified and highly automated approach, allowing developers to formally verify by model checking that a model transformation (specified by metamodeling and graph transformation techniques) from an arbitrary well-formed model instance of the source modeling language into its target equivalent preserves (language specific) dynamic consistency properties.

In contrast to related solutions (such as [4]) this approach can be adapted to arbitrary modeling languages taken from any enterprise engineering (and/or even mathematical) domains on a very high level of abstraction. As a result, the same visual notation (based on metamodeling and graph transformation) is used to capture the semantics of modeling languages and model transformations between them. Finally, the approach can be automated, during providing the transformation from the source into the target mathematical domain and subsequent generation of the model checking description to verify the correctness of the model transformation.

3 Proposed Approach

After the definition of different approaches to organize the M2M transformations and choice of the criteria of such transformations correctness, an automated approach can be described to formally verify the model transformation correctness of a specific source model into its target equivalent with respect to semantic properties.

In order to organize the automated formal verification of the M2M transformations, we have to describe the source and target models in a well-formed, strict manner. Such requirement guarantees the possibility to formalize the checking properties of semantic correctness of the transformation and generate a transition system in an automatic way.

Assuming a conversion between the two modeling languages A and B, to organize the automated formal verification of the M2M transformations the following algorithm have to be applied. This algorithm is a generalized and supplemented version of the algorithms described in [8] and [12].

1. **Specification of modeling languages.** First of all, as it was mentioned, both modeling languages (A and B) should be defined precisely using metamodeling and graph transformation techniques. For this, the approach described in [13] can be applied.
2. **Specification of model transformations.** The M2M transformation from A into B can also be specified by a set of graph transformation rules. It logically follows from the opportunity to represent any model in graph-oriented manner as a pair (E, R) of E entities and R relations between them. The rationale for the effectiveness of such a decision is given in [13] and [14]. It is important to note, that such transition to graph transformations is used to apply the automatic program generation facilities without affecting the independence of the verification technique in general.
3. **Automated model generation.** During this step, for a certain (but an arbitrary) well-formed model instance of the source language A is derived the corresponding target model by automatically generated transformation programs (for example, VIATRA). The correctness of this automated generation step is proved in [10].
4. **Generating transition systems.** At this phase, a behaviorally equivalent transition system is generated automatically for both the source and the target model on the basis of the provenly correct encoding presented in [10]. In our case we implement the transition system also as a set of OCL invariants, which state the correspondence between elements of the source and target models. Such definition of the transition system allows us to unify and automate the procedure of checking correctness of the model transformations and make it independent from the modeling language used. In more details the process of deriving OCL invariants from models' transformations is described in Sect. 3.2.
5. **Select a semantic correctness property.** After the definition of the transition system we should formulate the property of its correctness. For this goal one semantic property p (at a time) can be chosen in the source language A which is structurally expressible as a graphical pattern composed of the elements of the source metamodel. More details on using graphical patterns to capture static well-formedness properties can be found in [12].

6. **Model check the source model.** Since the property p of semantic correctness over the model A is chosen, we should check its appropriateness to the transition system derived. In this case, the discrepancy may be expressed in the following forms:

   a. Some inconsistencies detected in the source model itself (a verification problem occurred),

   b. Some informal requirements are not captured properly by property p (a validation problem occurred),

   c. The formal semantics of the source language is inappropriate as a counter example is found which should hold according to our informal expectations (also validation problem).

7. **Transform and validate the property.** Using the transformations system, the property p in the source language A is transformed into the property q in the target language B (manually, or using the same transformation program). Unfortunately, this vital validation step might not be fully automated, because it requires the participation of an expert, who proves that the property q is really the target equivalent of the property p or a strengthened variant.

8. **Model check the target model.** Finally, the transition system B is model-checked against the property q. The result of checking may be one of the following alternatives:

   a. If the verification succeeds, then we conclude that the model transformation is correct with respect to the pair (p, q) of properties for the specific pairs of source and target models having semantics defined by a set of graph transformation rules.

   b. Otherwise, the property p is not preserved by the model transformation and debugging can be initiated based upon the error traces retrieved by the model checker. As before, this debugging phase may fix problems in the model transformation or in the specification of the target language.

It is fair to note that the correctness of a model transformation can only be deduced if the transformation preserves every semantic correctness property used during the analysis. As a result, the procedure of verification of M2M transformation can be time-consuming. However, we leave the performance analysis beyond the scope of this study, addressing the works [5] and [12].

3.1 Defining Models Transformations Through Graphs and Invariants

Since the modeling language may represent an example of a domain-specific language (DSL), we assume to use a graph-oriented approach to the organization of model transformations, like described in the study [13]. Such approach is reasonable, since any model can be generalized as a set of interconnected entities in object-oriented manner with subsequent application of graph-transformations for its development or evolution.

Graph transformation (see [6] for theoretical foundations) provides a rule-based manipulation of graphs, which is conceptually similar to the well-known Chomsky grammar rules but using graph patterns instead of textual ones. From the formal point of view, any graph transformation rule is represented be a triple $Rule = (L, Neg, R)$, where L is the left-hand side graph, R is the right-hand side graph, *Neg* is (an optional) negative application condition.

In these conditions, the application of a rule to a model (graph) M results in replacing the pattern defined by L with the pattern of the R. From an algorithmic point of view, this means that we find a *match* of the L pattern in model M, check the negative application condition *Neg*, remove a part of model M, mapped to the pattern L and finally add new elements to the intermediate model *IM*, which exists in the R but cannot be mapped to the L yielding the derived model M.

Such mechanism is very close to the mechanism of finding inductive invariants, which describe the connection between components of two (or more) sets of objects and are denoted with inv_τ. For this type of invariants two types of specifications are defined, *next* and *inv*:

$$next_\tau.(p, q).F \triangleq [p \Rightarrow \mathcal{W}.F.q] \land inv_\tau.p.F \triangleq next_\tau.(p, p).F \land [\mathcal{J}.F \Rightarrow p]$$

Informally, $next_\tau.(p, q)$ means that whenever a transition is fired from a state that satisfies p, the resulting state satisfies q. Similarly, $inv_\tau.p$ specifies that p is true in any initial state and is preserved by every atomic transition. Therefore, by induction, p is true in every state. It should be noted that, since $[\mathcal{W}.F.q \Rightarrow q]$ because of possible stuttering $next_\tau.(p, q).F \Rightarrow [p \Rightarrow q]$.

According to the above definition, inductive invariant means, that there is a strong correspondence between elements of two sets of objects, which are connected during some relation (transformation). Such definition is very close to the relational approach for model transformation definition, when relationship between objects (and links) of the source and target language are declared. That results in the idea, that inductive invariant can be an effective mechanism for the definition of such model transformations and for the validation of the possibility of obtaining one model by transforming another.

In this case, graph transformation rules serve as elementary operations while the entire operational semantics of a language or a model transformation is defined by a model transformation system, where the allowed transformation sequences are constrained by a control flow graph (CFG) applying a transformation rule in a specific rule application mode at each node. From this point of view, the transition system consists of the operational invariants and can be associated with a subset $\mathcal{O}.F$ of $(\Sigma, F)^\omega$ of (in)finite sequences of states defined as follows.

An infinite computation $\sigma = \langle \sigma_0, \sigma_1, \ldots, \sigma_n, \ldots \rangle$ belongs to the set $\mathcal{O}.F$ if and only if

$$\begin{cases} \mathcal{J}.F.\sigma_0 \\ \forall i \in \mathbb{N} : \mathcal{W}.F.\{\sigma_{i+1}\}.\sigma_i \end{cases}$$

where $\{\sigma_{i+1}\}$ is the state predicate that evaluates to *true* for the state σ_{i+1} and to *false* for any other state.

Informally, $\mathcal{O}$ consists of those sequences of states that begin with an initial state that satisfies $\mathcal{J}$ (*Neg* negative application condition in our case) and in which each state has a successor in accordance with the transition $\mathcal{W}$ (*Rule* transformation rule in our case). The set $\mathcal{O}$ is nonempty because $\mathcal{J}$ is satisfiable and $\mathcal{W}$ includes stuttering steps.

Once the computations of a transition system are built, *next* and *inv* specifications are defined as expected:

$$next_{\mathcal{O}}.(p,q).F \triangleq \forall \sigma \in \mathcal{O}.F : \forall i \in \mathbb{N} : p, \sigma_i \Rightarrow q, \sigma_{i+1}$$
$$inv_{\mathcal{O}}.p.F \triangleq \forall \sigma \in \mathcal{O}.F : \forall i \in \mathbb{N} : p, \sigma_i$$

Informally, $next_{\mathcal{O}}.(p,q)$ means that, in any computation of the system, any state that satisfies p is immediately followed by a state that satisfies q. Although computations include stuttering steps, $next_{\mathcal{O}}.(p,q)$ does *not* imply that $[p \Rightarrow q]$. In the same way, $inv_{\mathcal{O}}.p$ means that any state of any computation of a system satisfies p. Naturally, $next_{\mathcal{O}}$ and $inv_{\mathcal{O}}$ are related in a way similar to the relationship between $next_{\tau}$ and inv_{τ}, namely: $inv_{\mathcal{O}}.p.F \equiv next_{\mathcal{O}}.(p,q).F \wedge [\mathcal{J}.F \Rightarrow p]$.

According to these principles, we can conclude, that validation of the model transformation correctness can be fully described through invariant mechanisms. Such definition can allow us to automate the process of formal validation of the model transformation, reducing it to verifying the presence of invariants of both types among defined model (graph) transformations.

3.2 Deriving OCL Invariants from QVT Transformations

Since we describe the model transformation using the graph-oriented approach (see [13] for more details) in QVT transformation language, the procedure to derive the OCL invariants need be implemented. Using the principals of inductive invariants, we need to describe the correspondence between different components of the source and the target models.

This is fully consistent with the concept of the QVT transformation language. In this language, a bidirectional transformation consists of a set of relations between two models. There are two types of relations: top-level and non-toplevel. The execution of a transformation requires that all its top-level relations hold, whereas non-top-level ones only need to hold when invoked directly or transitively from another relation [15].

Each relation defines two domain patterns, one for each model, and a pair of optional when and where OCL predicates. These optional predicates define the link with other relations in the transformation: the when clause indicates the constraints under which the relation needs to hold and the where clause provides additional conditions, apart from the ones expressed by the relation itself, that must be satisfied by all model elements in the relation [15].

Among all nodes in a domain pattern, one is marked as a root element. Definition of root nodes is purely for the sake of clarity, that does not affect the semantics of the matching process. When referring to other relations in when or where clauses, parameters can be specified, and thus it is possible to pass bound variables from one relation to another. Note that the bound objects received as parameters are necessary preconditions to enforce the pattern. According to these principles, when we talk about deriving the transformation system from the QVT transformation, we need to identify the invariants of both levels, Top-relation as well as Non-top relation to provide the whole consistence between the source and the target models. In what follows, we use OCL constraints to define the specific invariants of both types.

Definition 1: Let p be a top-relation with domain patterns $S = \{root_s, s_1, \ldots, s_n\}$, and $T = \{root_t, t_1, \ldots, t_m\}$, and $T_{when} \subseteq T$ be the set of elements of T referenced in p's 'when' section. Then, the following top-relation invariant takes place for the $S \rightarrow T$:

$$\mathbf{context}\, type(root_s)\, \mathbf{inv}\, p:$$
$$\left(\begin{array}{l} type(x_i) :: allInstances() \rightarrow forAll(x_i| \\ type(x_j) :: allInstances() \rightarrow forAll(x_j| \ldots \end{array} \right) \forall x_k \in (S \backslash \{root_s\}) \cup T_{when}$$
$$\mathbf{if}\, self.p - enabled(x_i, x_j, \ldots)\, \mathbf{then}$$
$$\left(\begin{array}{l} type(x_u) :: allInstances() \rightarrow exists(x_u| \\ type(x_v) :: allInstances() \rightarrow exists(x_v| \ldots \end{array} \right) \forall x_w \in T \backslash T_{when}$$
$$self.p - mapping(x_i, x_j, \ldots, x_u, x_v, \ldots) \ldots)) \mathbf{endif} \ldots))$$
$$\mathbf{context}\, type(root_s) :: p - enabled(x_i : type(x_i), \ldots)$$
$$\mathbf{body} : when\ and\ enabling\ conditions$$
$$\mathbf{context}\, type(root_s) :: p - mapping(x_i : type(x_i), \ldots)$$
$$\mathbf{body} : where\ and\ mapping\ conditions$$

Definition 2: Let p be a non-top relation with domain patterns $S = \{root_s, s_1, \ldots, s_n\}$, and $T = \{root_t, t_1, \ldots, t_m\}$, and $T_{when} \subseteq T$ be the set of elements of T referenced in p's 'when' section, and $P = \{a_1, \ldots, a_k\} \subseteq S \cup T$ the set of elements passed as parameters in the call to p from other relations.

Then, the following non-top relation invariant (a boolean operation) takes place for the $S \rightarrow T$:

$$\mathbf{context}\, type(root_s) :: p(a_1 : type(a_1), \ldots, a_k : type(a_k))$$
$$\left(\begin{array}{l} type(x_i) :: allInstances() \rightarrow forAll(x_i| \\ type(x_j) :: allInstances() \rightarrow forAll(x_j| \ldots \end{array} \right) \forall x_k \in (S \backslash \{root_s\} \backslash P) \cup T_{when}$$
$$\mathbf{if}\, self.p - enabled(x_i, x_j, \ldots)\, \mathbf{then}$$
$$\left(\begin{array}{l} type(x_u) :: allInstances() \rightarrow exists(x_u| \\ type(x_v) :: allInstances() \rightarrow exists(x_v| \ldots \end{array} \right) \forall x_w \in T \backslash T_{when} \backslash P$$
$$self.p - mapping(x_i, x_j, \ldots, a_1, \ldots, a_k x_u, x_v, \ldots) \ldots)) \mathbf{endif} \ldots))$$

After such extraction of the invariants from the QVT transformations, the correctness of the model transformation can be applied for solving two problems: (1) verification of correctness properties of transformations, that is, finding defects in them and (2) validation of transformations, that is, identifying transformations whose definition does not match the designer intent.

With application of OCL invariants both problems can be solved using existing OCL verification and validation tools for the analysis of model transformations. With these inputs, verification tools provide means to automatically check the consistency of the transformation model without user intervention. Checking consistency allows the verification of the executability of the transformation and the use of all validation scenarios. Other properties checked automatically by OCL analysis tools (e.g. redundancy of an invariant) lead to the verification of other properties, chosen as a correctness property, described in the previous sections.

4 Example: Transformations of Statecharts and Petri Nets

In order to show the feasibility of our approach in practice, we show its application in the case of transformation between UML Statecharts and Petri Nets models.

To do this, we will go through all the steps of the proposed algorithm, applying it to the specified languages.

4.1 Analysis of the UML Statechart and Petri Net Modeling Languages

UML Statecharts as the Source Modeling Language
The formalization of UML Statecharts was in details described in [7], therefore here we describe only a simple UML model as running example. In our case we analyze the UML models of a voting process which requires a consensus from the participants.

In the system (Fig. 1), a specific task is handled by several calculation units CalcUnit, which send their local decision to the Voter buffer (where decision is 'yes' or 'no'). The decision is considered accepted if all responses received by the Voter are 'yes'. At the final stage, the Voter notify all calculation units about decision taken (where decision is 'accept' or 'decline'). In what follows, we consider the system with two calculation units, that rather simplifies more general parameterized case.

Petri Nets as the Target Modeling Language
Petri Nets are often used to formally describe the dynamic semantics of the system. This popularity can be explained by the simplicity of this model, as well as the possibility of converting to other similar notations.

According to the metamodel of this modeling language (Fig. 2), a simple Petri Net consists of Places, Transitions, InArcs, and OutArcs as depicted by the corresponding classes. InArcs are leading from (incoming) places to transitions, and OutArcs are leading from transitions to (outgoing) places as shown by the associations. Additionally, each place contains an arbitrary (non-negative) number of tokens) [9].

Dynamic concepts, which can be manipulated by rules (i.e., attributes tokens, and fires) are printed in bold italic. The operational behavior of Petri Net models is captured by the notion of firing a transition. Example of algorithm for transition between is described in [7] and consists of four stages, which are responsible for applying the rules, adding new and removing unmatched nodes.

4.2 Defining the Model Transformation

Modeling Statecharts by Petri Nets
In this section we describe main rules, used to translate Statecharts components into the Petri Net model.

First of all, each state in Statechart is translated into a corresponding place in the Petri Net model. Using tokens in the place, we can identify, that the original state for this place was an active state. From this point of view, one token is allowed on each level of the state hierarchy (forming a token ring, or formally, a place invariant).

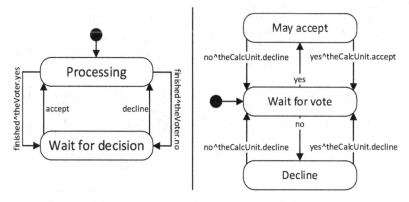

Fig. 1. Statemachines of CalcUnit (left) and Voter (right)

After the states, model messages from the event queues of a statemachine are translated into corresponding places. This stage of the transformation is not always straightforward, but we leave it out the scope of this study, assuming the approach described in [7].

Finally, each step in Statechart is transformed into a corresponding Petri Net transition. To do this, in fired transitions tokens are removed from source places (including event queue places) and new tokens are generated for all the target places and receiver message queues.

Applying previously provided rules to our Statechart, the following Petri Net can be derived (Fig. 3). In Fig. 3, for improving legibility, only a single transition (leading from state may_accept to wait_for_vote and triggered by the yes event) is shown. In this target model all original places of the Voter are replaced with the corresponding states and message queues for valid events, the initial state is marked by a token. Transitions have two incoming arcs as well, one from its source state.

Formalizing Model Transformations

In Sect. 3 we mentioned, that model transformations can be formalized using graph-oriented approach like [13]. Such formalization can be automated using special tools, for example VIATRA with a set of graph-transformation rules (in XMI or QVT) as its input.

The main element of such automation is the definition of inductive invariants, which establish correspondences between the elements of the source and target models. For example, in our case the following invariant for transforming Statechart states into Petri Net places can be derived (Fig. 4).

According to this pair of rules (Fig. 4), each initial state in the source model is transformed into a corresponding place containing a single token, while each non-initial state is projected into a place without a token.

Such triple structure of the invariants (and corresponding transformation rules) with reference elements allows us to organize the bidirectional transformations, that simplify the process of verification of model transformation correctness in the following stages.

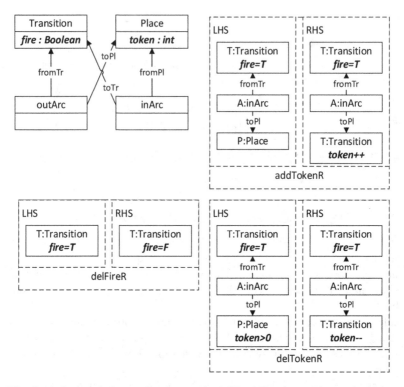

Fig. 2. A fragment of operational semantics of Petri Nets by graph transformation

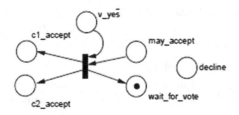

Fig. 3. A part of the Petri Net of the voter

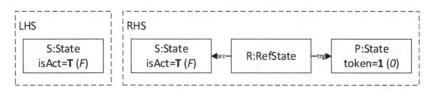

Fig. 4. Invariants for transforming active (*passive*) states into places

4.3   Verification of the Model Transformation

Generating Transition Systems

Transition systems are a common mathematical formalism that serves as the input specification of various model checker tools. In all practical cases, we have to restrict the state variables to have finite domains, since model checkers typically traverse the entire state space of the system to decide whether a certain property is satisfied [15].

In what follows, we use the SAL syntax for the concrete representation of transition systems. This system is derived automatically from graph-oriented definition of model transformations between source and target model using the approach, described in [5].

Formalizing the Correctness Property

Finally, we define the property, which is used to validate both source and target models. The only prerequisite for such a property is the ability to formalize it, that allow a designer to automate the validation process.

In our case the following property will be used for Statechart model. For all OR-states (non-concurrent composite states), only a single substate is allowed to be active at any time during execution. From the formal point of view, this property can be formalized by the following invariant:

$$\nexists O : ORState, S_1 : State, S_2 : State : subvertex(O, S_1) \land subvertex(O, S_2) \land$$
$$isAct(S_1) \land isAct(S_2) \land S_1 \neq S_1$$

Informally, it prohibits the simultaneous activeness of two distinct substates S_1 and S_2 of the same OR-state.

Unfortunately, this criterion is difficult to check in terms of the target Petri Net model, since both states, and message queues of objects, are transformed into places. In order to resolve this contradictory, the property can be concretized for the model-level, using specific states from our model. As a result, the invariant above will be re-written for all possible states of the original Statechart (Fig. 1), for example for states *wait_for_vote* and *may_accept* the following invariant is generated:

$$\neg(subvertex(O, wait\_for\_vote) \land subvertex(O, may\_accept) \land$$
$$isAct(wait\_for\_vote) \land isAct(may\_accept) \land wait\_for\_vote \neq may\_accept)$$

After this concretization we have three different, non-conflicting correctness properties, which are appropriate to be transferred to the target Petri Net model. Since the state hierarchy of Statecharts is not structurally preserved in Petri Net, the equivalents of the OR states are not projected into the target model. As a result, the corresponding property (see Table 1) contain only specific pairs of places having a token.

Table 1. Table of state transitions Petri nets.

Place	Place
wait_for_vote (token = 1)	may_accept (token = 1)
wait_for_vote (token = 1)	decline (token = 1)
decline (token = 1)	may_accept (token = 1)

At this point, we need to validate whether the equality (one) or inequality checks (more than one) are required in the property to be proved. We may conclude that checking equality is also sufficient.

As we mentioned before, constructing the pair of properties to be proved for property preservation is not always straightforward and cannot always be automated, since it requires a certain insight into the source and target languages and their transformation.

Model Checking the Target Model
At the final stage of the algorithm, taking into account the definition of Transition system *TS* with semantics defined as a Kripke structure), a correctness property p, the model checking problem can be defined as to decide whether p holds on all execution paths of the system.

Therefore, at this stage, the model checker is supplied with the transition system of the Petri Net model and the textual representation of the property q. As the places derived from the states of the same OR-state form a place invariant (with a single token circulating around), the model checker easily verifies even the strengthened property.

As a conclusion for our case study, the model transformation preserved the defined above correctness property for a specific source Statechart model and its target Petri Net equivalent.

5   Conclusion

In current research we demonstrated the model-level, modeling language independent and highly automated approach to formally verify the model transformations between different (in the general case) modeling languages. Proposed approach is based on the idea of finding invariants between entities of such modeling languages with the subsequent checking of them with dynamic consistency properties. Such consistency is a key element in ensuring semantic interoperability in the process of digital transformations. The ability to describe an enterprise from different points of view through consistent modeling languages allows stakeholders to achieve a single vision for the enterprise as a whole. Our approach can be one of the means to achieve such coherence. To demonstrate the feasibility of the approach, the case with transition from UML Statechart model into Petri Net model was analyzed.

In comparison with existing approaches like [8] and [10], which also use the ideas of automated model generation with subsequent correctness property checking, our approach doesn't depend on the modelling language and property chosen. Such independency follows from deriving invariants as stable logical structures from the model transformation rules. As a result, the verification procedure reduces to a simple check of two sets of OCL constraints between themselves.

Among the limitations on the proposed approach the state explosion problem may be noted. To resolve this limitation, we propose to improve the automated encoding into transition systems to improve the technics and extend it on larger scale model transformations.

References

1. Nonaka, I., Kodama, M., Hirose, A., Kohlbacher, F.: Dynamic fractal organizations for promoting knowledge-based transformation – a new paradigm for organizational theory. Eur. Manag. J. **32**(1), 137–146 (2014)
2. Heavin, C., Power, D.J.: Challenges for digital transformation – towards a conceptual decision support guide for managers. J. Decis. Syst. **27**(1), 38–45 (2018)
3. Mens, T., Czarnecki, K., Gorp, P.V.: A taxonomy of model transformations. Electron. Notes Theor. Comput. Sci. **152**, 125–142 (2006)
4. Degrandsart, S., Demeyer, S., Van den Bergh, J., Mens, T.: A transformation-based approach to context-aware modelling. Softw. Syst. Model. **13**(1), 191–208 (2014)
5. Bergmann, G., Ráth, I., Varró, G., Varró, D.: Change-driven model transformations. Softw. Syst. Model. **11**(3), 431–461 (2012)
6. Schürr, A.: Graph-transformation-driven correct-by-construction development of communication system topology adaptation algorithms. In: Schaefer, I., Karagiannis, D., Vogelsang, A., Méndez, D., Seidl, C. (eds.) Modellierung. LNI, pp. 15–29. Gesellschaft für Informatik, Bonn (2018)
7. Rahim, L.A., Whittle, J.: A survey of approaches for verifying model transformations. Softw. Syst. Model. **14**(2), 1003–1028 (2015)
8. Akehurst, D., Kent, S.: A relational approach to defining transformations in a metamodel. In: Jézéquel, J.-M., Hussmann, H., Cook, S. (eds.) UML 2002. LNCS, vol. 2460, pp. 243–258. Springer, Heidelberg (2002). https://doi.org/10.1007/3-540-45800-X_20
9. Bondavalli, A., Dal Cin, M., Latella, D., Majzik, I., Pataricza, A., Savoia, G.: Dependability analysis in the early phases of UML based system design. Int. J. Comput. Syst. - Sci. Eng. **16**(5), 265–275 (2001)
10. Küster, J.M., Abd-El-Razik, M.: Validation of model transformations – first experiences using a white box approach. In: Kühne, T. (ed.) MODELS 2006. LNCS, vol. 4364, pp. 193–204. Springer, Heidelberg (2007). https://doi.org/10.1007/978-3-540-69489-2_24
11. Amrani, M., et al.: A tridimensional approach for studying the formal verification of model transformations. In: Verification and Validation of Model Transformations (VOLT) (2012)
12. Hausmann, J.H., Heckel, R., Sauer, S.: Extended model relations with graphical consistency conditions. In: UML 2002 Workshop on Consistency Problems in UML-Based Software Development, pp. 61–74. Blekinge Institute of Technology (2002)
13. Ulitin, B., Babkin, E.: Ontology and DSL co-evolution using graph transformations methods. In: Johansson, B., Møller, C., Chaudhuri, A., Sudzina, F. (eds.) BIR 2017. LNBIP, vol. 295, pp. 233–247. Springer, Cham (2017). https://doi.org/10.1007/978-3-319-64930-6_17
14. Ruffolo, M., Sidhu, I., Guadagno, L.: Semantic enterprise technologies. In: Proceedings of the First International Conference on Industrial Results of Semantic Technologies, vol. 293, pp. 70–84 (2007)
15. Gogolla, M., Bohling, J., Richters, M.: Validating UML and OCL models in USE by automatic snapshot generation. J. Softw. Syst. Model. **4**(4), 386–398 (2005)

Multi-criteria Ranking Based on Joint Distributions

A Tool to Support Decision Making

Maria Ulan$^{(\boxtimes)}$, Morgan Ericsson, Welf Löwe, and Anna Wingkvist

Department of Computer Science and Media Technology,
Linnaeus University, 351 95 Växjö, Sweden
{maria.ulan,morgan.ericsson,welf.lowe,anna.wingkvist}@lnu.se

Abstract. Sound assessment and ranking of alternatives are fundamental to effective decision making. Creating an overall ranking is not trivial if there are multiple criteria, and none of the alternatives is the best according to all criteria. To address this challenge, we propose an approach that aggregates criteria scores based on their joint (probability) distribution and obtains the ranking as a weighted product of these scores. We evaluate our approach in a real-world use case based on a funding allocation problem and compare it with the traditional weighted sum aggregation model. The results show that the approaches assign similar ranks, while our approach is more interpretable and sensitive.

Keywords: Aggregation · Management by objectives · Ranking

1 Introduction

Making decisions is a regular part of everyday life. The average person makes many decisions a day, and it can lead to a phenomenon called *decision fatigue*, the deteriorating quality of decisions made by an individual after a long session of decision making [1]. For businesses, success is directly related to effective decision making. It influences almost every aspect of corporate life [2]. If done systematically, the decision-making process starts with determining relevant criteria and attaching weights to represent the relative importance of specific criterion compared to other criteria. It is followed by connecting numerical values to criteria representing the degree of how each decision alternative meets the particular criteria. Finally, these values are combined to determine the best choice. Ranking alternatives in an interpretable and well-defined way for several, possibly conflicting criteria is often a problem of critical concern [3].

Over the years several approaches for multi-criteria decision making have been proposed. Depending on decision maker is looking for an alternative which is the best in all criteria or not, approaches can be classified by three different scales, i.e., ordinal, cardinal or pairwise comparisons among alternatives [4]. For example, in *goal programming* approach decision maker is asked to express

© Springer Nature Switzerland AG 2019
M. Pańkowska and K. Sandkuhl (Eds.): BIR 2019, LNBIP 365, pp. 74–88, 2019.
https://doi.org/10.1007/978-3-030-31143-8_6

judgments in terms of goals, and focus on improving what (s)he considers the most important criterion until it reaches acceptable level of performance [5]. In approaches based on multi-attribute utility theory, *MAUT* [6–8] each alternative is given a score for each criterion. The *global score* takes into account all criteria and is obtained by aggregating the criteria scores. In approaches based on outranking relations [9–11] a so-called *preference degree* for each criterion is assigned to every ordered pair of alternatives. Then, a global preference degree is obtained by aggregating these preference degrees.

Note that for most of the approaches, aggregation plays a central role in the process. The main criticism of these and other decision making approaches is that they usually yield different results for the same problem [12]. It is called the *decision making paradox.*

Alternatively, a global score, preference degree, or ranking can be obtained by experts opinions. However, such an oracle is usually unavailable in everyday decision making and not even easy to obtain after when evaluating the consequences of a decision in a retrospective. Moreover, reasoning about and interpretation of scores, preferences or ranking obtained out of the box by experts in an ad-hoc manner is difficult to formalize [13].

Hence, there is a need to define an interpretable aggregation method in a formal way to provide a commonly understandable basis for decision making. To address this challenge, we introduce a weighted probabilistic product model, *WPPM*. It is a multi-criteria decision aid method for defining scores and their aggregation. We adapt the widely used weighted product approach for solving a multiple-criteria ranking problem based on joint distributions of experts opinions. In short, **the paper contributes** with **(i)** an approach to aggregate assessments of criteria of a decision alternative to a comparable global score, **(ii)** a mathematically sound and intuitive interpretation of this aggregation, and **(iii)** an experimental assessment of the accuracy and the sensitivity of the approach in a real-world multi-criteria decision problem.

The remainder of the paper is structured as follows. We provide the foundations in Sect. 2. We summarize related work in Sect. 3. We introduce the *WPPM* approach in Sect. 4. We evaluate and compare this approach to alternatives in Sect. 5. Finally, we discuss and conclude the results in Sect. 6.

2   Foundations

The philosophy behind the so-called *Management by Objectives* or *MBO* can be interpreted as measuring the work process against stated objectives [14]. Managers specify the objectives, and employees should achieve these objectives but are free to decide how to organize their work. However, *MBO* requires periodic objectives-oriented evaluation. Decision makers widely use the *MBO* model because of its simplicity and potential for systematic improvement. In simple words, the objectives are known from the beginning and should be measurable. Hence, the criteria for evaluation are defined, and it is clear how to compare and rank the alternatives for any specific criterion. Decisions grow in complexity when decision-makers should consider several criteria simultaneously. Criteria are assessed by metrics and indicators or are obtained from expert opinions. We refer to the process as *measurement* and the results as *metric values*. The aggregation of metrics, i.e., making them comparable and integrating them into a single score, is non-trivial and leaves options.

Mathematical models are widely used to explain aspects of some phenomena numerically. The degree to which an alternative satisfy a specific criterion can be expressed using probabilities. The probability density function, *PDF*, and its corresponding cumulative density function, *CDF*, provide a statistical overview of the assessed metric values of a criterion, modeled by a random variable X of this criterion. We use the *PDF* to find the probability that the metric value x of criterion X is within an interval and the *CDF* to find the probability for X to be less than or equal x, respectively. The *CDF* of a random variable X is the function $F_X(x) = P(X \leq x)$, and the connection between *PDF* and *CDF* can be expressed as $P(a < X \leq b) = F_X(b) - F_X(a)$.

3   Related Work

The degree to which an alternative satisfies a set of criteria can be expressed as a mapping between a set of alternatives to a measurement scale. Some studies suggested to consider *membership functions* of fuzzy sets of alternatives to express partial scores [15]. Dombi summarized the criticism of fuzzy decisions and proposed the *theory of evaluation* that suggests aggregation operators as an alternative to the fuzziness measures [16]. Yager [17] introduced weighted averaging operators, *OWA*, for reordering the alternatives before their aggregation. Saaty [11] used the simpler geometric mean instead.

Aggregation operators are widely used to aid in the decision-making process, and they can mainly be classified as a measure of similarity, weighted sum, and weighted product [18]. Ranking of alternatives obtained from aggregation aid in objective evaluation processes in different domains. Such a ranking can be obtained as a measure of closeness to the ideal alternative, used, e.g., for the evaluation of universities [19], companies [20], and knowledge management systems [21]. Rankings can also be obtained by Saaty's analytic hierarchy process *AHP* [11] used, e.g., for the evaluation of municipal solid waste facility sites [22] and sustainable chemical process design options [23] and many more. Note that *AHP* assumes criteria to be independent. This (often too strong) assumption can be resolved by applying analytic network process *ANP* [24]. Rankings can also be obtained by applying linear additive models. This has been used, e.g., for the evaluation of highway investment proposals [25], logistics suppliers [26], and banks [27].

In general, it is difficult to interpret such overall rankings, since these aggregation approaches compare and add values of different criteria directly, which corresponds to comparing and adding apples and oranges.

In this paper, we suggest supporting a multi-criteria decision-making process by ranking the set of alternatives based on numerical representations of performance and their joint distributions with respect to several criteria. Comparing

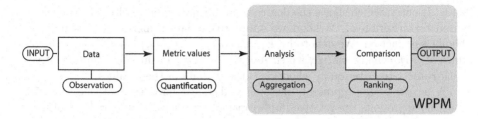

Fig. 1. Decision making process scheme

and integrating performances in different criteria is sound as we use probabilities instead of actual values.

4 The Assessment Approach

For this research, we assume that the metrics values of criteria are given. We consider a joint distribution of these values with respect to several criteria and assign a probabilistic score. This way, we aggregate the values of individual criteria into a global score. Once the global scores are computed, the alternatives can trivially be ranked by the score.

Consider a decision maker who needs to choose among a set of alternatives with respect to multiple criteria. Since a decision can be evaluated only if the decision maker's objectives are known, we consider the criteria as given by which performance in achieving these objectives can be measured. We rest on a well-known model of decision making proposed by Simon [28] and adapt it for multi-criteria ranking. The process is decomposed into four steps with specific goals, see Fig. 1. The first step is *Observation*, i.e., data collection for each alternative and criterion. The second step is *quantification*, i.e., measurement assigning numerical metrics values for these alternatives based on several criteria. The third step is *aggregation*, i.e., assigning scores to metrics values of each alternative and criterion and combining the scores into a global score for each alternative. Fourth, *ranking* compares different alternatives based on their global scores. Finally, as an output, the decision maker can find the best alternative and rank alternatives from worst to best. We propose *WPPM* as a method to aid in aggregation and ranking the goals.

4.1 Formal Problem Definition

We consider two different types of preferences in decision making: the decision criteria and the importance of each criterion.

Let $C = \{c_1, \ldots, c_n\}$ be a set of n criteria. These criteria are well defined and each represents a separate property. Let $A = \{a_1, \ldots, a_m\}$ be a set of m decision alternatives. Each alternative should be evaluated based on the criteria C. Measurements evaluate each alternative, quantified and represented as a $m \times n$ *performance matrix* of metrics values. We denote by $e_j(a_i)$ for $\forall i \in \{1, m\}, \forall j \in \{1, n\}$

an (i, j)-entry, which shows the degree of performance for an alternative a_i measured for criterion c_j. W.l.o.g, we assume that larger metrics values indicate higher satisfaction. We denote by $E_j = [e_j(a_1), \ldots, e_j(a_m)]^T \in \mathcal{E}_j^m$ the j-th column of *performance matrix*, which represents metrics values for all alternatives with respect to criterion c_j where $\mathcal{E}_j$ is the domain of these values.

A *weight vector* represents decision makers' preferences related to criteria. Each w_i represents the relative importance of criterion c_i compared the others:

$$w = [w_1, \ldots, w_n]^T, \text{ where } \sum_{i=1}^{n} w_i = 1 \tag{1}$$

We do not study how the metric values are obtained and nor how the weights are determined. We assume that they are provided by an appropriate measurement process and the decision maker, respectively.

4.2 WPPM: Weighted Probabilistic Product Model

For each alternative $a_i \in A$ and criterion $c_j \in C$, we define a score $s_j(a_i)$, which indicates the degree to which this alternative satisfies that criterion, i.e., meets the requirements for this criterion. Formally, for each criterion c_j we define a score function s_j:

$$e_j(a) : A \mapsto \mathcal{E}_j$$
$$s_j(e) : \mathcal{E}_j \mapsto [0, 1] \tag{2}$$

Based on the score functions s_j for each criterion, our goal is to define an overall score function that, for any alternative, indicates the degree to which this alternative satisfies all criteria. Formally, we are looking for a function:

$$F(s_1, \ldots, s_n) : [0, 1]^n \mapsto [0, 1] \tag{3}$$

Such an aggregation function takes an n-tuple of criteria scores and returns a single overall score. We require the following properties:

1. If an alternative does not meet the requirements for one of the criteria, the overall score should be close to zero.

$$F(s_1, \ldots, s_n) \to 0 \text{ as } s_j \to 0 \tag{4}$$

2. If all scores of one alternative are greater or equal than all scores of another alternative, the same should be true for the overall scores.

$$s_1(e_1(a_k)) \geq s_1(e_1(a_l)) \wedge \ldots \wedge s_n(e_n(a_k)) \geq s_n(e_1(a_n)) \Rightarrow$$
$$F(s_1(e_1(a_k)), \ldots, s_n(e_n(a_k))) \geq F(s_1(e_1(a_l)), \ldots, s_n(e_n(a_l))) \tag{5}$$

3. If the alternative perfectly meets all but one criterion, the overall score is equal to that criterion's score.

$$F(1, \ldots, 1, s_j, 1, \ldots, 1) = s_j \tag{6}$$

Analysis and Aggregation. We propose to express the degree of satisfaction with respect to a criterion using probability. We define the score function of Eq. (2) as follows

$$s_j(e_j(a)) = Pr(E_j \leq e_j(a)) = CDF_{e_j}(a) \tag{7}$$

In other words, this score represents a probability of finding another alternative with evaluation value smaller or equal to the given value. For multi-criteria case we can specify a joint distribution in terms of n marginal distributions and so-called *copula* function [29]:

$$Cop(CDF_{e_1}(a), \ldots, CDF_{e_n}(a)) = Pr(E_1 \leq e_1(a), \ldots, E_n \leq e_n(a)) \tag{8}$$

The *copula* function Cop satisfies the signature (3) and fulfills the required properties (4), (5), and (6).

We assume the criteria to be orthogonal, i.e., metrics values of different criteria are mutual statistically independent. Under this assumption, we can use a so-called *independence copula*, e.g., the *Archimedian copula* that can be expressed as product of the criterion scores of Eq. (7):

$$Cop(s_1, \ldots, s_n) = \prod_{j=1}^{n} s_j \tag{9}$$

Finally, we can take into account weight vectors (1). We propose to adapt the *copula* to be a weighted product of criteria scores. Weights represent dependencies in terms of the relative importance of a specific criterion compare to other criteria. This does not contradict the assumption of independence of metric values. We define an aggregation *WPPM* as a composition of criteria score functions as follows:

$$WPPM = \prod_{j=1}^{n} s_j^{w_j} \tag{10}$$

From a practical point of view, probabilities can be calculated empirically, and each score can be obtained as a ratio of the number of alternatives with lower than a given metric value to the number $|A|$ of alternatives. Hence, the overall computational complexity is $O(n \times |A|)$; scalability is not an issue.

We assume that larger metrics values indicate higher experts preferences. Note that it is not a limitation since we can use $CCDF = 1 - CDF$ instead if smaller values correspond to higher preferences for a metric. Note that *copula* function allows to combine an arbitrary number of marginal distributions, hence *WPPM* approach works for any number of criteria.

Comparison and Ranking. We consider one alternative a_l to be better than or equally good as another alternative a_k, i.e., experts prefer a_l or consider a_l to be an indifferent alternative compared to a_k with respect to the criteria set

C, if the total score according to Eq. (10) of a_l is greater than or equal the total score of a_k:

$$a_l \succeq a_k \Leftrightarrow WPPM(a_l) \geq WPPM(a_k) \qquad (11)$$

Aggregation $WPPM$ is defined as a composition of product, exponential, and CDF functions, which are increasing function. Hence, the score which is obtained by $WPPM$ allows to rank set A of alternatives with respect to criteria set C:

$$Rank(a_l) \leq Rank(a_k) \Leftrightarrow WPPM(a_l) \geq WPPM(a_k) \qquad (12)$$

The scores in the $[0, 1]$ interval are calculated empirically as fractions. Hence, we also need to consider the number of decimal places before rounding the results. For example, a notation $0.XY$, where X and Y represents numerical digits allows distinguishing only 10^2 different numbers. Thus, using the widely popular approach of rounding the results up to 2 decimal places can lead to misinterpretation of scores and false rankings. For a large enough amount of alternatives, $n > 100$ in the example, some alternatives can have the same result after rounding, while their actual scores are different. We suggest rounding the results up to k decimal places only if the number of alternatives $n \leq 10^k$ and, otherwise, to use a scale $[0, 100]$ of integers to represent the scores in percentages.

4.3   Decision Process and Interpretation

Consider a decision maker who is interested in a multi-criteria ranking of a set of alternatives A. (S)he defines a weight vector and is given a performance matrix that quantifies the appropriateness of alternatives according to the criteria on different scales. (S)he studies the distributions of metrics values E_j for all alternatives for each criterion c_j. (S)he sets, for each alternative $a_i \in A$, the criterion score s_j as the CDF of the distribution of E_j and the metric value $e_j(a_i)$. (S)he sets the total score as a weighted product of criteria scores and ranks the alternative in descending order according to the total score.

This $WPPM$ approach allows the decision maker to express the preference for an alternative as the probability to observe something with an equal or worse score or metrics values, based on all alternatives observed. Low (high) ranks correspond to high (low) probabilities. This interpretation is the same on all levels of aggregation, from metrics value to criterion score to the total score.

5   Evaluation

We evaluate the proposed $WPPM$ approach and compare it to the weighted sum model WSM. We compare the approaches in terms of interpretability and sensitivity. We measure the difference between rankings obtained by these approaches and study the agreement between aggregated scores.

We use a real-world case, a funding allocation problem provided by *Vinnova*.[1] We study anonymous data of the grant call *Innovative Startups*. While

---

[1] Vinnova, a Swedish government agency under the Ministry of Enterprise and Innovation https://www.vinnova.se/en/.

we do neither judge the goal nor the decision criteria of the call, we give some background for better understanding. The goal of the call is to test novel, high reward, high-risk ideas before companies become profitable. The call is open for new, small, and independent companies, and it gets around 600 application twice a year. All applications are assessed by at least three independent external experts appointed with relevant knowledge and experience, researchers from academia and practitioners from industry. The decision criteria are the following six: Gender *Equality* strategy, Will the *Team* able to execute? Does the composition of the team allow for new ideas? Does the team have adequate and sufficient knowledge, experience, ambition, and contacts/network? *Achievability*, i.e., how likely is it that the project achieves the promised objective? *Sustainability* potential, i.e., is the ability of the innovation to persist, *Economy* growth potential and competitiveness, *Originality* and innovation.

We decompose the decision making process into the following three steps: *Measurement:* each application is evaluated by experts, and the experts express their opinion (metric value) for each criterion. *Aggregation:* criteria scores are combined into a single total score, taking into account criteria weights. *Ranking:* applications are ranked by the total score.

We consider each application as an alternative to assess. We obtain scores based on the expert evaluations results for the criteria mentioned above. We formulate an objective as follows: the decision maker requires a well-defined and interpretable total score to be able to compare applications.

5.1   Dataset Characteristics

We study the data from one of the latest call, where 558 applications were assessed by experts according to six criteria: *Equality, Team, Achievability, Sustainability, Economy, Originality* using a scale 0–5: 0 - beyond poor, 1 - poor, 2 - fair but needs improvement, 3 - good, 4 - very good, and 5 - excellent.

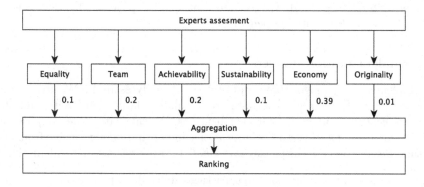

Fig. 2. Innovative startups call decision making process

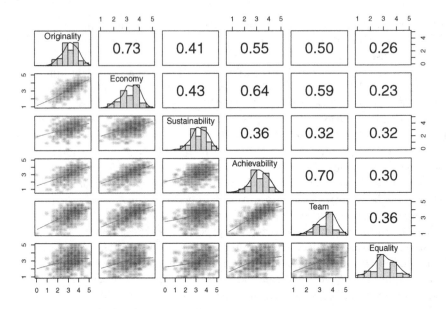

Fig. 3. Innovative startups criteria evaluations

Some criteria are more important than others. For each criterion the weight indicates its importance compared to other criteria as illustrated by Fig. 2.

For each application, the metrics of specific criteria are calculated as averages of several expert opinions on a $[0, 5]$ scale. We measure the pairwise degree of association between these values, i.e., how well a monotonic function describes their relationship. Therefore, we use *Spearman's rho* [30] as a correlation coefficient. We show how these values are distributed and their pairwise scatter plots in Fig. 3. We can observe that correlation varies from weak to moderate, but the sample size is not big enough to make any claims about possible dependencies between criteria in general. We assume that weights provided by the decision maker also regard potential dependencies.

5.2 Implementation Aspects

We implemented all algorithms and statistical analyses in *R*. We use the *R* package *dplyr*[2] for filtering the data to calculate relative sensitivity and the packages *ggplot2*[3] and *psych*[4] for visualizations. We calculate scores empirically as CDFs by using multi-thread computations and optimized algorithms from the package *Emcdf*.[5] We use the package *rankdist*[6] for rankings distance calculations.

---

[2] dplyr, https://cran.r-project.org/web/packages/dplyr/dplyr.pdf.

[3] ggplot2, https://ggplot2.tidyverse.org/reference/.

[4] psych, https://CRAN.R-project.org/package=psych.

[5] Emcdf, https://github.com/cran/Emcdf.

[6] rankdist, https://CRAN.R-project.org/package=rankdist.

5.3 Evaluation Method

We apply two models for multi-criteria decision making on to the dataset that leads to different aggregation approaches. In *WSM*, the total score is calculated by the weighted sum of metrics from the experts:

$$\mathbf{WSM} = 0.1 \times Equality + 0.2 \times Team + 0.2 \times Achievability$$
$$+ 0.1 \times Sustainability + 0.39 \times Economy + 0.01 \times Originality$$

In *WPPM*, the total score is calculated as the weighted product of *CDFs* of criteria scores calculated from the experts' metrics:

$$\mathbf{WPPM} = s_{Equality}^{0.1} \times s_{Team}^{0.2} \times s_{Achievability}^{0.2} \times s_{Sustainability}^{0.1} \times s_{Economy}^{0.39} \times s_{Originality}^{0.01}$$

Agreement. We measure agreement between total scores obtained by *WPPM* and *WSM* using *Spearman's correlation* and *Bland-Altman* statistics [31,32]. We study the correlation between *WSM* and *WWPM* to assess the ordering of the *WPPM* and *WSM* values, their relative spacing, and possible functional dependency. We put values of *WPPM* into *WSM* scale by using an non-linear exponential regression model.

Moreover, we calculate two rankings of the applications based on the two approaches by simply ordering the values from smallest to largest. We assigned the same rank for applications in case their total scores are equal. We measure a distance between the two rankings based on the *Kendall tau distance*, which counts the number of pairwise disagreements between two lists [33].

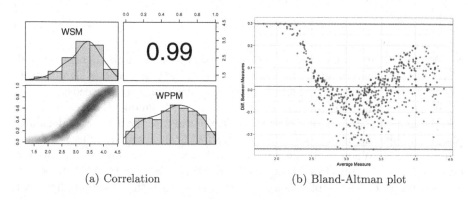

(a) Correlation   (b) Bland-Altman plot

Fig. 4. Agreement between *WPPM* and *WSM* total scores (Color figure online)

Sensitivity. We also study a variety of values for both methods to understand the percentage of applications that have the same total score and, as a consequence, the same rank. The *overall sensitivity* is the ratio of unique total scores and number of applications. We compare *WSM* and *WPPM* in terms of their *relative sensitivity*, i.e., the capability of one approach to a show higher sensitivity for a subset of applications that shares the same score obtained by the other approach. First, we consider the unique total scores for *WSM*. For each of these scores, we extract a sample of applications that share this *WSM* score, and set a *relative sensitivity* of *WSM* as the ratio of 1 to sample size. Then, we compare it with corresponding *relative sensitivity* of *WPPM*, which equals to ratio of unique *WPPM* scores to sample size. Second, we mirror this and start with unique total scores for *WPPM* and compare it with the *relative sensitivity* of *WSM*.

5.4   Results

We observe a strong correlation between *WPPM* and *WSM*, cf. Fig. 4(a). In the Bland-Altman plot, cf. Fig. 4(b), each alternative (application) is represented by a point with the average of the *WSM* and *WPPM* scores as the x-value and the difference between these two scores as the y-value. The blue line represents the mean difference between scores and the red lines the 95% confidence interval $(mean \pm 1.96SD)$. We can observe that measurements are mostly concentrated near the blue line $y = 0.007$ and only a few of them are close to the red lines $y = -0.265$ and $y = 0.296$, i.e., 95% of the differences are within a range of $\frac{0.296-(-0.265)}{5-(-5)} = 5.61\%$ of the possible difference range. The *Kendall tau distance* equals to 0.037, which means that only 4% of pairs differ between the two rankings. We conclude that approaches *WSM* and *WPPM* agree and may be used interchangeably.

Sensitivity. Figure 5 shows the *overall sensitivity* for different numbers of decimal places the scores are rounded to. We observe that *WPPM* becomes significantly more sensitive than *WSM* when the number of decimal places exceeds 4.

When starting with the sets of applications with unique *WSM* scores, we observe some variation in the *relative sensitivities* in case the number of decimals places is 2, but the relative sensitivity of *WPPM* is always greater than or equal than of *WSM*. When rounding to 3 decimal places the results show that for every sample of applications that share the same *WSM* score, *WPPM* scores can differentiate these applications. When starting with the sets of applications with unique *WPPM* scores, we observe that *WSM* shows higher sensitivity than *WPPM* in case the number of decimal places is 2. However, when the number of decimal places is greater or equal to 3, *WSM* has the same sensitivity as *WPPM* has. This means that *WSM* is not capable of differentiating the applications that score equally according to the *WPPM* approach.

We summarize descriptive statistics of sensitivities in the *boxplots* of Fig. 6. They show the minimum, the 25th percentile, the median, the 75th percentile,

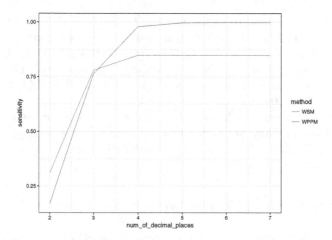

Fig. 5. WSM and WPPM overall sensitivity

and the maximum of *WPPM* and *WSM* sensitivities, resp. For each method, the sensitivities are computed as one over the number of applications with the same score rounded to $2\ldots 8$ decimal places.

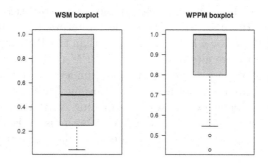

Fig. 6. Comparing WSM and WPPM sensitivities

Altogether, we observe that *WPPM* is the more sensitive approach. It can distinguish more applications than *WSM*.

Interpretability. We claim that a well-defined (mathematical) concept should exist that is supporting the decision making process beyond the plain numerical calculation of scores and ranks. We argue that the interpretability of results is higher if calculations just implement such a concept instead of constitute the concept. Probability theory provides such a concept for the *WPPM* approach: we can interpret a *WPPM* score from $[0, 1]$ for an application a as a probability to find another application that is less preferable than a or at most as preferable as

a in all criteria. It is harder to interpret a *WSM* score from $[0, 5]$. We might want to apply the *center of mass* concept from basic physics or the *central tendency* concept from basic statistics. This is, however, questionable as the criteria do not have the same nature, i.e., they are "apples" and "oranges": For example, how to interpret the result of adding evaluations values of *Originality* to *Equality* or *Sustainability* to *Team*, etc.

The decision makers from Vinnova feel comfortable with a probabilistic interpretation. However, they prefer not more than four decimal digits to choose among the applications. Note that the probabilistic score can be expressed as percentages on a $[0, 100]$-scale.

6 Conclusions and Future Work

The paper defines an approach that provides a sound basis for sensitive and interpretable multi-criteria decision making. It introduces *WPPM* scoring and provides its mathematical foundations: probabilistic scores are obtained based on the distributions of criteria and aggregated using weighted products. The paper evaluates the approach using a real-world case where the decision maker's objective is to obtain ranks of alternative funding applications based on the aggregation of multiple ranking criteria. The paper compares the *WPPM* approach with the popular alternative of using a weighted sum aggregation *WSM*. The paper concludes that the approaches do not differ statistically in the ranking of alternatives. However, *WPPM* has clear interpretation while *WSM* has not. Moreover, *WPPM* has a higher *sensitivity* than the *WSM* approach, which allows to distinguish more alternatives with *WPPM* that are considered equivalent with *WSM*. This leads to better and more understandable decisions.

The proposed approach is not limited to a specific decision-making problem. It is ready to be implemented in decision making software systems supporting enterprise decision management (EDM) or business decision management (BDM). It is future work to study the effects of the suggested approach on EDM/BDM.

We also plan to conduct simulation experiments to study a deviation between *WSM* and *WPPM* sensitivities depending on the number of alternatives. We assume that criteria are statistically independent or that weights regard mutual dependency. We plan to extend our approach to consider both dependencies and weights. In general, there is no objective or optimal solution for defining the weights of criteria. However, the suggested decision highly depend on these weights. The present paper assumes that decision makers chose the appropriate weights based on their knowledge and expertise and that these weights indicate the importance of criteria objectively. In the future, we plan to extend our approach to consider another type of weights. Such a weight should represent the capacity of a criterion to separate alternatives and can be extracted from data. Finally, objectives-oriented evaluations also need to reason why specific objectives are achieved or not. The interpretable *WPPM* approach based on probabilistic scores and joint distributions could provide a basis for reasoning.

Based on that, we further plan to extend our approach to quantify the effort needed to achieve quantitative multi-criteria objectives or to improve towards them. This way, we could suggest focusing the on some criteria that lead to overall improvements with lesser efforts.

Acknowledgments. This research was supported by *The Knowledge Foundation* within the project "Software technology for self-adaptive systems" (ref. number 20150088). We are also grateful to Jan Sandred at *Vinnova*, for contributing with a real-world dataset, fruitful discussions, and feedback.

References

1. Iyengar, S., Lepper, M.: When choice is demotivating: can one desire too much of a good thing? J. Pers. Soc. Psychol. **79**(6), 995–1006 (2000)
2. Simon, H.: Rational decision making in business organizations. Am. Econ. Rev. **69**(4), 493–513 (1979)
3. Figueira, J., Greco, S., Ehrgott, M.: Multiple Criteria Decision Analysis: State of the Art Surveys, vol. 78. Springer Science & Business Media, Berlin (2005). https://doi.org/10.1007/b100605
4. Triantaphyllou, E.: Multi-criteria decision making methods. In: Multi-criteria Decision Making Methods: A Comparative Study, pp. 5–21. Springer, Boston (2000). https://doi.org/10.1007/978-1-4757-3157-6_2
5. Lee, S.M., et al.: Goal Programming for Decision Analysis. Auerbach Publishers, Philadelphia (1972)
6. Von Winterfeldt, D., Fischer, G.: Multi-attribute utility theory: models and assessment procedures. In: Wendt, D., Vlek, C. (eds.) Utility, Probability, and Human Decision Making, pp. 47–85. Springer, Dordrecht (1975). https://doi.org/10.1007/978-94-010-1834-0_3
7. Fishburn, P.: Utility Theory for Decision Making. Wiley, New York (1970)
8. Keeney, R., Raiffa, H.: Decisions with Multiple Objectives: Preferences and Value Trade-offs. Cambridge University Press, New York (1993)
9. Roy, B.: The outranking approach and the foundations of electre methods. In: Bana e Costa, C.A. (ed.) Readings in Multiple Criteria Decision Aid, pp. 155–183. Springer, Heidelberg (1990). https://doi.org/10.1007/978-3-642-75935-2_8
10. Brans, J.P., Vincke, P., Mareschal, B.: How to select and how to rank projects: the promethee method. Eur. J. Oper. Res. **24**, 228–238 (1986)
11. Saaty, T.: Decision making with the analytic hierarchy process. Int. J. Serv. Sci. **1**(1), 83–98 (2008)
12. Triantaphyllou, E., Mann, S.: An examination of the effectiveness of multi-dimensional decision-making methods: a decision-making paradox. Decis. Support Syst. **5**(3), 303–312 (1989)
13. Budescu, D., Rantilla, A.: Confidence in aggregation of expert opinions. Acta Psychol. **104**(3), 371–398 (2000)
14. Drucker, P.: The Practice of Management. Routledge, London (2012)
15. Dubois, D., Prade, H.: Criteria aggregation and ranking of alternatives in the framework of fuzzy set theory (1984)
16. Dombi, J.: Basic concepts for a theory of evaluation: the aggregative operator. Eur. J. Oper. Res. **10**(3), 282–293 (1982)

17. Yager, R.: On ordered weighted averaging aggregation operators in multicriteria decision making. IEEE Trans. Syst. Man Cybern. **18**(1), 183–190 (1988)
18. Velasquez, M., Hester, P.: An analysis of multi-criteria decision making methods. Int. J. Oper. Res. **10**(2), 56–66 (2013)
19. Wu, H.Y., Chen, J.K., Chen, I.S., Zhuo, H.H.: Ranking universities based on performance evaluation by a hybrid MCDM model. Measurement **45**(5), 856–880 (2012)
20. Tansel, Y.: A topsis based design of experiment approach to assess company ranking. Appl. Math. Comput. **227**, 630–647 (2014)
21. Li, M., Jin, L., Wang, J.: A new MCDM method combining QFD with topsis for knowledge management system selection from the user's perspective in intuitionistic fuzzy environment. Appl. Soft Comput. **21**, 28–37 (2014)
22. De Feo, G., De Gisi, S.: Using an innovative criteria weighting tool for stakeholders involvement to rank MSW facility sites with the AHP. Waste Manag. **30**(11), 2370–2382 (2010)
23. Othman, M., Repke, J.U., Wozny, G.: Incorporating negative values in AHP using rule-based scoring methodology for ranking of sustainable chemical process design options. Comput. Aided Chem. Eng. **28**, 1045–1050 (2010)
24. Saaty, T.L.: Theory and Applications of the Analytic Network Process: Decision Making with Benefits, Opportunities, Costs, and Risks. RWS Publications, USA (2005)
25. Pearman, A., Mackie, P., May, A., Simon, D.: The use of multicriteria techniques to rank highway investment proposals. In: Lockett, A.G., Islei, G. (eds.) Improving Decision Making in Organisations, pp. 157–165. Springer, Heidelberg (1989). https://doi.org/10.1007/978-3-642-49298-3_15
26. Chen, C.T., Pai, P.F., Hung, W.Z.: An integrated methodology using linguistic promethee and maximum deviation method for third-party logistics supplier selection. Int. J. Comput. Intell. Syst. **3**(4), 438–451 (2010)
27. Podviezko, A.: Augmenting multicriteria decision aid methods by graphical and analytical reporting tools. In: Niedrite, L., Strazdina, R., Wangler, B. (eds.) BIR 2011. LNBIP, vol. 106, pp. 236–251. Springer, Heidelberg (2012). https://doi.org/10.1007/978-3-642-29231-6_19
28. Simon, H.: The New Science of Management Decision. Harper & Brothers, New York (1960)
29. Nelsen, R.: An Introduction to Copulas. Springer Science & Business Media, Berlin (2007). https://doi.org/10.1007/0-387-28678-0
30. Spearman, C.: "General intelligence," objectively determined and measured. Am. J. Psychol. **15**(2), 201–292 (1904)
31. Bland, J.M., Altman, D.: Measuring agreement in method comparison studies. Stat. Methods Med. Res. **8**(2), 135–160 (1999)
32. Stöckl, D., Cabaleiro, D.R., Van Uytfanghe, K., Thienpont, L.: Interpreting method comparison studies by use of the Bland-Altman plot: reflecting the importance of sample size by incorporating confidence limits and predefined error limits in the graphic. Clin. Chem. **50**(11), 2216–2218 (2004)
33. Kendall, M.: Rank Correlation Methods. Griffin, London (1948)

Towards Ecosystemic Stance in Finnish Public Sector Enterprise Architecture

Jarkko Nurmi[✉], Katja Penttinen, and Ville Seppänen

Faculty of Information Technology, University of Jyvaskyla,
P.O. Box 35, 40014 Jyväskylä, Finland
{jarkko.s.nurmi,katja.i.penttinen}@student.jyu.fi,
ville.r.seppanen@jyu.fi

Abstract. Governments and organizations in both public and private sector are operating in fields of ever-growing uncertainty and complexity. To study this complex environment, the concept of ecosystems has been suggested, interpreting organizations as intertwined systems among layers of evolving ecosystems. While offering possibilities, operating in an ecosystemic environment might prove to be challenging, and the change from traditional governance structures might be difficult to manage, requiring holistic yet detailed view. Enterprise Architecture (EA) has been an interest of academics and practitioners for few decades, offering one of the most prominent solutions to managing complex organizations. Recently, it has been discussed that EA should further evolve to respond to the interconnectedness of organizations', thus extending the focus of enterprise architecting from intra-organizational to the ecosystems level. Based on data from 26 in-depth practitioner interviews in Finland, we discuss how EA should be developed to better support Finnish public sector ecosystems. Our data indicates that qualities such as organizational capabilities, holistic view, co-creation and needs-based utilization are essential features of public sector ecosystem EA.

Keywords: Enterprise architecture · Public sector · Ecosystem

1 Introduction

As the world alters towards networked and complex structures, the changes within the organizations and in the environment are becoming more frequent, yet more difficult to perceive. The underlying complexity is prone to increase, making it near impossible for governments to achieve public policy endeavors by dividing complex issues into smaller pieces [4, 13]. Contrariwise, embracing holism and the interconnections among organizations might be a key to solve some of the problems occurring, as ecosystems-enabled co-creation is seen as a key innovation in public service delivery [6]. To study this complex environment, the concept of an ecosystem has been suggested as *"the alignment structure of the multilateral set of partners that need to interact in order for a focal value proposition to materialize"* [1, p. 40]. Public administration structures and actors such as cities [55] and state [5] are increasingly interpreted as service systems and ecosystems. As an example, [13, p. 110] argue, that *"the society could be defined*

© Springer Nature Switzerland AG 2019
M. Pańkowska and K. Sandkuhl (Eds.): BIR 2019, LNBIP 365, pp. 89–103, 2019.
https://doi.org/10.1007/978-3-030-31143-8_7

as a complex set of relationships based on the continuous sharing of resources and on the combination of several expectations culminating in the building of new value", thus making society a domain which *"cannot be analyzed in the light of a mechanistic approach; it requires the adoption of a holistic perspective"*. Ecosystems have attracted interest in private and public sector, and both new models of public services delivery and new business models have been suggested. Ecosystemic perspective can enhance understanding of complex contexts with systems-level thinking [9] and could be beneficial in the public sector, bringing forth benefits such as avoidance of duplication, enhanced transparency, faster service delivery and increased flexibility [49]. Further, a United Nations e-government survey stresses the need for a holistic approach to governance, bringing forth ecosystemic stance as a crucial strategy to achieve holism. In the same vein, the World Economic Forum has envisioned some features of future world government, where the cornerstones are such as networked governance, interconnection and collaboration [49].

Whilst interpreting public administration as an ecosystem could bring forth benefits, the transition from traditional government structures might prove to be challenging and difficult to manage, requiring holistic yet detailed view. As [9] note, prior research has found that while technology creates opportunities in ecosystem service innovation, its complexity is prone to increase, necessitating the integration on people, processes, technology and information. Here, Enterprise Architecture (EA) could have a vital role. EA has been an interest of academics and practitioners for a few decades, offering one of the most prominent solutions to managing organizations. EA is traditionally used in modelling of organizations in current and future states and has gained attention as an approach for achieving IT-business alignment [2], bringing numerous other potential benefits along (e.g. [19, 31, 53]).

Changes in business-environments have sparked a discussion of further evolving EA to respond to the challenges related to interconnectedness of organizations [17]. While EA can be used to examine organizations and its elements, i.e. processes, systems and information, it has been argued, that current EA methodologies are not suitable in bridging internal and external environments, and in involving various stakeholders for building successful ecosystems [3, 18, 45]. EA might need a reconceptualization on methods and tools, to provide requisite coherence and adaptability in reacting internal and external change demands [30]. As the scope and purpose of EA seems to be expanding from mechanistic IT-business alignment to a holistic design of an organization in an ecosystemic environment (ibid), a systemic stance on enterprise architecture seems to have a growing interest among scholars and practitioners [10, 33]. Well-known scholars have explicitly stated the need to study the relations between systemic thinking and EA. As an example, Kappelman and Zachman [28, p. 93] state, that "[...] *the EA trend of applying holistic systems thinking, shared language, and engineering concepts, albeit in the early stages of their application, is here to stay"*. Further, Rahimi et al. [46, p. 138] discuss the *"importance of systems thinking and, especially, of adopting the open systems principle, for managing EA design and evolution"*. Recently, EA has been applied in networked [4, 14, 50] and ecosystemic [21, 36, 45] settings. Systemic and ecosystemic stance on public administration, and government architectures have been discussed especially in the context of e-government [25] and smart cities [7, 26, 36, 37], as well as other endeavors [e.g. 15, 29].

Although EA has been used to enhance interoperability of inter- and intra-organizational IT systems in the public sector, the means of extending the focus of enterprise architecting from intra-organizational to the ecosystems level is an area not yet sufficiently studied.

EA in the public sector differs from the private sector context, due to differences in usage - while in the private sector EA is often used in one organization, the scope in the public sector is much larger. Especially in the public sector, EA initiatives seem to face challenges in practice. Thus, as noted in prior studies, further research about EA in the public sector is also needed [16, 48, 51, 54]. The somewhat mature usage of government EA makes Finland a viable area to study EA usage in the public sector. Finland introduced government enterprise architecture in 2006 and has since 2011 mandated the use of EA in public sector organizations. In 2017, Ministry of Finance, the key actor governing public EA efforts in Finland, published first drafts of ecosystems model for public administration EA. In Finnish public administration, the state government and local government co-exist, comprising 12 ministries, about 50 special agencies, and some 200 regional state agencies. Prevailing reform in Finnish Social and Health services aims at to form 18 counties and an ecosystem including shared IT services as the common platform for currently siloed and fragmented data resources.

Our research question: "How enterprise architecture should be developed to better support Finnish public sector ecosystems?" is answered with thematic analysis of data from 26 in-depth practitioner interviews, conducted in different levels of Finnish public administration. While EA is much used in the public sector, its power in organizational interoperability and coherence is yet to be seen, and new ways of designing, developing and governing public administration EA are needed. Our data indicates that qualities such as organizational capabilities, holistic view, co-creation and needs based utilization are essential features of public sector ecosystem EA.

The remainder of this paper is structured as follows. In the following sections, the main concepts of this study - ecosystem and EA - are briefly introduced. Section 3 explains the methods of this study, and in Sect. 4, we offer the results of our study. Results are discussed with concluding remarks in Sect. 5.

2   Background

2.1   Enterprise Architecture in the Public Sector

Enterprise architecture has been defined and used in manifold ways. An "enterprise" indicates to the scope of the examination, and can be defined e.g. as an organization, a part of the organization or several organizations forming a whole. According to ISO/IEC/IEEE 42010:2011, "architecture" is defined as *"fundamental concepts or properties of a system in its environment embodied in its elements, relationships, and in the principles of its design and evolution"*. Although the definitions of EA are numerous, with no common definition, it's scope and purpose seem to be increasingly extending from the purpose of IT-business alignment towards a tool of holistic organizational design and development in the system-in-environment setting [40].

Prior research discusses government EA as an efficient tool to overcome the challenges and problems related to e.g. interoperability, integration and complexity of e-government systems. [e.g. 19, 35]. In the public sector, government-as-a-whole architectures have been studied using various terminology, such as government architecture [23], government enterprise architecture [42, 49] and national enterprise architecture [24, 34]. [44] cites earlier studies, and states, that public sector policymakers initiate EA programs to enhance productivity, improve interoperability and improve the standard of service systems.

Although EA has been used in public sector in more than 20 countries [47], the efforts have not been only successful, numerous problems have occurred and many government organizations have performed poorly in their EA efforts. As an example, [16] discuss the problems and their root causes of EA in the public sector. They conclude, that previous research has recognized numerous problems, including problems related to the organization, EA project teams, EA users, and EA itself. Examples include complex structures, minimum collaboration among agencies, lack of broader understanding and guidance, lack of capabilities and skills, overemphasizing IT perspective, and lack of shared understanding of EA itself. [52] studied key issues in EA adoption in the public sector, concluding that there are three broad categories: resistance towards EA, relevant EA goals, and EA practices in use. These include issues such as lack of practical skills required in EA development, reluctancy to adopt new ways of working and general image problem of EA, due to e.g. troublesome implementation and technical representation.

Public administration in Finland has been in continuous change as in all Western Countries, if not globally. Although EA has emerged as a prominent tool to manage the change, the proof of its success in organizational interoperability and coherence is yet to be seen. In Finnish public administration, the state government and local government co-exist, comprising 12 ministries at the state level, steering their branches along of about 50 specialized central agencies. The semi-independent local governments consist of about 300 municipalities, which are self-governing units by Constitution, with the right to tax the residents. The municipalities have formed collaborative networks and joint ownerships with third-party vendors, which creates a complex ecosystem per se. Altogether, the Finnish public administration forms a complex ecosystem of organizations of high complexity, diverse goals and services, as well as some common infrastructure. In addition to that, various cross-organizational management forms, such as policy programs, and other endeavors are ongoing via various forms of organizations. Prevailing reform in Finnish Social and Health services aims to an ecosystem that will include shared IT services as the common platform for currently siloed and fragmented data resources. 18 counties are to be formed, with the liability to produce social and health care service.

In order to enable and ensure the interoperability of public administration, The Act on Information Management Governance in Public Administration (634/2011) has since 2011 necessitated the use of EA in public administration. Finnish public sector authorities must plan and describe their EA and adhere to the created and maintained EA, descriptions, and definitions of interoperability. Public sector organizations should use the Finnish national EA (FINEA) method and its guidelines in EA planning and management. In practice, the implementation and use of the method have been challenging [44, 52].

2.2 Ecosystems in the Public Sector

Having emerged from the field of biology, different types of ecosystems have been widely discussed in various academic disciplines, such as marketing, strategy, social sciences, innovation management, engineering and information technology, gaining popularity especially in recent years [27]. Ecosystem have been defined and classified in manifold ways, and different kinds of ecosystems include business ecosystem, innovation ecosystem, service ecosystem, ecosystem as a standalone concept as well as various others. Some common elements among different types of ecosystems include focal roles, co-specialization, co-evolution and co-opetition, interdependence, loosely coupled hierarchical structure, shared vision, system level business model and modularity [20]. Adner [1, p. 40] offers one definition for an ecosystem, that is both reasonably cited, and seems like a suitable metaphor for public administration: an ecosystem is *"the alignment structure of the multilateral set of partners that need to interact in order for a focal value proposition to materialize"*. In the public administration, diverse actors, i.e. state administration, civil service department, city officials and so forth come together, not to generate profit, but something of value - such as wellbeing of citizens. Similarly, [22] have identified three streams of ecosystems literature; business ecosystems stream, innovation ecosystems stream and platform ecosystems stream. While the first one centers on a firm in an environment and the second concerns an innovation or a value proposition among the constellation of actors supporting, the third discusses actors organized around a platform (ibid). So, the innovation ecosystems stream, discussing a focal value proposition, is focused on the system of service provision, not the individual enterprises.

As a structure, ecosystems can be interpreted in four nested and interrelated levels [38]: micro-, meso-, macro- and mega-level. At micro-level, service-for-service exchanges through actor-to-actor structures are allowed. Indirect interaction occurs at meso-level, involving actors in the same ecosystem. At the macro level, complex networks, such as institutional arrangements, arise, enabling or constraining activities at micro-, and meso-levels. Interdependencies between co-existing ecosystems occur at mega-level (ibid).

Ecosystems have been studied, to some extent, in the context of public administration and service provision. As an example, [9] show with a case study, that national health information system can be interpreted as an ecosystem, where public and private health care organizations act in meso-level, and the whole ecosystem represents a macro-level. Systemic stance on government EA is further discussed by e.g. [25], who examine the use of EAs in the Dutch public administration from a complex adaptive systems perspective. Based on the analysis of 11 cases, they derive eight architectural design principles, including development of modular architectures, stimulation of sharing and formation of coalitions. Further examples include the study by [35], who discuss developing a government EA framework to support the requirements of big and open linked data with the use of cloud computing. [8] provides an overview on different types of ecosystems and their characteristics and proposes views for the modelling of ecosystems with insights to three aspects: goal modelling, ecosystem modelling and platform modelling.

3   Methods of Study

This study is part of a longitudinal research project, researching the implementation of the Finnish national enterprise architecture method (the whole project is reported in [44]). The research constituted of two rounds of interviews, and the data used in this research was collected from 26 semi-structured interviews during the summer 2017. The selection of interviewees was based on purposeful sampling [43] in order to capture variation in the data in terms of both assumed information intensiveness and stakeholder population. The interviewees were asked to sign a written informed consent and were allowed to discontinue participating at any given time of the study. Transcribed interviews were stored securely, and the results of the interviews are reported anonymously. Further, the questions were presented in a manner that excludes interviewer bias [32]. The interviewees represented stakeholders from different levels and sectors of Finnish public administration and IT companies, with representatives from state administration (4), administrative sector (3), civil service department (4), cities (5) as well as managers (5) and workers (6) from private IT companies. The interviewees had an average of 15 years of experience in EA-related activities, ranging from 3 to 40 years.

The interview questions were divided into four parts: questions of (1) background information of interviewees, (2) previous situations (3) current situation and (4) future of EA. The questions covered macro- and micro-level issues. The past- and future-related questions covered issues of FINEA and the interviewees' perceptions of how it has affected their own work. The current situation questions were different for the interviewees from the public and private sectors. The interviewees from the public sector were asked questions about EA in the organizations they represented, and the interviewees from the private sector we asked questions about their public sector client organizations. To enhance repeatability (i.e. reliability), example questions are offered in the Appendix.

The interviews lasted from 36 to 100 min, the average being 63 min. The interviews were audio recorded, and transcribed. The quotations were translated into English and edited for brevity, thus removing hesitations, words and such, which were not essential for overall understanding of the data. We conducted a thematic analysis consisting of six phases: familiarization, initial coding, search of themes, reviewing potential themes, defining and naming themes, and producing the report [11]. The coding was done with the ATLAS.ti software, using both inductive and deductive approaches. To minimize the impact of individual bias, all authors did participate in the analysis, although no intercoder reliability was tested.

4   Results

During the data analysis, we were able to form four major themes of importance: co-creation, capabilities, holistic view and needs-based utilization. Summary of the themes and their incidence by stakeholder groups is presented in Table 1. There were also minor themes that were mentioned only few times. Among them were interoperability, cost savings, EA framework, digitalization and governance. Next, we explain the meaning of the formed themes and illustrate them with excerpts from the interviews.

Table 1. Themes considered important in developing public sector ecosystem EA

Theme	State	Administrative sector	Civil service department	City	IT company manager	IT company worker
Capabilities	◑	◐	◑	O	◐	●
Co-creation	◐	◐	◑	◑	O	◐
Holistic view	●	◐	●	◐	◐	◑
Needs-based utilisation	◑	◑	◑	◐	◑	◐

O = not mentioned, ◐ = rarely mentioned, ◑ = occasionally mentioned, ● = frequently mentioned.

4.1 Capabilities

Capability concept was added in the latest FINEA version and is defined as combinations of: (a) operations models and processes, (b) employees and skills, and (c) information and systems. Of these, the most mentioned in our data were resources that most often mean employees' time that they can use in EA. Interviewee from state government said: "Organizations should invest enough in it [EA], give enough resources, to see what the benefits in their own operations are". Without proper resources, the benefits will be modest. Skills and competence were also mentioned, and the interviewees emphasized both technical and business capabilities. While IT consultants mentioned capabilities often, the managers of the companies discussed capabilities only rarely. Moreover, while other public sector interviewees mentioned capabilities rarely or occasionally, city personnel gave no mention of this issue.

4.2 Co-creation

Co-creation has recently received a lot of attention in the public sector. In the beginning of the FINEA work, co-creation was quite unfamiliar. Especially, the stakeholders from civil service departments, cities and employees of IT companies have realized the value of co-creation in EA. A public sector representative said: "We have come far in ten years, and the need for co-creation has been recognized and understood". This theme constitutes of things like achieving a common understanding, communication, dialogue, co-operation and different kinds of groups for people doing EA. Senior specialist of a city describes their cross-sectoral operations: "We have got governance over the operations in our city. Without communication and forum, this work would be impossible. This is the biggest value". In their city, EA is connected in the project management model and in the strategy. They have an EA group and architects do co-creation with operations personnel. Representative of another city mentioned that they do an operations model picture in cooperation with substance or process owner and this leads into understanding of what really needs to be done. When discussing about stakeholders and co-operation with private actors, one public sector representative stated that "[...] and then there are enterprises with which we have this ecosystem thinking. If we would not have mutual architecture, we could not have mutual and decentralized development". This viewpoint on co-operation was also shared by the private sector interviewees, one of which noted that: "I think that in public adminis-tration there is, at least to some extent, thinking of being this platform-type of platform for third party vendors and private actors". Although many interviewees mentioned, that co-creation is of value, some felt that it has not been enhanced by EA: "The reality in cross-organizational cooperation seems to be more wretched than before and EA has not been able to bring anything to the table". Further, IT company managers gave no mentions about co-operation.

4.3   Holistic View

Holistic view is the big picture that comes through EA's four viewpoints: information, business, information systems and technology. These four architecture domains are in FINEA framework and in many generally known EA models, such as TOGAF. Holistic view was the most often mentioned issue in our interviews. It was considered to have many benefits and potential uses, such as identify structures, understand different stakeholders, and help in co-operation, governance, risk management, and cyber security. Interviewee from the state government describes the idea well: "To be able to make a holistic view of this complex public administration and its functions that consists of different segments and their relationships. And to be able to give structure and understand different actors and co-operate with stakeholders. And the services and systems and to be able to form a holistic view, it helps in many ways in decision making [...] management [...]. It has potential in this. And in my opinion, we need more of this [...] in this change in society [...] to make the complex whole simpler". Another state interviewee continued, that: "We chose from the beginning to look public administration as a whole [...] it requires systematic and systemic thinking". Further it was noted that "EA has been good in endorsing thinking of public administration as, in a way, one organization". Although the holistic view was recognized as one of the important aspects of EA, and public administration was regularly looked from this viewpoint, also organization-specific EA-work was valued: "On the other hand there are the things in common [in public administration], but also some that are organization-specific. It is kind of a buzzword, but there is an ecosystem". When asked about different viewpoints of EA work in public sector, the state administration interviewee noted that: "[we look at EA] rather in the macro-level. Of course, it is important to examine the architecture from the viewpoint on an organization. But we are more looking on what is shared in public administration [...] the strategic objectives of the whole-of public administration, at this moment, begins from digitalization and also from developing an ecosystems-model. We are developing the next version of the public administration enterprise architecture [...] it has been developed for a year with various stakeholders, and emphasis is on developing public, citizen-oriented services. It is about cost-efficiency, avoidance of overlapping and utilizing collected data at large".

Further, a private sector interviewee noted, that "The world is complex and always changing, these frameworks and their methods tend to age, and new ones are needed".

4.4 Needs-Based Utilization

There is a constant struggle to get enough resources for EA work and development work in general. This is the main reason why needs-based utilization came up in all stakeholder groups. Needs-based utilization is an important issue in successful EA in the public sector. If EA project starts without setting proper goals and understanding of the problem area, the result is often excessive modelling which is waste of resources. In Finland the FINEA is mandated by law, which has led to EA work that is done to fulfil regulations. Hence, motivation is a problem. Many interviewees saw needs-based utilization as a means to motivate and to help in setting relevant goals for EA. Interviewee from state administration noted that: "This is the most important thing in EA work, do not start without answering a couple of why questions... then things get easier, you do better EA and know redundant work". According to interviewees, it is important to think what are the problems that need to be solved with EA work and then use the method as a tool. Interviewee from the administrative sector says: "[...] rigid EA work, where current and future stare are modelled similarly, textbook like, it is a lot of redundant work. And we have modelled many things that are insignificant in the big picture".

5 Discussion and Concluding Remarks

Enterprise architecture has been one of the leading ways of modelling the structures of an organization, and based on the interviews, one that currently is used. Still, the results of this study indicate that new ways of designing, developing and governing public administration are needed. In addition, new ways of interpreting government EA are needed - ones that can justify themselves in the world of growing complexity, speed of change and interrelations among actors. As prior noted, Finland introduced government EA in 2006 and has since 2011 mandated the use of EA in public sector organizations. In 2017, first drafts of ecosystems model for public administration EA were published, replacing the formerly used domain-based model. The former model was described as rigid, siloed, hierarchical and such that it does not enable cross-domain co-creation [39]. Further, the domain-based model is described to "*not represent the reality, as actors form ecosystems instead of hierarchies*" [39, p. 6], and being unable to foster the forming of ecosystems. Although the new ecosystems model may better enable successful EA work in the Finnish public sector, it does not discuss in detail, how EA work should be done, and which qualities are important for public sector EA to be successful. Based on our data, we argue, that Finnish public sector EA should foster holistic view, co-creation, needs-based utilization and capabilities as prominent possibilities to successful EA-work.

Interpreting public sector as an ecosystem might enhance successful implementation and usage of EA. While holistic view of an organization has traditionally been one of the key features of enterprise architecture, it can be argued that it is not altogether clear what holistic means in the government EA, or in different levels and sectors of public administration. As prior discussed, [16] looked into the problems and their root causes of EA in the public sector, one of these being minimum collaboration among agencies, an issue also mentioned as a problem in the domain-based model of FINEA [4141]. The idea of ecosystems is exploiting the resources and capabilities of different actors in a given time. As stated by [1], ecosystems are "the alignment structure of the multilateral set of partners that need to interact in order for a focal value proposition to materialize". Similarly, our results indicate that capabilities, needs-based utilization and holistic co-creation have a vital role in public sector EA work. If the public sector is interpreted as an ecosystem, government EA could be adapted in co-created projects where the capabilities of different actors are exploited in order to materialize a given goal. When EA projects are done when needed, and connect to a focal value proposition, a lot of unnecessary modelling can be omitted.

In practice, extending the scope of EA to the level of ecosystems has been prior discussed by e.g. [12, 17, 41], and our results are in line with these studies. [17] discuss the stages from EA to Extended Enterprise Architecture, to Collaborative Network Enterprise Architecture and Focused Business Ecosystem Architecture and, finally, to Business Ecosystem Architecture These ideas are further discussed by [41], who enhance ideas of Drews and Schirmer and conclude with a tentative management model for the government ecosystem architecture, and [12] who, by discussing four case studies and identifying six architectural perspectives, offer an ecosystem architecture metamodel.

As prior noted, there were notable differences in terms of how often, if at all, the issues were mentioned by different interviewee groups. The city personnel did not mention capabilities and IT managers did not consider co-creation as a notable issue. Although, judging from the data, it is not evident, where these distinct differences come from, and especially, why the city personnel did not mention capabilities at all, some speculation is possible. In 2017, there was an ongoing trend of talking about capabilities in the context of EA, especially by some of the private sector EA consultants, which might have affected to the answers given by IT company workers. Also, Archimate is much used in the Finnish public administration, it is the recommended notation in FINEA. Capabilities as elements were introduced in Archimate 3.0, and were added to FINEA in spring 2017, just before our interviews. It might be possible that private sector interviewees were more familiar with the concept than those working in cities. State personnel might have been familiarized with the concept while working with the new versions of FINEA. This may also reflect the different maturity levels of capability driven EA design in public and private organizations. As for the lack of discussion on co-creation by the IT company managers, less can be speculated. The differing opinions between private and public sector interviewees, as well as differences between public sector personnel are important, and should be further studied in a separate study. In an effort to contribute to stream of studies on public sector EA, as well as those discussing developing EA to be better utilized in ecosystemic environments, we answered the following research question: "How enterprise architecture should be developed to better support Finnish public sector ecosystems?". We concluded that while EA is widely used in the public sector, new ways of designing, developing and governing public administration EA are needed. Our interviewees, 26 professionals from different levels of Finnish public and private sectors, recognized organizational capabilities, holistic view, co-creation and needs-based utilization as important factors in government EA. Based on the results, we propose the following guidelines to be used in the public sector ecosystem EA:

- EA work utilizes capabilities of organizations' participating in the ecosystem
- Development work is done in co-creation mode
- Partners of the ecosystem form a holistic view
- EA modelling is utilized needs-based

The aim of the ecosystem is to create value to participating partners and citizens. This contradicts the traditional view of EA, as a structure of one organization. Instead the EA in ecosystem is based in the interrelationships and interactions of the participating organizations. We argue, that EA should be further developed with these thoughts in mind.

This study mainly concerns public sector EA in Finland, and the interviewees were based on a single country. Therefore, different aspects might be emphasized elsewhere, and there might occur differing opinions concerning important and redundant qualities of EA. As discussed, EA is used in public sector internationally, and is also mandated by law in some countries other than Finland. Although the findings of this study may have significance in other contexts, more research is definitely needed, for example in other countries. Especially constructive studies, as well as case studies, forming and testing new ways of conducting EA, would be valuable. Further, some features of EA in public administration ecosystem are probably common also in the private sector. The generalizability of our results in wider contexts is hopefully to be validated by future research.

Appendix

For background information we asked for interviewees: name, organization, job description, duration of work in EA field. We also asked them to describe their EA work and their viewpoint to EA work (government-as-a-whole or own organization). Second, we asked backward questions:

- What do you think about the public sector EA method?
- Have you used the method in your work?
- The results of the interviews ten years ago included 1. implementation ability and governance, 2. structures of government and 3. advancement of interoperability as key challenges. In your opinion, are these still challenges?
- Has EA work increased cross-sectoral co-operation?
- Are you familiar with the law that mandates the use of EA? Has the law affected EA work?

- Ten years ago, there was not a mutual understanding about what EA means and what are the main goals of the EA work. In your opinion, is there currently a mutual understanding?

Third, we asked about current EA work:

- Is EA work done in your organization/client-organization? Why/why not?
- What kind of strategic goals are set for EA work?
- What are the stakeholder groups of EA?
- In your opinion, what is important in EA work?
- In your opinion, what is redundant in EA work?
- What is learned from EA work?
- How does EA support the digitalization of the public sector?

Fourth, we asked about the future of EA:

- What are the next steps of EA work in your organization/client-organization?
- How should the EA method be further developed?
- How information security should be noticed in forthcoming co-operation and public information systems?
- In your opinion, what kind of future EA work has in public sector?

Last, we asked: Is there something you would like to add?

References

1. Adner, R.: Ecosystem as structure: an actionable construct for strategy. J. Manag. **43**(1), 39–58 (2017)
2. Alaeddini, M., Asgari, H., Gharibi, A., Rad, M.R.: Leveraging business-IT alignment through enterprise architecture—an empirical study to estimate the extents. Inf. Technol. Manage. **18**(1), 55–82 (2017)
3. Aldea, A., Iacob, M.E., Wombacher, A., Hiralal, M., Franck, T.: Enterprise architecture 4.0–A vision, an approach and software tool support. In: 2018 IEEE 22nd International Enterprise Distributed Object Computing Conference (EDOC), pp. 1–10. IEEE, October 2018
4. Bakhtiyari, R.Z.: Applying enterprise architecture to business networks. Doctoral dissertation, Queensland University of Technology (2017)
5. Barile, S., Lusch, R., Reynoso, J., Saviano, M., Spohrer, J.: Systems, networks, and ecosystems in service research. J. Serv. Manage. **27**(4), 652–674 (2016)
6. Bason, C.: Leading Public Sector Innovation: Co-creating for a Better Society. Policy Press, Bristol (2018)
7. Bastidas, V., Bezbradica, M., Helfert, M.: Cities as enterprises: a comparison of smart city frameworks based on enterprise architecture requirements. In: Alba, E., Chicano, F., Luque, G. (eds.) Smart Cities. LNCS, vol. 10268, pp. 20–28. Springer, Cham (2017). https://doi.org/10.1007/978-3-319-59513-9_3
8. Benedict, M.: Modelling ecosystems in information systems–a typology approach. In: Proceedings of the Multikonferenz Wirtschaftsinformatik, pp. 453–464 (2018)

9. Beirão, G., Patrício, L., Fisk, R.P.: Value cocreation in service ecosystems: investigating health care at the micro, meso, and macro levels. J. Serv. Manage. **28**(2), 227–249 (2017)
10. Bernus, P., et al.: Enterprise engineering and management at the crossroads. Comput. Ind. **79**, 87–102 (2016)
11. Braun, V., Clarke, V., Terry, G.: Thematic analysis. Qual. Res. Clin. Health Psychol. **24**, 95–114 (2014)
12. Burmeister, F., Drews, P., Schirmer, I.: An ecosystem architecture meta-model for supporting ultra-large scale digital transformations. In: ACIS (2019)
13. Caputo, F., Walletzky, L., Štepánek, P.: Towards a systems thinking based view for the governance of a smart city's ecosystem: a bridge to link smart technologies and big data. Kybernetes **48**, 108–123 (2018)
14. Carter, B.: Systems theory based architecture framework for complex system governance (2016)
15. Carter, B., Moorthy, S., Walters, D.: Enterprise architecture view of complex system governance. Int. J. Syst. Syst. Eng. **7**(1–3), 95–108 (2016)
16. Dang, D.D., Pekkola, S.: Systematic literature review on enterprise architecture in the public sector. Electron. J. e-Govern. **15**(2) (2017)
17. Drews, P., Schirmer, I.: From enterprise architecture to business ecosystem architecture: stages and challenges for extending architectures beyond organizational boundaries. In: 2014 IEEE 18th International Enterprise Distributed Object Computing Conference Workshops and Demonstrations (EDOCW), pp. 13–22. IEEE, September 2014
18. Goerzig, D., Bauernhansl, T.: Enterprise architectures for the digital transformation in small and medium-sized enterprises. Proc. CIRP **67**(1), 540–545 (2018)
19. Gong, Y., Janssen, M.: The value of and myths about enterprise architecture. Int. J. Inf. Manage. **46**, 1–9 (2019)
20. Han, J., Lowik, S., de Weerd-Nederhof, P.: Uncovering the conceptual boundaries of the ecosystems: origins, evolution and future directions (2017)
21. Hedges, J., Furda, A.: The emerging role of the ecosystems architect. Software engineering for variability intensive systems: foundations and applications, p. 131 (2019)
22. Jacobides, M.G., Cennamo, C., Gawer, A.: Towards a theory of ecosystems. Strategic Manage. J. **39**, 2255–2276 (2018)
23. Janssen, M., Flak, L.S., Sæbø, Ø.: Government architecture: concepts, use and impact. In: Wimmer, M.A., Janssen, M., Scholl, H.J. (eds.) EGOV 2013. LNCS, vol. 8074, pp. 135–147. Springer, Heidelberg (2013). https://doi.org/10.1007/978-3-642-40358-3_12
24. Janssen, M., Hjort-Madsen, K.: Analyzing enterprise architecture in national governments: the cases of Denmark and the Netherlands. In: 40th Annual Hawaii International Conference on System Sciences, HICSS 2007, p. 218a. IEEE, January 2007
25. Janssen, M., Kuk, G.: A complex adaptive system perspective of enterprise architecture in electronic government. In: Proceedings of the 39th Annual Hawaii International Conference on System Sciences, HICSS 2006, vol. 4, p. 71b. IEEE, January 2006
26. Kakarontzas, G., Anthopoulos, L., Chatzakou, D., Vakali, A.: A conceptual enterprise architecture framework for smart cities: a survey based approach. In: 2014 11th International Conference on e-Business (ICE-B), pp. 47–54. IEEE, August 2014
27. Kapoor, R.: Ecosystems: broadening the locus of value creation. J. Organ. Design **7**(1), 12 (2018)
28. Kappelman, L.A., Zachman, J.A.: The enterprise and its architecture: ontology & challenges. J. Comput. Inform. Syst. **53**(4), 87–95 (2013)

29. Katuu, S.: Using enterprise architecture as a means of understanding institution technology ecosystems. In: Proceedings of the ICMLG 2018 16th International Conference on Management Leadership and Governance. Academic Conferences and Publishing International, May 2018

30. Korhonen, J.J., Lapalme, J., McDavid, D., Gill, A.Q.: Adaptive enterprise architecture for the future: towards a reconceptualization of EA. In: 2016 IEEE 18th Conference on Business Informatics (CBI), pp. 272–281. IEEE, August 2016

31. Kurek, E., Johnson, J., Mulder, H.: Measuring the value of enterprise architecture on IT projects with CHAOS research. MSCI, Orlando, USA (2017)

32. Kvale, S.: To validate is to question. In: Kvale, S. (ed.) Issues of Validity in Qualitative Research, pp. 73–92. Studentlitteratur, Lund (1989)

33. Lapalme, J., Gerber, A., Van der Merwe, A., Zachman, J., De Vries, M., Hinkelmann, K.: Exploring the future of enterprise architecture: a Zachman perspective. Comput. Ind. **79**, 103–113 (2016)

34. Lemmetti, J., Pekkola, S.: Understanding enterprise architecture: perceptions by the finnish public sector. In: Scholl, H.J., Janssen, M., Wimmer, M.A., Moe, C.E., Flak, L.S. (eds.) EGOV 2012. LNCS, vol. 7443, pp. 162–173. Springer, Heidelberg (2012). https://doi.org/10.1007/978-3-642-33489-4_14

35. Lnenicka, M., Komarkova, J.: Developing a government enterprise architecture framework to support the requirements of big and open linked data with the use of cloud computing. Int. J. Inf. Manage. **46**, 124–141 (2019)

36. Lnenicka, M., Machova, R., Komarkova, J., Pasler, M.: Government enterprise architecture for big and open linked data analytics in a smart city ecosystem. In: Uskov, V.L., Howlett, R. J., Jain, L.C. (eds.) SEEL 2017. SIST, vol. 75, pp. 475–485. Springer, Cham (2018). https://doi.org/10.1007/978-3-319-59451-4_47

37. Mamkaitis, A., Bezbradica, M., Helfert, M.: Urban enterprise: a review of smart city frameworks from an enterprise architecture perspective. In: 2016 IEEE International Smart Cities Conference (ISC2), pp. 1–5. IEEE, September 2016

38. Manna, R., Ciasullo, M.V., Cosimato, S., Palumbo, R.: Interplaying ecosystems: a mega-level analysis of education and labour ecosystems. The TQM J. **30**, 572–588 (2018)

39. Ministry of Finance: Ecosystems Model for Finnish Public Sector Enterprise Architecture. In: Finnish (2017). https://wiki.julkict.fi/julkict/juhta/juhta-tyoryhmat-2016/jhka-tyoryhma/jhka-2.0/jhka-2-0-10-ekosysteemimalli/at_download/file

40. Nurmi, J., Penttinen, K., Seppänen, V.: Examining enterprise architecture definitions–implications from theory and practice. IRIS (2018)

41. Nurmi, J., Seppänen, V., Valtonen, K.: Ecosystem architecture management in the public sector - from problems to solutions. CSIMQ **19**, 1–18 (2019)

42. Ojo, A., Janowski, T., Estevez, E.: Improving government enterprise architecture practice–maturity factor analysis. In: 2012 45th Hawaii International Conference on System Science (HICSS), pp. 4260–4269. IEEE, January 2012

43. Patton, M.Q.: Qualitative Evaluation and Research Methods. SAGE Publications Inc, London (1990)

44. Penttinen, K.: The long and winding road of enterprise architecture implementation in the Finnish public sector. JYU Dissertations, no. 48 (2018)

45. Pittl, B., Bork, D.: Modeling digital enterprise ecosystems with ArchiMate: a mobility provision case study. Serviceology for Services. LNCS, vol. 10371, pp. 178–189. Springer, Cham (2017). https://doi.org/10.1007/978-3-319-61240-9_17

46. Rahimi, F., Gøtze, J., Møller, C.: Enterprise architecture management: toward a taxonomy of applications. Commun. Assoc. Inform. Syst. **40**(1), 7 (2017)

47. Ramos, K.H.C., de Sousa Jr., R.T.: Bibliometric analysis of enterprise architecture in the public administration. Int. Inform. Inst. Tokyo Inform. **18**(2), 501 (2015)
48. Rouhani, B.D., Mahrin, M.N.R., Nikpay, F., Ahmad, R.B., Nikfard, P.: A systematic literature review on enterprise architecture implementation methodologies. Inform. Softw. Technol. **62**(2015), 1–20 (2015)
49. Saha, P.: A methodology for government transformation with enterprise architecture. In: Advances in Government Enterprise Architecture, pp. 1–29. IGI Global (2009)
50. Santana, A., Fischbach, K., Moura, H.: Enterprise architecture analysis and network thinking: a literature review. In: 2016 49th Hawaii International Conference on System Sciences (HICSS), pp. 4566–4575. IEEE, January 2016
51. Scholl, H.J., Kubicek, H., Cimander, R.: Interoperability, enterprise architectures, and IT governance in government. In: Janssen, M., Scholl, H.J., Wimmer, M.A., Tan, Y. (eds.) EGOV 2011. LNCS, vol. 6846, pp. 345–354. Springer, Heidelberg (2011). https://doi.org/10.1007/978-3-642-22878-0_29
52. Seppänen, V., Penttinen, K., Pulkkinen, M.: Key issues in enterprise architecture adoption in the public sector. Electron. J. e-govern. **16**(1) (2018)
53. Shanks, G., Gloet, M., Someh, I.A., Frampton, K., Tamm, T.: Achieving benefits with enterprise architecture. J. Strateg. Inf. Syst. **27**(2), 139–156 (2018)
54. Simon, D., Fischbach, K., Schoder, D.: An exploration of enterprise architecture research. Commun. Assoc. Inform. Syst. **32**, Article 1 (2013)
55. Visnjic, I., Neely, A., Cennamo, C., Visnjic, N.: Governing the city: unleashing value from the business ecosystem. Calif. Manag. Rev. **59**(1), 109–140 (2016)

Data Mining Methodologies in the Banking Domain: A Systematic Literature Review

Veronika Plotnikova$^{(\boxtimes)}$, Marlon Dumas, and Fredrik P. Milani

Institute of Computer Science, University of Tartu, J. Liivi 2, 50409 Tartu, Estonia
{veronika.plotnikova,marlon.dumas,fredrik.milani}@ut.ee

Abstract. Data mining and advanced analytics methods and techniques usage in research and in business settings have increased exponentially over the last decade. Development and implementation of complex Big Data and advanced analytics projects requires well-defined methodology and processes. However, it remains unclear for what purposes and how data mining methodologies are used in practice and across different industry domains. This paper addresses the need and provides survey in the field of data mining and advanced data analytics methodologies, focusing on their application in the banking domain. By means of systematic literature review we have identified 102 articles and analyzed them in view of addressing three research questions: for what purposes data mining methodologies are used in the banking domain? How are they applied ("as-is" vs adapted)? And what are the goals of adaptations? We have identified that a dominant pattern in the banking industry is to use data mining methodologies "as-is" in order to tackle Customer Relationship Management and Risk Management business problems. However, we have also identified various adaptations of data mining methodologies in the banking domain, and noticed that the number of adaptations is steadily growing. The main adaptation scenarios comprise technology-centric aspects (scalability), business-centric aspects (actionability) and human-centric aspects (mitigating discriminatory effects).

Keywords: Data mining · Banking · Literature review

1 Introduction

The use of data mining methodologies have gained significant adoption in business settings, in particular in the financial services sector [1]. However, little is known about what and how data mining methodologies are applied. There are studies that surveyed data mining techniques and applications across domains, yet, they focused on data mining process artefacts and outcomes (eg. [2]), but not on end-to-end process methodology. There are some studies that have surveyed data mining methodologies in hospitality [3], accounting [4], education [5], and manufacturing [6] industries, but no comprehensive studies have been

© Springer Nature Switzerland AG 2019
M. Pańkowska and K. Sandkuhl (Eds.): BIR 2019, LNBIP 365, pp. 104–118, 2019.
https://doi.org/10.1007/978-3-030-31143-8_8

conducted on financial companies. In particular, studies in banking domain were so far narrow in scope - either addressed only specific data mining techniques, typically in connection with concrete business problem or product domain (eg. credit cards [7]), or tackled the technique in combination with required software toolset [8]. Data mining process methodology in this research was not addressed.

Given this gap, we investigate the application of data mining methodologies in the banking domain[1]. This is achieved by tackling the following research questions: for what purposes data mining methodologies are used in the banking domain? (RQ1), how are they applied ("as-is" vs adapted)? (RQ2), and what are the goals of adaptations? (RQ3).

The research questions are addressed by the means of a systematic literature review (SLR). As part of SLR, existing studies have been categorized by deriving taxonomy, and examined in depth by analyzing typical data mining methodologies application scenarios. The paper provides two distinct contributions: (1) it identifies and classifies data mining methodologies application scenarios and business problems addressed in banking industry settings, (2) it examines data mining methodologies adaptations, documenting associated reasons, goals and benefits. In doing so, the paper identifies gaps in 'de-facto' standard data mining methodologies that manifest themselves when applied in banking. Further, it provides evidence and insights to built upon further research activities with respect to data mining frameworks applications in banking domain.

The work is structured as follows. Section 2 provides the background while Sect. 3 presents the research design. The findings are presented in Sect. 4 while Sect. 5 concludes.

2   Background

The section provides a brief overview of data mining concept, existing data mining methodologies and their evolution.

Data mining methodologies can be defined as a set of rules, processes, algorithms that are designed to generate actionable insights, extract patterns, and identify relationships from large data sets [9]. As such, data mining methods commonly involve extraction, processing, and modeling data by means of methods and techniques.

The data mining methods are commonly represented as a high level process [10,11] that defines a set of activities and tasks, inputs and outputs required, accompanied with guidelines on how to perform the steps [10]. The foundations for structured data mining were first proposed by [12–14] with the introduction of Knowledge Discovery in Databases (KDD). This approach consists of nine steps. The first concerns learning the application domain by which is meant

---

[1] We use the term *banking domain* to refer to: (1) traditional businesses providing universal banking and insurance products and services (eg. lending, transactions, capital markets, asset management, etc.) to all types of clientele (private, corporate, financial institutions and firms), and (2) niche players, disruptors (FinTech, monoline banks etc.) specialized in specific banking, insurance products and services.

understanding the domain and identifying the goals of data mining. The second step focuses on creating the dataset while the third works with data cleaning and processing. The fourth step, data reduction and projection, concerns finding useful features to represent the data. In the fifth step, the target outcome is defined while in the sixth step, the methods and models to use on the dataset, with consideration to the objectives, are selected. In the seventh step, the work of mining the data is performed followed by the eight step where the results are interpreted and finally, are used as basis for decisions (ninth step).

The KDD approach gained traction in industrial and academic settings [11, 15], and it was also used as basis for refinements aiming to address specific gaps. However, such approaches received limited attention [11,15] with the exception of SEMMA (Sample, Explore, Modify, Model and Assess). The latter has been widely adopted due to its incorporation into SAS data mining tool [16].

An industry-driven methodology called Cross-Industry Standard Process for Data Mining (CRISP-DM) was introduced in 2000 as an alternative to KDD [11]. CRISP-DM is considered as 'de-facto' standard for data mining methodology and commonly used as a reference framework by which other methodologies are benchmarked against [10]. While CRISP-DM builds upon KDD, it consists of six phases that are executed in iterations [11]. The iterative executions of CRISP-DM stands as the most distinguishing feature when compared to KDD. CRISP-DM, much like KDD, aims at providing practitioners with guidelines to perform data mining on large data sets and designed to be domain-agnostic [10]. As such, it is widely used by industry and research communities [11].

CRISP-DM has six phases with a total of 24 tasks and outputs. The first phase is to understand the business domain, the project objectives, and converting business requirements into data mining problem definition. In the second phase, the objective is to gain an initial understanding of the data. The third phase focuses on data preparation while in the fourth phase various modelling techniques are selected and applied. In the fifth phase, the models are evaluated to ensure that they can achieve the objectives. In the final (sixth) phase, the models are deployed and results organized, presented, and distributed. Similarly to KDD, CRISP-DM has been used as basis for new data mining approaches which largely addressed deployment, use of insights [17] or project management and organizational factors [18]. CRISP-DM has also been modified to specific domains such as Industrial Engineering [19] and Software Engineering [20].

3   Research Design

The main research objective of this paper is to study how data mining methodologies are applied in the banking domain. We apply systematic literature review (SLR) method as it ensures trustworthy, rigorous, and auditable methodology, as well as supports synthesis of existing evidence, identification of research gaps, and provides framework to appropriately position new research activities [21]. Our SLR followed the guidelines proposed by [21].

To formulate the research questions, we started from the traditional set of "W" questions, specifically "Why?", "What?" and "How?". The "Why" question led us to RQ1 (for what purposes are data mining methodologies used in the banking domain?). We then raised the "What" question ("What data mining methodologies are used in the banking domain?"), but discarded this question after a preliminary analysis - we found that all major data mining methodologies (e.g. CRISP-DM, SEMMA, etc.) are used in this domain and there are little insights to be derived from analyzing this question further. Next, we raised the "How?" question, which led us to RQ2 (are data mining methodologies in the banking domain used "as-is" or are they adapted?). An initial exploration of this question led us to the preliminary conclusion that indeed data mining methodologies are sometimes adapted, which in turn led us to pose a third research question: With what goals are data mining methodologies adapted for the banking domain (RQ3)?

According to the guidelines for conducting SLR [21] we derived and validated search terms and strings, identified types of literature, selected electronic databases, and defined the screening procedures.

The search string were derived from the research questions and included the terms "data mining" and "data analytics" as these are often used interchangeably. The terms "methodology", "framework" and "banking" were added resulting in the search string being defined as ("data mining methodology") OR ("data mining framework") OR ("data analytics methodology") OR ("data analytics framework") AND ("banking"). Validation of the search string according to [22], led to adding the search string of ("CRISP-DM") OR ("SEMMA") OR ("ASUM") AND ("banking") in order to capture case study papers. The search strings were applied to Scopus, Web of Science, and Google Scholar databases. Multidisciplinary indexed/non-indexed electronic databases were selected to ensure wide data sources coverage, and to include studies from both academic (peer reviewed) and practitioners communities ("grey" literature). Specifically, our "grey" literature search covered industry reports, white papers, technical reports, and research works not indexed by Scopus or Web of Science.

Based on the SLR best practices [21,23], we designed a multi-step screening procedures (relevancy and quality) with associated set of *Screening Criteria* (exclusion and inclusion criteria), and *Scoring System*. The exclusion criteria served to eliminate studies in languages other than English, duplicating texts, as well as publications shorter than 6 pages, or the ones not accessible (by University subscriptions). Papers that passed all exclusion criteria were retained and assessed according to relevance criteria. Each paper was considered relevant if it was: (1) about data mining approach within the banking domain, and (2) introduced or described data mining methodology/framework or modification of existing approaches. Finally, quality screening was conducted for full texts evaluation. For that we developed a *Scoring Metrics* as proposed in [22]. Papers were given the score of 3 if all steps of the data mining process were clearly presented and explained. Further, to merit a score of 3, the paper must have also presented proposal on usage, application, or deployment of solution in organization' s business process(es) and IT/IS system, and/or discuss prototype or full solution implementation. If description of some process steps were missing, but without impacting the holistic view and understanding of the work performed, the paper was given a score of 2. Only papers scoring "2" or "3" were included in the final primary studies corpus.

The initial number of studies retrieved amounted to 693 of which 167 were academic and 526 "grey" literature. Having performed the screening based on exclusion criteria, 509 studies remained and were subject to relevance screening. 141 papers were finally identified as relevant and moved into quality assessment phase, and 41 peer-reviewed papers and 61 studies from "grey" literature received a score of 2 or higher. By means of SLR we identified primary texts corpus with 102 relevant studies. Figure 1 below exhibits yearly published research numbers with the breakdown by "peer-reviewed" and "grey" literature starting from 1997.

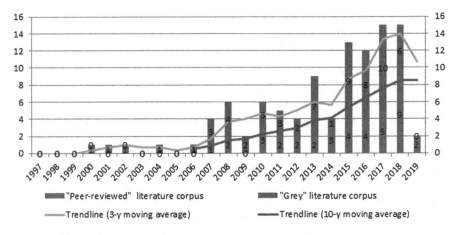

Fig. 1. SLR derived texts corpus - data mining methodologies peer-reviewed research and "grey" literature for period 1997–2019 (no. of publications).

Temporal analysis of texts corpus resulted in two observations. Firstly, we note that research on application of data mining methodologies within the banking domain began more than a decade ago - in 2007. Research efforts made prior to 2007 were infrequent and irregular, with 3–4 years gap periods between publications. Secondly, we note that research on data mining methodologies within banking domain has grown since 2007, an observation supported by the 3-year and 10-year constructed mean trendlines. In particular, we also note that the number of publications have roughly tripled over the last decade, hitting all-time high in 2018 with 22 texts released.

4   Findings and Discussion

In this section, we present results of publications analysis, address the research questions and discuss threats to validity.

RQ1 - For What Purposes are Data Mining Methodologies Used in the Banking Domain? In-depth analysis of text corpus revealed that data mining methodologies are predominantly being employed in the banking domain for two main purposes - customer-oriented and risk-oriented (see Fig. 2a below).

We identified 47 customer-oriented studies which address various aspects related to customer behavior modelling. A typical example is profiling according to usage pattern of different digital channels, [24][2] authors profiled Internet bank users, while [25] focuses on patterns of electronic transactions based on demographic and behavioural features. In the field of Customer Relationship Management (CRM), the most common business problem analyzed relate to identifying and predicting customers who are likely to churn [26], customer loyalty and retention [27], customer segmentation [28], and customer value identification [29]. Further, smart and improved customer targeting in sales campaigns [30] and improved targeting and customer prioritization decision support are also popular business problem [31]. A few studies consider efficiency aspects of bank's infrastructure such as Automated Teller Machines (ATMs) and branch networks (eg. [32]).

The second most commonly analyzed area is Risk Management, predominantly, credit risk. We identified 34 studies that focus on modelling tasks for supporting a variety of risk management processes including credit risk scoring and default prediction [33], prediction of financial distress [34], and credit decisions for private and corporate customers (especially, small and medium enterprises as in [35]). Further, identification and prevention of fraud behavior [36] and AML (anti-money laundering) risks [37] are addressed as well. Finally, other risk management topics, such as market risk, as well as asset management [38], trading strategies [39], overall economic analysis and predictions [53] are also addressed.

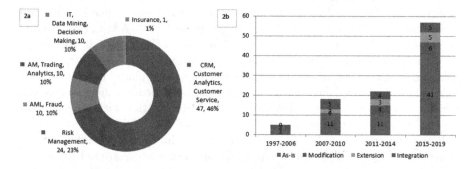

Fig. 2. Applications of data mining methodologies in banking: (a) breakdown by purposes; (b) breakdown by adaptation paradigms

---

[2] Due to space limitation, examples of key texts are presented throughout the analysis. All texts corpus is available at https://figshare.com/articles/MasterListxlsx/ 8206604.

RQ2 - How are Data Mining Methodologies Applied ("as-is" vs Adapted)? The second research questions addresses the extent to which data mining methodologies are used "as-is" versus adapted. Our review identified two distinct paradigms on how data mining methodologies are applied. The first is "as-is" where the data mining methodologies are applied as stipulated. The second is with "adaptations", i.e., methodologies are modified by introducing various changes to the standard process model when applied. Furthermore, our review led us to identify three distinct adaptation scenarios namely "Modification", "Extension", and "Integration":

Scenario "Modification" - introduces specialized sub-tasks and deliverables in order to address a specific use cases or business problems. Modifications typically concentrate on granular adjustments to the methodology at the level of sub-phases, tasks or deliverables within the existing CRISP-DM or KDD stages.

Scenario "Extension" - primarily proposes significant extensions to CRISP-DM resulting in either fully-scaled and integrated data mining solutions, data mining frameworks as a component or tool for automated IS systems or adapted to specialized environments. Adaptations where extensions have been made elicit and explicitly presents various artefacts in the form of system and model architectures, process views, workflows, and implementation aspects. Key benefits achieved are deployment, implementation and leveraging of data mining solutions as integral components of IS systems and business processes. Also, data mining process methodology is substantially changed and extended in all key phases to accommodate new Big Data technologies, tools and environments [47,53].

Scenario "Integration" - 'Integration' primarily concentrates on either combining CRISP-DM with data mining methodologies originated from other domains (e.g. Business Information Management, Business Process Management, BI [58]), adjusting to specific organizational aspects [62], and discrimination-awareness with respect to customers [56]. Adaptations in the form of integration typically introduces various types of ontologies and ontology-based tools, business processes, business information, and BI-driven framework elements. Key benefits are improved at the deployment phase, improved usage of data and discovered knowledge, higher business processes effectiveness and efficiency. Key gap filled in is lack of CRISP-DM integration with other organizational and domain frameworks.

We also noted that publications discussing "as-is" implementations have grown strongly but at the same time, adaptations are also gaining ground (as exhibited in Fig. 2b). Further, there is balanced development and distribution of the research among "Modification", "Extension" and "Integration" paradigms. We can hypothesize that existing reference methodologies do not accommodate and support increasing complexity of data mining projects and IS/IT infrastructure, as well as banking domain specific requirements and as such need to be adapted.

RQ3 - What are the Goals of Adaptations? We address the third research question by analyzing each of adaptation scenarios in depth.

Modification. This adaptation scenario was identified in 12 publications where modifications overwhelmingly consist of specific case studies. However, the major differentiating point compared to "as-is" case studies is clearly the presence of specific adjustments towards standard data mining process methodologies. Yet, the proposed modifications and their purposes do not go beyond traditional CRISP-DM phases. They are granular, specific and executed on tasks, sub-tasks, and at the level of deliverables. This is in clear contrast to "extensions" where one of the key proposals are new phases, such as including a new IS/IT systems implementation and integration phase. Also, with modifications, authors describe potential business applications and deployment scenarios at a conceptual level, but typically do not report or present real implementations to the IS/IT systems and business processes. Further, in the context of banking domain, this research subcategory can be classified with respect to business problems addressed (presented in the Fig. 3[3].)

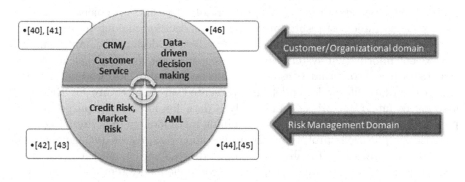

Fig. 3. Data mining methodologies in banking - 'Modification' scenario example texts mapping to business problems

Extension. "Extension" scenario was identified in 10 publications and we noted that it was executed for the two major purposes:

1. To implement fully scaled, integrated data mining solution and regular, repeatable knowledge discovery process - address model, algorithm deployment, implementation design (including architecture, workflows and corresponding IS integration). Also, complementary goal is to address changes to business process to incorporate data mining into organization activities
2. To implement complex, specifically designed systems and integrated business applications with data mining model/solution as component or tool.

---

[3] Due to space limitations, two most cited texts references are presented if number of texts per category exceed two, all texts corpus is available at https://figshare.com/articles/MasterListxlsx/8206604.

Typically, this adaptation is also oriented towards Big Data specifics, and is complemented by proposed artefacts such as Big Data architectures, system models, workflows, and data flows.

We also conclude that the first purpose focuses on implementation of specific data mining models and associated frameworks and processes. For example, apart from classification model and evaluation framework, [47] proposes a knowledge-rich financial risk management process while [48] introduces framework for machine-learning audits. [49] presented data mining-based solution for AML implemented as a tool with respective IS architecture and investigative process. [50] focused on combined data mining concept introducing multiple data sources, methods and features, all incorporated in the real-time prototyped solution. [51] focused on actionable data mining by presenting post-processing data mining framework which enables automated actions generation. In the similar vein, [52] presented large-scale data mining framework extended to incorporate social media data including adaptions to parallel processing. The major benefit achieved by these adaptations, apart from resolved business problem or research gap, is the usefulness of results produced in the decision-making process.

In contrast, the second purpose concentrates on design of complex, multi-component information systems and architectures. For instance, [53] have constructed a framework that considers socio-economic data, its processing methods, a new data life-cycle model, and presented an architecture for Big Data systems to integrate, process and analyze data for forecasting purposes. [54] proposed refinements of reference data mining methodology to address Big Data analytics, applications prototyping and its evaluation, project management and results communication. Finally, [55] proposed cross-border market monitoring and surveillance system with 3 subsystem components, system and data flows. In this research, authors discuss and present useful architectures, algorithms and tool sets in addition to methods and techniques which alone are not sufficient to create deployable systems and tools. The key benefits provided are broad context enabling practical implementations of complex, integrated data mining solutions. The specific list of studies mapped to each of the given purposes along with key artefacts is presented in Fig. 4 below.

Integration. Integration of data mining methodologies were found in 14 publications. Our analysis shows that these adaptations are at the highest abstraction level and typically executed with the goals to (1) introduce discrimination-awareness in data mining, (2) integrate/combine with other organizational frameworks, and (3) integrate/combine with other well-known frameworks, process methodologies and concepts. Example list of studies with artefacts is presented in Fig. 4[4] and further discussed.

Discrimination-aware data mining (DADM), as proposed by [56], includes tool support for "correct" decision process. The major benefit is increased correctness and usefulness of results in the decision-making process, monitoring, avoidance of discrimination and transparency.

---

[4] All texts corpus with complete mappings is available at https://figshare.com/articles/MasterListxlsx/8206604.

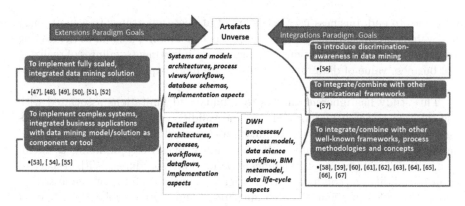

Fig. 4. Data mining methodologies in banking - 'Extension' and 'Integration' scenarios adaptation goals, their artefacts and example texts mapping

[57] author combined data mining methodology with organizational context to instill and improve data-driven decision-making. Further, [58] integrated data mining with business process frameworks and models (also proposed by [59]). [60] integrated data mining with BIM (Business Information Modelling) while [61] merged data mining with BI. All with the purpose to improve usage of data, business processes effectiveness and deployment of data mining solutions. These works are complemented by number of publications [62,63] specifically tackling actionability of data mining results, which aim to reduce likelihood of data mining project producing high quality knowledge with limited or no business benefit. Authors propose shift to domain-driven data mining paradigm by integrating such new key component as domain intelligence, human-machine cooperation, in-depth mining, actionability enhancement, and iterative refinement process. Emphasis on data-mining business requirements, model sharing and resuse from business user perspective is also tackled by introducing ontology-based data mining model management approach [64]. Identical problems are addressed from organizational point of view by [65], which focused on Big Data Analytics governance framework. Finally, number of innovative research papers focused on integrating data mining with technical concepts and frameworks from other domains, for example, relational (symbolic) data mining methods [66] and game theory [67].

To summarize, from "extension" and "integration" research we have identified three important banking domain specific factors, which require adjustments of existing data mining process frameworks and models. Firstly, potential discrimination in the context of credit decision-making requires financial services companies to adapt data mining to achieve transparency. Secondly, large number of accumulated data and associated complex IS/IT architectures, require to adapt data mining process to address complex data mining models deployment patterns and implement them as component of complex systems and business applications. Thirdly, actionability of data mining results, adaptation of analytics outcomes to end, business-user needs are of utmost importance to achieve business value realization. We can hypothesize that in banking domain as the leading adopter of data mining solutions with significant investments, failures of realizing full business value of data mining projects are more explicit and observable and need to be addressed.

This study has inherent threats to validity and limitations associated with the selected research method (SLR). The validity threats include incompleteness of search results (internal validity[5]) and general publication bias (external validity[6]). We have mitigated internal validity by strictly adhering to inclusion criteria, and performing significant validation procedures. With respect to external validity, we conducted trial searches to ensure validity of search strings and proper identification of potential papers. Our initial publications harvest size reached almost 700 texts originated from indexed peer-review research and "grey" literature thus mitigating external validity risk. Further, the key limitation of the SLR method for this study is that banking industry internal practices are not frequently disclosed in academic literature. We mitigated the negative impact by inclusion of "grey" literature where reporting on existing industry practices by professionals is common.

5   Conclusion

In this study we have examined data mining methodologies usage in the banking domain. By means of Systematic Literature Review we have identified 102 relevant studies of peer-reviewed and "grey" literature which have been evaluated in depth to address three research questions: for what purposes data mining methodologies are used in the banking domain? (RQ1), how are they applied ("as-is" vs adapted)? (RQ2), and what are the goals of adaptations? (RQ3).

Tackling RQ1 (For what purposes?) we have discovered that data mining methodologies are applied regularly since 2007 and their usage has tripled. Further, data mining in financial services domain is primarily used for two main purposes - to address Customer Relationship Management and Risk Management related business problems.

Answering RQ2 (How?), we have identified that over the last decade data mining methodologies have been primarily applied "as-is" without modifications. Yet, we have also discovered emerging and persistent trend of using data mining methodologies in banking with adaptations. Further, we have distinguished three adaptations scenarios ranging from granular modifications on tasks, subtask and deliverables level and ending up with merging standard data mining methodologies with other frameworks.

Addressing RQ3 (What are the adaptations goals?), we have examined the adaptation objectives, banking domain specific factors behind such adaptations,

---

[5] The internal validity stems from subjective screening and rating of studies when applying relevancy and quality criteria.

[6] The threats to external validity relate to the extent by which the results can be generalized beyond the scope of this study.

and as a result have identified three such aspects. Firstly, discriminatory awareness and transparent decision-making (human-centric aspect) require data mining process adaptation. Secondly, actionability of data mining results (business-centric aspect) plays a central role in the banking domain. Thirdly, we have also identified that standard data mining methodologies lack deployment and implementation aspects (technology-centric aspects) required to scale and transform data mining models into software products and components integrated into Big Data Architectures. Therefore, adaptations are used to integrate data mining models and solutions in complex IT/IS systems and business processes of the banking industry. This study highlighted the needs and established ground for future work to develop refinements of existing data mining methodologies for the banking domain which would address three above mentioned concerns.

References

1. Forbes Homepage. https://www.forbes.com/sites/louiscolumbus/2017/12/24/53-of-companies-are-adopting-big-data-analytics/4cf12a2139a1. Accessed 26 May 2019
2. Liao, S.H., Chu, P.H., Hsiao, P.Y.: Data mining techniques and applications - a decade review from 2000 to 2011. Expert Syst. Appl. **39**(12), 11303–11311 (2012)
3. Mariani, M., Baggio, R., Fuchs, M., Hoepken, W.: Business intelligence and big data in hospitality and tourism: a systematic literature review. Int. J. Contemp. Hospit. Manage. **30**(12), 3514–3554 (2018)
4. Amani, F., Fadlalla, A.: Data mining applications in accounting: a review of the literature and organizing framework. Int. J. Acc. Inform. Syst. **24**, 32–58 (2017)
5. Murnion, P., Helfert, M.: A framework for decision support for learning management systems. In: 10th European Conference on e-Learning ECEL-2011, Brighton, UK (2011)
6. Bi, Z., Cochran, D.: Big data analytics with applications. J. Manage. Anal. **1**(4), 249–265 (2014)
7. Wongchinsri, P., Kuratach, W.: A survey - data mining frameworks in credit card processing. In: 13th International Conference on Electrical Engineering/Electronics. Computer, Telecommunications and Information Technology (ECTI-CON), pp. 1–6. IEEE, Chiang Mai (2016)
8. Hassani, H., Huang, X., Silva, E.: Digitalisation and big data mining in banking. Big Data Cogn. Comput. **2**(18), 1–14 (2018)
9. Morabito, V.: The Future of Digital Business Innovation: Trends and Practices. Springer, Switzerland (2016). https://doi.org/10.1007/978-3-319-26874-3
10. Mariscal, G., Marban, O., Fernandez, C.: A survey of data mining and knowledge discovery process models and methodologies. Knowl. Eng. Rev. **25**(2), 137–166 (2010)
11. Marban, O., Mariscal, G., Segovia, J.: A data mining and knowledge discovery process model. In: Julio, P., Adem, K. (eds.) Data Mining and Knowledge Discovery in Real Life Applications, pp. 438–453. Paris I-Tech, Vienna (2009)
12. Fayyad, U.M., Piatetsky-Shapiro, G., Smyth, P.: From data mining to knowledge discovery in databases. AI Mag. **17**(3), 37–54 (1996a)
13. Fayyad, U.M., Piatetsky-Shapiro, G., Smyth, P.: The KDD process for extracting useful knowledge from volumes of data. Commun. ACM **39**(11), 27–34 (1996b)

14. Fayyad, U.M., Piatetsky-Shapiro, G., Smyth, P.: Knowledge discovery and data mining: towards a unifying framework. In: Proceedings of the Second International Conference on Knowledge Discovery and Data Mining (KDD-96), Portland, Oregon, USA, pp. 82–88 (1996c)

15. Kurgan, L.A., Muslek, P.: A survey of knowledge discovery and data mining process models. Knowl. Eng. Rev. **21**(1), 1–24 (2006)

16. SAS Institute: Data Mining Using SAS Enterprise MinerTM: A Case Study Approach. SAS Institute Inc., Cary, 1166NC (2013)

17. Cios, K.J., Kurgan, L.A.: Trends in data mining and knowledge discovery. In: Pal, N.R., Jain, L. (eds.) Advanced Techniques in Knowledge Discovery and Data Mining. Advanced Information and Knowledge Processing, pp. 1–26. Springer, London (2005). https://doi.org/10.1007/1-84628-183-0_1

18. Moyle, S., Jorge, A.: RAMSYS - a methodology for supporting rapid remote collaborative data mining projects. In: ECML/PKDD01 Workshop: Integrating Aspects of Data Mining, Decision Support and Meta-learning (IDDM-2001) (2001)

19. Solarte, J.: A proposed data mining methodology and its application to industrial engineering. Ph.D. Thesis, University of Tennessee (2002)

20. Marban, O., Segovia, J., Menasalvas, E., Fernandez-Baizan, C.: Toward data mining engineering: a software engineering approach. Inform. Syst. **34**(1), 87–107 (2009)

21. Kitchenham, B.: Procedures for performing systematic reviews. Keele University Technical Report 1038TR/SE-0401, ISSN:1353–7776; NICTA Technical Report 0400011T.1, 1–28 (2004)

22. Kitchenham, B., Charters, S.: Guidelines for performing systematic literature reviews in software engineering. EBSE Technical Report No. EBSE-2007-01 (2007)

23. Brereton, P., Kitchenham, B.A., Budgen, D., Turner, M., Khalil, M.: Lessons from applying the systematic literature review process within the software engineering domain. J. Syst. Softw. **80**(4), 571–583 (2007)

24. Mansingh, G., Rao, L., Osei-Bryson, K.M., Mills, A.: Application of a data mining process model: a case study-profiling internet banking users in Jamaica. In: AMCIS, p. 439 (2010)

25. Etaiwi, W., Biltawi, M., Naymat, G.: Evaluation of classification algorithms for banking customer's behavior under apache spark data processing system. Proc. Comput. Sci. **113**, 559–564 (2017)

26. Kumar, D.A., Ravi, V.: Predicting credit card customer churn in banks using data mining. Int. J. Data Anal. Tech. Strategies **1**(1), 4–28 (2008)

27. Bahari, T.F., Elayidom, M.S.: An efficient CRM-data mining framework for the prediction of customer behaviour. Proc. Comput. Sci. **46**, 725–731 (2015)

28. Tsiptsis, K.K., Chorianopoulos, A.: Data Mining Techniques in CRM: Inside Customer Segmentation. Wiley, Hoboken (2011)

29. Moeini, M., Alizadeh, S.H.: Proposing a new model for determining the customer value using RFM model and its developments (case study on the Alborz insurance company). J. Eng. Appl. Sci. **100**(4), 828–836 (2016)

30. Neysiani, B. S., Soltani, N., Ghezelbash, S.: A framework for improving find best marketing targets using a hybrid genetic algorithm and neural networks. In: 2nd International Conference on Knowledge-Based Engineering and Innovation (KBEI), pp. 733–738. IEEE (2015)

31. Ghosh, S., Hazra, A., Choudhury, B., Biswas, P., Nag, A.: A comparative study to the bank market prediction. In: Perner, P. (ed.) MLDM 2018. LNCS (LNAI), vol. 10934, pp. 259–268. Springer, Cham (2018). https://doi.org/10.1007/978-3-319-96136-1_21

32. Met, I., Tunali, G., Erkoç, A., Tanrikulu, S., Dolgun, M.O.: Branch efficiency and location forecasting: application of Ziraat bank. J. Appl. Financ. Bank. **7**(4), 1–13 (2017)

33. Khemakhem, S., Ben Said, F., Boujelbene, Y.: Credit risk assessment for unbalanced datasets based on data mining, artificial neural network and support vector machines. J. Modell. Manage. **13**(4), 932–951 (2018)

34. Geng, R., Bose, I., Chen, X.: Prediction of financial distress: an empirical study of listed Chinese companies using data mining. Eur. J. Oper. Res. **241**(1), 236–247 (2015)

35. Gulsoy, N., Kulluk, S.: A data mining application in credit scoring processes of small and medium enterprises commercial corporate customers. Wiley Interdisc. Rev.: Data Min. Knowl. Discov. **9**(3), e1299 (2019)

36. Adeyiga, J.A., Ezike, J.O.J., Omotosho, A., Amakulor, W.: A neural network based model for detecting irregularities in e-banking transactions. Afr. J. Comput. ICTs **4**(2), 7–14 (2011)

37. Colladon, A.F., Remondi, E.: Using social network analysis to prevent money laundering. Expert Syst. Appl. **67**, 49–58 (2017)

38. Liu, X., Ye, Q.: The different impacts of news-driven and self-initiated search volume on stock prices. Inf. Manage. **53**(8), 997–1005 (2016)

39. Al-Radaideh, Q. A., Assaf, A. A., Alnagi, E.: Predicting stock prices using data mining techniques. In: The International Arab Conference on Information Technology (ACIT 2013) (2013)

40. Smith, K.A., Willis, R.J., Brooks, M.: An analysis of customer retention and insurance claim patterns using data mining: a case study. J. Oper. Res. Soc. **51**(5), 532–541 (2000)

41. Karimi-Majd, A.M., Mahootchi, M.: A new data mining methodology for generating new service ideas. Inform. Syst. e-Bus. Manage. **13**(3), 421–443 (2015)

42. Montiel, J., Bifet, A., Abdessalem, T.: Predicting over-indebtedness on batch and streaming data. In: 2017 IEEE International Conference on Big Data (Big Data), pp. 1504–1513. IEEE (2017)

43. Rajan, M.: Credit scoring process using banking detailed data store. Int. J. Appl. Inform. Syst. (IJAIS) **8**(6), 13–20 (2015)

44. Luo, X.: Suspicious transaction detection for anti-money laundering. Int. J. Secur. Appl. **8**(2), 157–166 (2014)

45. Resta, M.: VaRSOM: a tool to monitor markets' stability based on value at risk and self-organizing maps. Intell. Syst. Acc. Financ.Manage. **23**(1–2), 47–64 (2016)

46. Kaddouri, A.: Why human expertise is critical for data mining. Int. J. Comput. Inform. Technol. **2**(1), 99–108 (2013)

47. Peng, Y., Wang, G., Kou, G., Shi, Y.: An empirical study of classification algorithm evaluation for financial risk prediction. Appl. Soft Comput. **11**(2), 2906–2915 (2011)

48. Clark, A.: The machine learning audit - CRISP-DM framework. ISACA **1** (2018)

49. Le Khac, N.A., Markos, S., Kechadi, M.T.: A data mining-based solution for detecting suspicious money laundering cases in an investment bank. In: Second International Conference on Advances in Databases, Knowledge, and Data Applications, pp. 235–240. IEEE (2010)

50. Sridevi, P., Reddy, N.: Informative knowledge discovery using multiple data sources, multiple features and multiple data mining techniques. IOSR J. Eng. **31**, 20–25 (2013)

51. Yang, Q.: Post-processing data mining models for actionability. In: Cao, L., Yu, P.S., Zhang, C., Zhang, H. (eds.) Data Mining for Business Applications, pp. 11–30. Springer, Boston (2009). https://doi.org/10.1007/978-0-387-79420-4_2

52. Yuan, H., Lau, R. Y., Xu, W., Pan, Z., Wong, M.: Mining individuals' behavior patterns from social media for enhancing online credit scoring. In: 22nd Pacific Conference on Information Systems (PACIS) Proceedings, Japan, p. 163 (2018)

53. Blazquez, D., Domenech, J.: Big data sources and methods for social and economic analyses. Technol. Forecast. Soc. Chang. 130, 99–113 (2018)

54. Angée, S., Lozano-Argel, S.I., Montoya-Munera, E.N., Ospina-Arango, J.D., Tabares-Betancur, M.S.: Towards an improved ASUM-DM process methodology for cross-disciplinary multi-organization big data and analytics projects. In: Uden, L., Hadzima, B., Ting, I.H. (eds.) KMO 2018. Communications in Computer and Information Science, vol. 877, pp. 613–624. Springer, Cham (2018). https://doi.org/10.1007/978-3-319-95204-8_51

55. Diaz, D., Theodoulidis, B., Abioye, E.: Cross-border challenges in financial markets monitoring and surveillance: a case study of customer-driven service value networks. In: 2012 Annual SRII Global Conference, pp. 146–157. IEEE (2012)

56. Berendt, B., Preibusch, S.: Better decision support through exploratory discrimination-aware data mining: foundations and empirical evidence. Artif. Intell. Law 22(2), 175–209 (2014)

57. Debuse, J.C.W.: Extending data mining methodologies to encompass organizational factors. Syst. Res. Behav. Sci.: Off. J. Int. Federat. Syst. Res. 24(2), 183–190 (2007)

58. Pivk, A., Vasilecas, O., Kalibatiene, D., Rupnik, R.: On approach for the implementation of data mining to business process optimisation in commercial companies. Technol. Econ. Dev. Econ. 19(2), 237–256 (2013)

59. Lessmann, S., Listiani, M., Voß, S.: Decision support in car leasing: a forecasting model for residual value estimation. In: 31st International Conference on Information System (ICIS) Proceedings, St. Louise, p. 17 (2010)

60. Priebe, T., Markus, S.: Business information modeling: a methodology for data-intensive projects, data science and big data governance. In: 2015 IEEE International Conference on Big Data (Big Data), pp. 2056–2065. IEEE (2015)

61. Balkan, S., Goul, M.: A portfolio theoretic approach to administering advanced analytics: the case of multi-stage campaign management. In: 44th Hawaii International Conference on System Sciences, pp. 1–10. IEEE (2011)

62. Cao, L., Zhang, C.: The evolution of KDD: towards domain-driven data mining. Int. J. Pattern Recogn. Artif. Intell. 21(04), 677–692 (2007)

63. Cao, L.: Domain-driven data mining: challenges and prospects. IEEE Trans. Knowl. Data Eng. 22(6), 755–769 (2010)

64. Li, Y., Thomas, M.A., Osei-Bryson, K.M.: Ontology-based data mining model management for self-service knowledge discovery. Inform. Syst. Front. 19(4), 925–943 (2017)

65. Lawler, J., Joseph, A.: Big data analytics methodology in the financial industry. Inform. Syst. Educ. J. 15(4), 38–51 (2017)

66. Kovalerchuk, B., Vityaev, E.: Symbolic methodology for numeric data mining. Intell. Data Anal. 12(2), 165–188 (2008)

67. Qin, Z., Wan, T., Dong, Y., Du, Y.: Evolutionary collective behavior decomposition model for time series data mining. Appl. Soft Comput. 26, 368–377 (2015)

Multi-component Infrastructure for e-Lectures

A Viable Solution for Small and Medium-Sized Organizations

Vera G. Meister⬤, Wenxin Hu$^{(\boxtimes)}$⬤, Emre Arkan⬤,
and Hannes Günther⬤

Technische Hochschule Brandenburg,
14770 Brandenburg a. d. H, Brandenburg, Germany
{vera.meister,wenxin.hu}@th-brandenburg.de

Abstract. e-Lectures dominate course material in many e-learning environments. Even small and medium-sized organizations with significant constraints in budget and other resources need a way to make their e-lectures systematically and easily accessible. The paper presents an innovative prototypical approach to a viable multi-component infrastructure for e-lectures. The selection and customization of the components is discussed from the state of the art and aligned to requirements of small and medium-sized organizations. In order to measure the overall performance, computer experiments were carried out according to scientifically sound procedures. The affordability of the multi-component system was finally examined applying an argumentative-deductive analysis. The paper therefore serves as an implementation guidance in similar environments.

Keywords: e-Lecture · Video management system ·
Semantic content management · Dual video cast · Video deployment

1 Introduction

Due to significantly lowered barriers for the production and delivery of videos and not least due to the didactic proximity to classical lecture formats, e-lectures dominate course material in many e-learning environments, particularly in nearly all MOOCs (Massive Open Online Courses) [1, p. 3]. While in MOOCs as well as in administrated university courses the e-lectures are integrated in learning management systems (e.g. Moodle, to name a widely distributed open source tool) the problem of giving open and course-independent access to e-lectures remain not well addressed. There are several reasons why such prominent streaming platforms like YouTube or Vimeo should not be used directly: cluttering by advertisement, limited opportunities for structuring, lack of support for certain production and delivery styles.

The market offers a wide range of video management systems for businesses, but they are not cost-viable at all for small and medium-sized organizations [2]. In addition, these systems cannot solve all the above problems, particularly in terms of structuring and delivery styles. On the other hand, there is a great variety of open source components and technologies as well as high-performance services at affordable prices which can be combined to an accordingly customized system.

© Springer Nature Switzerland AG 2019
M. Pańkowska and K. Sandkuhl (Eds.): BIR 2019, LNBIP 365, pp. 119–134, 2019.
https://doi.org/10.1007/978-3-030-31143-8_9

The paper presents the experiences and insights from several years of developing a multi-component system for e-lectures at a small university with 2,600 students and 250 employees. The system is openly accessible and is not only used at the home university but also at cooperating institutions. Because of its generic structure, it can be used in any educational environment, not just universities. A schema.org-based business knowledge schema serves as a central structuring artifact. All in all, the infrastructure encompasses a wide range of different components: (i) the hardware for video production in a style flexibly combining talking head with screencasts, (ii) a Vimeo[1] account for storing videos and providing streaming services, (iii) OntoWiki[2] as the back end of the e-lecture management system, (iv) a web-based user interface[3] based on OntoWiki's site extension feature providing structured access to e-lectures, (v) the OpenHPI[4] dual player software for customizable and synchronous delivery of talking head and screencast videos, (vi) a streaming app providing metadata and control features for consuming e-lectures[5], and (vii) a business process for populating the relevant databases with new e-lecture data and files implemented in Camunda BPM[6].

Research methods applied in this paper are prototyping for the system development, computer experiments for performance measurements, and argumentative-deductive analysis for proving the overall affordability in the given environment. Quantitative and/or qualitative research on the didactic value of e-lectures and on the general use of semantic technologies in e-learning environments (see e.g. [1, 3–5]) are outside the focus of this work. The rest of the paper is structured as follows. Section 2 discusses the main concepts and definitions, mainly e-lecture, video management system, and knowledge schema. Section 3 provides a deeper insight into the state of the art of e-lecture platforms. The research questions and methods applied are stated and explained in Sect. 4. Section 5 addresses in detail the system design and prototypical implementation. Section 6 is concerned with the evaluation of the system. The paper closes with a summary and an outlook on future work in Sect. 7.

2 Main Concepts and Definitions

The main concepts to be defined in this section are e-lecture, video management system, and knowledge schema. Since these concepts are subject to different interpretations, the following definitions are intended to ensure a uniform understanding within the framework of this work.

Following [6] we call *e-lecture* any digital learning resource in lecture format, which is recorded in a studio in the absence of the intended audience. In differentiation to this, [6] names a lecture recorded in a real context as life digitized lecture.

---

[1] https://vimeo.com/de/upgrade.

[2] http://ontowiki.net/.

[3] https://fbwtube.th-brandenburg.de/.

[4] https://github.com/openHPI/video-player.

[5] See e.g. http://univera.de/FHB/fbwTube/?id=DFW_EN&chapter=0.

[6] https://camunda.com/products/bpmn-engine/.

The e-lectures at hand combine flexibly a so-called talking head video and a screencast video, which is genuinely supported by the recording technology used. Compared to a comprehensive typology of 18 video production styles, including eight types of e-lectures, (comp. [1]) the chosen lecture style is close to picture-in-picture, where the screencast integrates a smaller video of the speaker. But it is more flexible because the user of the streaming app can adjust the presentation canvasses according to his or her needs. This style is proven to be very effective by the successful MOOC platform openHPI [7, p. 13]. Table 1 shows the resulting characteristic when applying the classification criteria from [3, p. 73] to the e-lectures considered in this article.

Table 1. Characteristics of e-lectures in the context of the paper

Criterion	Characteristic
Recording method	Combination of camera and screencast
Content mediation	Classical lecture
Recording location	Studio setting
Duration	5–20 min, collected in series
Integration of the lecturer image	Flexibly sizable separate video

A *video management system* (VMS) is a specific type of content management system (CMS) where videos are the main content provided. According to [8], a CMS assures the division of content, layout, and structure. The video content is stored at ideally powerful video (streaming) servers. The layout ensures a consistent and concise appearance, and the structure comes from the implemented data models. Another characteristic of CMS are the roles and corresponding rights provided to user agents. Three of them are of relevance in the given context: consumer, editor, and service. Consumer and editor are humans, whereas a service is a technical agent. It "uses" the CMS via application programming interfaces (API).

The last concept to define in this section is *knowledge schema*. One of the basic sets of concepts in the field of Information Systems comprises data, information and, knowledge (comp. e.g. [9]). The content provided in a CMS can be characterized as information. The structure of content representation depends on the implemented data model which, may range from lightweight metadata structures to formal schemata. A knowledge schema is a domain-specific, semantically rich and standards-based conceptualization which may constitute the structure of an information system. In the case at hand, we use a RDF-based knowledge schema for shaping the VMS back end.

3 State of the Art

In order to assess the adequacy of the prototype described in Sect. 5, the state of the art for VMS shall be summarized in this section. Therefore, leading solutions from three categories of VMS will be scrutinized: (i) major VMS platforms like YouTube or Vimeo, (ii) non-semantic VMS, and (iii) semantic VMS, where the term semantic refers to Semantic Web technologies. Since the paper deals with systems for small and medium-sized organizations, high-priced systems from categories (ii) and (iii) are not considered. Instead, the focus is on open source solutions.

Major VMS Platform Vimeo. In general, Vimeo can be used as an organizational VMS with customizable roles and domains where videos may be embedded. Videos can be proactively grouped in albums and/or channels. This grouping doesn't provide ordered list features. Further, videos can be tagged with a title and a description. Each video is provided with a URL for streaming. Creation and modification dates as well as duration and some other streaming features are captured automatically. Finally, several pictures including their metadata are created, e.g. for thumbnails (comp. [10]). More complex didactic relations, e.g. between lectures and lecturers or study programs, are not implementable. The main exclusion criterion in the given context, however, is that Vimeo does not support the synchronous display of two videos.

Non-semantic VMS. A low-threshold architecture for a non-semantic VMS combines an easy to implement open source CMS (e.g. WordPress) with an appropriate video player. This is how the problem of dual synchronous video display can be solved. Content can be arranged in predefined categories, enriched by human-readable metadata and probably tagged. Basic search functions are limited to string matching in textual data. With the help of plugins, a facetted searching or filtering can be implemented. However, specific relations between the categories are not feasible and therefore no complex queries are possible (comp. e.g. [11]).

Semantic VMS. Since 2014, the TIB AV Portal [12] has been a very powerful, open VMS for quality-checked scientific e-lectures from six scientific disciplines. The portal relies genuinely on semantic technologies and services such as automatic video analysis and semantic tagging. Basic lecture metadata is entered along the schema for non-textual materials (NTM). Further structured data is created by automatic annotation of video content. The NTM schema is based on the collection-related interests of libraries and less on didactic issues. Relationships between e-lectures and courses or degree programs are not offered, but relations to subject areas and subjects can be established along controlled vocabularies. The VMS is equipped with rich filtering and search functions. Content delivery by a dual video player is not supported.

Another approach to providing video content via semantic platforms is offered by freely configurable semantic wiki systems such as Semantic MediaWiki (SMW) [13] and OntoWiki. Both are available as open source. OntoWiki not only allows but requires the use of individual knowledge schemata to build semantic content structures, whereas SMW as an extension to MediaWiki – the software that powers Wikipedia – inherits from it all wiki-typical classes and functions but allows the import of additional RDF data. OntoWiki's benefits are genuinely structured, nested views and rich browsing functions. Equipping OntoWiki with a VMS interface nevertheless requires the implementation of a sophisticated site extension. Both systems are mainly programmed in PHP. It should be noted that SMW has a vibrant development community issuing regularly new software releases, while the development of OntoWiki has been frozen on stable version 1.0 in 2017 in favor of newer technologies.

If one weighs up all the advantages and limitations presented against each other and at the same time considers the following two requirements to be indispensable: (i) implementation of the semantic structure of the educational domain in the back end and (ii) support of the dual delivery format in the user interface, the implementation of OntoWiki as back end for the VMS appears to be the means of choice.

4   Research Questions and Methodology

The engagement with e-lectures and a related infrastructure began in 2014 as an individual initiative of the author - a professor at Brandenburg University of Applied Sciences (BUAS). As explained in the previous section, there is no ready-made solution for the case under consideration. Therefore, from the very beginning, the project had a research character. Main research questions where stated as follows:

1. Which components are required for a viable infrastructure for e-lectures that is driven by semantic technology and allows dual display of talking head and screencast videos?
2. Which level of performance can achieve this multi-component infrastructure for
3. e-lectures in comparison to other production processes and VMS?
4. What types of resources does the implementation of the system in question require and what does it look like compared to large VMSs?

Main research method applied in this work is prototyping. The state-of-the-art analysis in the previous section showed the absence of easy-to-implement solutions that meet the stated requirements. Therefore, the development process was characterized by intensive literature and source studies, experimental developments and well-founded reflections. At the same time, the implemented parts of the system were continuously used in teaching and thus subjected to regular practical tests. The knowledge gained in this way influenced further developments. The results of prototyping are demonstrated and critically reflected in Sect. 5 and thus give an answer to research question 1. In order to solve research questions 2, computer experiments were carried out according to scientifically sound procedures. Finally, research question 3 was subjected to an argumentative-deductive analysis. The results of these experiments and analyses are described in Sect. 6.

5   Prototypical Implementation

After the general discussion of the problem and the state of the art, the prototypical multi-component solution for e-lectures will be scrutinized in detail in this section. The main design and development steps will be explained, and the direct results reflected. The successively growing system is in productive use since 2015. As already explained in Sect. 1, the system consists of seven components. They will be discussed in a system-oriented logic in Sects. 5.2–5.6. The following section provides an introductory description of the system's core architecture.

5.1 System Design

As first asset of the overall system, the university acquired the so-called TeleTask Recording System[7] together with lightening equipment and a streaming server. After a series of discouraging tests, the server was replaced by an external streaming service. Another disappointing experience was the built-in delivery format of the e-lectures. An acceptable adaptation to our corporate design was not possible with the preconfigured settings. A direct manipulation of the built-in software was also prohibited. We agreed with the manufacturer – a subsidiary of Hasso Plattner Institute (HPI) by University of Potsdam – to reconfigure the software for direct export of the two e-lecture videos (talking head and screencast). Then we were able to build our own customized interface reusing the HPI open source dual player software. This historical part of the system is visualized in the upper right part of Fig. 1. The e-lectures now could be used via URLs provided in Moodle, i.e. in the context of specific courses. Figure 7 shows the appearance of e-lectures in that environment. At that point, the first of two crucial requirements were met.

Over time, the collection has grown to almost 200 e-lectures with a total duration of approx. 40 h. The individual e-lectures are arranged in series, which correspond to a class. They are currently used in eight courses and in all four major study programs of the Department of Economics at BUAS and in addition, at four foreign partner universities. Therefore, a need for a VMS arose that would not only enable efficient management of e-lectures but would also provide easy access to that material beyond specific courses and study programs.

Right from the start, the goal was to base the VMS on a domain-specific knowledge schema. First, the possibilities of the CMS Drupal were tested, which had a semantic plugin in its version 8. Since earlier good experience had been gained with a semantic catalog application, another prototype was then built from scratch. Both prototypes could not meet the requirements. Finally, an OntoWiki project was set up and successfully implemented. Figure 1 shows the implemented IT architecture of the e-lecture system in an abstract graphic. OntoWiki acts as back end with Virtuoso as data storage.

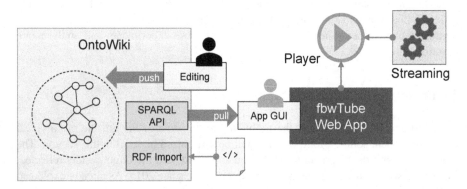

Fig. 1. Abstract architecture of the e-lecture system

---

[7] https://www.tele-task.de/about/.

Data on new e-lectures are imported as RDF files and edited in the back end as required. The VMS business logic and user interface were implemented on the base of a so-called site extension. By browsing, searching and filtering, users pull data from OntoWiki via its SPARQL API. On click on an e-lecture link, the dual player application starts in a new tab and loads the video streams from Vimeo.

5.2 Production Studio

Budget bottlenecks in smaller organizations affect not only money and human resources, but also premises and other equipment. Therefore, the video recordings were first carried out in a seminar room (comp. [14]). The recording equipment had to be set up and dismantled each time. In addition, it was not possible to illuminate the speaker as desired. Fortunately, a small basement room could be occupied after one year. With the help of a photo expert, the headlights could be installed as intended.

The equipment of the studio is completed by a desk for the recording assistant, a sideboard for the lecturer as well as a touch screen presentation computer for the handling of learning material or resources. Camera and computer are cable connected with the recording box via device interfaces. The lecturer uses a wireless microphone which is pre-tuned to be recorded by the box. All components are visible on Fig. 2.

On wish list remain an additional sound system with multiple microphones to record group teaching or discussions and a camera with better resolution for brighter talking head videos. To improve the resolution of screencasts, a new recording box

Fig. 2. e-Lecture production studio with dual cast equipment

with HDMI interfaces must be acquired. According to the manufacturer, an upgrade of the box in use is not possible. That would be a large investment, which actually cannot be made solely from the university's own resources. Another useful add-on would be a teleprompter to allow the lecturers to look directly into the camera more often. Such an additional screen could be implemented without much effort.

5.3   Knowledge Schema

As stated at the beginning and repeatedly confirmed, a domain-specific knowledge schema should form the structure-giving backbone for the VMS. In this role, it allows flexible traversing of the entire graph and thus valuable queries and views in the user interface as well as at the back end. In addition, it is planned to publish metadata about the e-lectures in the system openly on the web by using semantic annotation based on schema.org. That's why the classes, relations and attributes were taken from the schema.org vocabulary as completely as possible. Basic structuring relations and attributes were taken from RDFS, namely `subClassOf`, `label`, and `comment`. Apart from that, all domain-specific predicates come from schema.org.

The situation with the relevant classes is more problematic. Videos and e-lectures can be interpreted as subclasses of the schema.org top-level class `CreativeWork`. There is an explicit subclass `VideoObject` which initially was part of the domain schema. It is defined as a class of video files, in the situation at hand MP4 files for the talking head or the screencast of a single e-lecture. In the course of the development, it becomes clear, that this level of granularity will yield no benefits. Therefore, the class was omitted from the schema. Strictly speaking, an e-lecture (in Fig. 3 depicted as `DoubleClip`) is a series of two corresponding video objects and therefore they form a subclass of `CreativeWorkSeries`. The same applies to the other granularity levels, namely series of e-lectures for a single class (modeled as `VideoLecture`) and series of these series represented as `LectureSeries`. The schema.org class `MovieSeries` does not fit properly for any of these classes, therefore the mentioned proprietary classes are introduced.

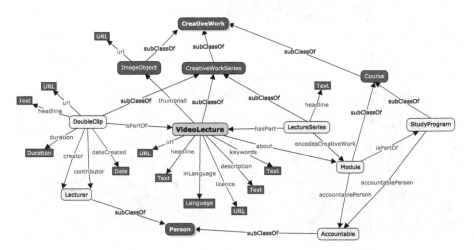

Fig. 3. Knowledge schema for the e-lecture system (Color figure online)

Similar problems arose at modeling courses and study programs. Both appear as subclasses of schema.org's `Course` and are modeled for distinction purposes as `Module` and `StudyProgram`. Lastly, subclasses for `Person` were introduced: `Lecturer` and `Accountable`. Figure 3 shows the schema at a conceptual level. The elements taken from schema.org are represented in red color.

5.4 Back End

The knowledge schema discussed in the last section provides the navigation structure for the OntoWiki system, which finally was chosen as back end resource. At the left side in Fig. 4 a snippet of that schema is visualized, namely the subclasses of Creative Work Series: Double Clip, Video Lecture and Lecture Series. OntoWiki depicts on the surface `rdfs:labels` wherever they are available. The schema itself and the bulk data on e-lectures can be imported directly in OntoWiki as soon as they are available in RDF. All data – schema data as well as productive data – are stored in the associated Virtuoso Triple Store. The populated knowledge base allows editors to browse, to edit and to request structured data from the graph via user interface functions and widgets [15]. In the center of Fig. 4 the data for a specific video lecture are depicted. On the right side a window element labelled as "Instances linking here" lists the corresponding e-lectures (Double Clips) as well as the lecture series this video lecture is part of. All resources are clickable and therefore further explorable.

Fig. 4. OntoWiki back end with exposure of e-lecture data

After extending OntoWiki with the help of the site extension for creating a VMS user interface, new items are automatically added to the OntoWiki Navigation Classes: `Navigation` for the specification of the Web app navigation and `WebPages` for the definition of all pages (templates) used in the app. Static pages like Imprint or Privacy can be edited directly in the back end. The following listing shows an excerpt of RDF data in Turtle format for the video lecture exposed in Fig. 4.

```
vide:DFW_EN    a          vidp:VideoLecture ;
  rdfs:label             "DFW_EN" ;
  schema:headline        "Digital Forms and Workflows"@en ,
  schema:inLanguage      "en" ;
  schema:thumbnail       vide:DFW_EN ;
  schema:about           vide:WIBW ;
  schema:url "http://univera.de/FHB/fbwTube/?id=DFW_EN".
```

5.5   User Interfaces

In this section two technically independent user interfaces will be discussed. The first represents the front end of the VMS, the second acts as the dual player interface. Tele-Task runs a sophisticated VMS with multiple filtering functionalities and a powerful search embedding the dual player directly in the application[8]. We decided to connect two separate applications mentioned above, as this is much easier to implement.

Another decision which differentiates the presented here VMS user interface from others is the omission of the common, often unaesthetic thumbnails and the use of clear, expressive, and theme-related logos instead. Thematically close video lectures can be tagged with the same logo and therefore show their proximity at one glance. For every video lecture, concise metadata are provided: language, number of associated e-lectures, total duration, lecturer(s), and description teaser (Fig. 5). Several surface

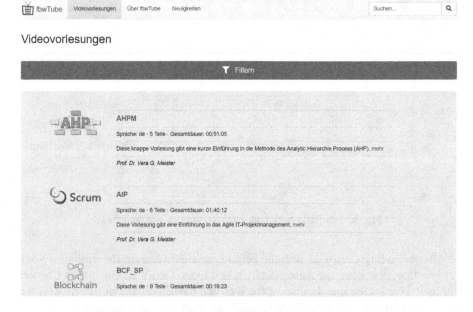

Fig. 5. Main page of the OntoWiki-based VMS user interface

---

[8] https://www.tele-task.de/series/.

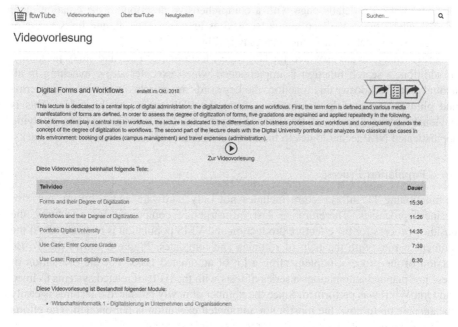

Fig. 6. Details page of the VMS interface with links to e-lectures

Fig. 7. Dual player interface with sizable videos, metadata and control elements

elements link to a details page with a comprehensive description, the creation date, courses where the video lecture can be used as learning material, and links to the e-lectures itself which open in the dual player (Figs. 6 and 7).

Filter functions are provided for languages, lecturers, courses and study programs. In addition, a search function is implemented which executes string matching in all textual data. To booster this function, the keywords are enriched with prominent terms and phrases extracted by text mining from the PDF scripts of the video. This is obviously more direct and therefore cheaper and less error-prone than applying sophisticated NLP technologies to the unstructured data of screencasts or audio tracks.

5.6   Population Process

A functioning IT infrastructure includes not only hardware and software, but also business processes. Therefore, as last infrastructure component for e-lectures, the business process for the e-lecture production and VMS population is considered. At the moment it runs with the help of routines and templates. Figure 8 shows the To-Be version of the process, implementing a lot of automated tasks. For the evaluation of these pre-planned automations a series of tests with the APIs of related systems (Vimeo and OntoWiki) was performed. Since the number of newly produced e-lectures is easily manageable up to now, the mostly not-automated execution is fair enough. The efforts for automation would far exceed the expected time savings.

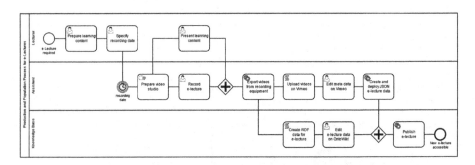

Fig. 8. To-Be production and population process for e-lectures

The most suitable candidate for automation is the activity "Create and deploy JSON e-lecture data". This file delivers structured metadata and necessary links for a video lecture consisting of several e-lectures to be displayed in the dual player. The necessary data can be captured partly from the Vimeo API and partly from the recording equipment. The following listing presents an excerpt of such a file (see also Fig. 7).

```
{
  "courses":[
  {
    "title": "Information Systems - Digitalization in
              Enterprise and Organization",
    "lectureTitle": "Digital Forms and Workflows",
    "lecturer": "Prof. Dr. Vera Meister",
    "lecturerMail": "vera.meister@th-brandenburg.de",
    "chapters": [
    {
      "title": "Forms and their Degree of Digitization",
      "videos":
      {
        "url_teacher": "https://vimeo.com/296600095",
        "url_presentation": "https://vimeo.com/296600051"
      }
    }, …
```

6 Evaluation

In the last section, the components of an infrastructure for e-lectures built on semantic technologies and supporting the synchronous recording and dual display of talking head and screencast videos were presented and discussed in detail. Therefore, research question 1 is answered. The remaining research questions 2 and 3 are partially addressed in the last section and will be consolidated in this section. Performance measures of the implemented infrastructure for e-lectures are presented in Sect. 6.1 whereas the affordability of the overall system for small and medium-sized organizations is proved in Sect. 6.2.

6.1 Performance Measures

The performance of the overall system (comp. Fig. 1) depends on the performance of its four presentation-related parts: (i) the video streaming service by Vimeo, (ii) the SPARQL queries in OntoWiki, (iii) the VMS pages (main and details), and (iv) the dual player software. Since the system is in use mainly at a small university, issues of scaling to a huge number of parallel requests is not in the focus. The performance of the services offered by Vimeo can be considered as verified (comp. e.g. [16]). The performance of the other three components is mainly represented by the response and loading times respectively. According to [17], a loading time of 3 s is considered a benchmark.

The response time for the SPARQL queries is measured directly in OntoWiki. Table 2 shows the results of a test series for all queries used in the VMS pages. Even the aggregation of all queries takes less than 1 s.

Table 2. Response times for SPARQL queries in OntoWiki (measured in ms)

Test number	1	2	3	4	5	6	7	8	9	10	Ø
aboutQuery	2	2	2	2	2	2	2	2	2	2	2
clipInfo	35	49	45	61	48	45	52	45	44	45	46,9
filterLecturer	3	3	2	2	2	2	3	2	3	3	2,5
filterModule	3	4	2	3	3	2	3	3	3	3	2,9
filterStudyProgram	4	3	3	2	2	3	3	2	2	2	2,6
moduleInfo	2	2	2	2	2	2	2	2	2	2	2
videoDurationContributor	21	21	22	20	20	21	21	22	21	21	21
videoInfo	10	9	9	10	9	10	10	9	11	9	9,6
videoLectureSearchFilter	752	638	726	594	649	702	616	663	670	556	656,6
Aggregated times	**832**	**731**	**813**	**696**	**737**	**789**	**712**	**750**	**758**	**643**	**746,1**

As in [18], dotcom-tools[9] were selected to measure in random computer experiments the loading times of the VMS pages and the dual player software. Two different browsers and two different mobile operating systems were chosen for testing. The tests have been conducted using six different server locations in Europe: London, Paris, Amsterdam, Frankfurt, Warsaw, and Madrid. The results are listed in Table 3.

Table 3. Loading times for VMS pages and dual player software (in seconds)

Tested site/software	Mozilla Firefox	Google Chrome	iOS	Android	Ø
VMS main page	4,3	4,5	3,8	4,7	4,3
VMS main page with filter	3,4	3,8	2,6	3,4	3,3
VMS exemplary details page	2,1	2,0	2,0	2,1	2,1
Dual player software	2,8	3,2	2,8	2,1	2,7

The measurements show that the main page of the VMS exceeds the benchmark of 3 s, while the other features remain below it. For comparison, two other VMSs were examined: TeleTask operated by the University of Potsdam and TIB AV operated by the University of Hanover. Their main pages loaded on average 2 s.

6.2 Affordability

In order to demonstrate the affordability of the presented multi-component infrastructure for e-lectures in the case at hand, all necessary cost items are listed by category and quantified where possible or necessary. Direct comparability with other solution alternatives is difficult because there are too many influencing factors. In the present case, a large part of the investment costs was covered by public grants. The digitalization of teaching is currently a politically strongly promoted issue. It can be assumed that funding of various origins will be available in similar cases.

---

[9] https://www.dotcom-tools.com/website-speed-test.aspx.

Since e-lectures are a didactic offer – i.e. part of the genuine business of a university – the costs of core and support services, which are provided anyway, are not counted separately. In addition to the preparation of materials by the lecturer, this includes the maintenance of servers and software applications. The process of recording itself is designed to take 2 h of studio time for a 90-min lecture. The teacher is supported by a student assistant whose work is the only additional cost. She or he handles the post-processing and publication of the recorded e-lectures, which takes another 2 h. This will result in additional costs of approx. 50 € for such a recording.

The external service costs for the Vimeo subscription amount to € 180 per year. The largest cost block includes the investment costs, which consist of the following items: the acquisition costs for the recording system and the additional studio equipment (approx. 16.000 €) as well as the costs for the customization of the back-end software and the development of the front-end applications by student assistants (approx. 10.000 €). Internal costs for the room and usual equipment, such as chairs, tables and PCs, are not considered.

If the lifetime of the entire system is calculated at 7 years, the annual depreciation is approx. 3,700 €. In the present case, 80% of the acquisition costs and 100% of the labor costs for customization and development were covered by public grants. Thus, the actual imputed costs per year amount to € 460. Together with the Vimeo service costs, this amounts to 640 €. Both values are significantly lower compared to the license fee of € 16,000, which must be paid, for example, for the MOOC House service platform offered by HPI[10].

7   Conclusion and Future Work

The paper examined the viability of an infrastructure for e-lectures in small and medium-sized organizations. This is an issue of relevance as e-lectures are an important instrument of digital teaching. Via a VMS, the offer can be made accessible across departments and courses. A prototype consisting of seven different components was developed and evaluated in terms of performance and affordability. The latter could be proven. The system has been in operation since the beginning of 2019. Work must continue improving performance, the loading times of the main pages must be short-ened. Improvement of the search function and of the publication process are also planned. Finally, the VMS pages shall be enriched with automatically published semantic annotations to improve the retrievability of e-lectures on the Web.

References

1. Hansch, A., et al.: Video and Online Learning: Critical Reflections and Findings from the Field. HIIG Discussion Paper Series No. 2015(02), pp. 1–34. HIIG, Heidelberg (2015)
2. Gartner Inc.: Reviews for Enterprise Video Content Management. https://www.gartnercom/reviews/market/enterprise-video-content-management. Accessed 19 May 2019

---

[10] https://mooc.house/.

3. Handke, J.: Handbuch Hochschullehre Digital – Leitfaden für eine moderne und mediengerechte Lehre. Tectum Verlag, Marburg (2015)
4. Mouromtsev, M., d'Aquin, M.: Open Data for Education – Linked, Shared, and Reusable Data for Teaching and Learning. Springer International, Switzerland (2016)
5. Wang, Y., Wang, Y.: A survey of semantic technology and ontology for e-learning. In: Semantic Web – Interoperability, Usability, Applicability. IOS Press Journal (2019)
6. Demetriadis, S., Pombortsis, A.: e-Lectures for flexible learning: a study on their learning efficiency. Educ. Technol. Soc. **10**(2), 147–157 (2007)
7. Meinel, C., Willems, C.: openHPI – Das MOOC-Angebot des Hasso-Plattner-Instituts. Technische Berichte des HPI, N° 79, Universitätsverlag Potsdam (2013)
8. Lehner, F.: Wissensmanagement, 3rd edn. Hanser, München (2009)
9. Davenport, T., Prusak, L.: Working Knowledge – How Organizations Manage What They Know. Harvard Business School Press, Boston (2000)
10. Vimeo API. https://developer.vimeo.com/api/reference. Accessed 19 May 2019
11. WordPress Online Manual. https://codex.wordpress.org/. Accessed 19 May 2019
12. Arnold, P., et al.: Handbuch E-Learning, 5th edn. Bertelsmann, Bielefeld (2018)
13. Semantic Media Wiki. https://www.semantic-mediawiki.org/. Accessed 19 May 2019
14. Meister, V., Hu, W.: Videovorlesungen in der Wirtschaftsinformatik – Systemanalyse und Reflexionen. In: Barton, T., et al. (eds.) Angewandte Forschung in der Wirtschaftsinformatik 2016, pp. 304–317. Mana-Buch, Heide (2016)
15. Frischmuth, P., Martin, M., Arndt, N.: OntoWiki 1.0: 10 Years of Development – What's New in OntoWiki. In: SEMPDS 2016 (2016). http://ceur-ws.org/Vol-1695/paper11.pdf
16. Bartuskova, A., Krejcar, O., Sabbah, T., Selamat, A.: Otherwise, the reference is complete and correct, see eg. https://www.researchgate.net/publication/312062238_Website_speed_testing_analysis_using_speedtesting_model
17. Kissmetrics. https://blog.kissmetrics.com/wp-content/uploads/2011/04/loading-time.pdf. Accessed 20 May 2019
18. Bartuskova, A., Krejcara, O., Sabbahb, T., Selama, A.: Website speed testing analysis using speedtesting model. Jurnal Teknologi **78**(12–3), 121–134 (2016)

Enterprise Architecture Oriented Requirements Engineering for Open Data Usage in Schools

Mubashrah Saddiqa[1(✉)], Marite Kirikova[2], and Jens Myrup Pedersen[1]

[1] Department of Electronic Systems, Aalborg University, Fredrik Bajers Vej 7,
9220 Aalborg, Denmark
`{mus,jens}@es.aau.dk`
[2] Computer Science Department, Riga Technical University, Kalku 1,
Riga 1658, Latvia
`marite.kirikova@rtu.lv`

Abstract. Open Data has been considered as a key to scientific innovations. These openly licensed data-sets can be accessed, used, rebuild, and shared by anyone and anywhere. Mostly, Open Data is discussed in relation to its production, storage, licensing and accessibility, but less often - in relation to its practical subsequent uses, e.g. as an educational resource. In general, Open Data can be used as an open educational resource to develop transversal skills among school students. This paper presents an Enterprise Architecture Oriented Requirements Engineering (EAORE) approach for Open Data usage as an educational resource in Danish public schools. The aim of this research work is to identify requirements of Danish public schools for the development of an Open Data interface. The EAORE approach represents how Enterprise Architecture (EA) models guide overall Requirements Engineering (RE) process for Open Data usage in Danish public schools.

Keywords: Enterprise architecture · Requirements engineering ·
Open Data · Open Data interface · Educational resource

1 Introduction

Open Data is openly available data-sets permitting citizens to freely use, modify, and share them for any purpose [1]. Open Data is data-sets, that are open to everyone, i.e. citizens, businesses, non-profits, public administrations, and technologists. It is a source that promotes democracy, transparency, civic engagement, efficient public services, and economic growth. Open Data opportunities and benefits could increase significantly, if citizens were able to use that data effectively and efficiently [4,5]. Hence, citizens' active engagement is vital to harness the power of Open Data. However, in general, Open Data debates and research focus more on the technical side, e.g. collection, storage, availability, licensing and have overlooked the public issues and its consequent uses [2,3],

M. Pańkowska and K. Sandkuhl (Eds.): BIR 2019, LNBIP 365, pp. 135–147, 2019.
https://doi.org/10.1007/978-3-030-31143-8_10

e.g. which data-sets public needs, how Open Data can be used as an educational resource, and how citizens can be engaged in exploiting available Open Data? In order to equip the future generation with future essential learning skills, it is important to engage the younger generation of school students with Open Data. Open Data can act as a key, to develop digital and data literacy skills, enhance critical thinking, and civic awareness among higher education students [9]. Hence, Open Data is not only a potential resource of opportunities for public (e.g. to improve public services, to bring transparency etc.); it could also act as 21st century raw material to develop digital and data skills among public school students, and as a source to inform them about their communities. Yet, the educational use of these openly available data-sets are not fully exploited, specifically in the schools, e.g. to facilitate teaching activities using Open Data as part of different subjects.

Many open data-sets are available on Open Data portals, that could be used as part of basic teaching materials. Public schools could experiment with these openly available data-sets not just to grow public engagement but to develop digital and data skills, and to foster civic awareness among younger students by providing useful local information through Open Data. For instance, pollution level, noise level and water quality data-sets can provide the current situation of local areas as part of chemistry subject. Students can further discuss why the levels are high or low, and how they could improve the situation [6]. Open data-sets can also be used as educational resources, to support different other teaching subjects, and permit students to work with the actual data-sets and to develop new learning skills [10]. Hence, many countries start taking initiatives, and launch different projects to introduce the possible opportunities of Open Data [32] to the younger generation of students. The research work described in this paper is affiliated to the part of the Copenhagen Community Drive project [29] with particular focus on the city's many types of data and how to put them into use especially in an educational context. The project focuses on how existing Open Data could facilitate the educational process in Danish public schools and how we can integrate technology in schools in a way that benefits students' digital and learning skills.

In order to facilitate educational activities using Open Data, appropriate open data-sets, e.g. environmental, geographical and traffic data-sets should be visualized in simple graphs, e.g. bar, pie or line [28]. However, the use of data also requires a lot of effort by the teachers and they may need data analytics skills to fragment the bigger data-sets into smaller data-sets and make visualizations. To stimulate the use of Open Data in Danish public schools, our idea is to integrate an Open Data interface in schools, where teachers and students can relate their subjects to actual information of their local areas, and compare the data with other communities in the form of simple visualizations. However, for the development of such an interface, it is important to identify teachers and students requirements. To the best of our knowledge, there exist no guidelines for the RE process for Open Data usage in schools as an educational resource. This paper attempts to make a first step towards defining a best practice for such situations using Enterprise Architecture Oriented Requirements Engineering (EAORE).

The characteristics and challenges of our research question *"How EA guides RE process to derive teachers/students' needs and requirements to stimulate the use of Open Data as an educational resource in Danish public schools?"* have formed the basis for the development of Enterprise Architecture (EA) models using EAORE approach. We believe that the obtained results are sufficiently general and might be interesting for other researchers working in the domain of Open Data applications. We are aiming to develop EA models using EAORE, which helps to elicit requirements for the successful development of Open Data interface for schools. The interface could enable teachers to relate their subjects with the actual information, e.g. pollution level, noise level or traffic congestion near the schools. We integrate RE and architecture design to investigate the problem, specify solutions, and validate them for the development of Open Data interface that allows teachers to use open Data as an educational resource at public schools.

The structure of this paper is as follows: In Sect. 2, we discuss the research method and related work, where we demonstrate the theoretical boundaries of RE and EA. In Sect. 3, we provide a frame for EAORE in the context of Open Data usage in schools; and in Sect. 4, we provide the conclusions and point to our future work plans.

2   Research Methods and Related Work

The research methods applied in this work consists of the following steps:

1. Analyze open data-sets of target domains.
2. Identify Open Data impact domains that may facilitate teaching.
3. Analyze available data visualization tools.
4. Survey Danish schools to learn teachers and students perspective on Open Data.
5. Envision a possible solution for Open Data usage in schools.
6. Propose an approach for the identification of requirements for the envisioned solution.

Denmark is famous for its Open Data initiatives, and has a national portal[1] for Open Data where cities, organizations, and researchers publish useful data for public. This data is used to develop different mobile applications and improve public services to bring benefit to the citizens of Denmark. In order to use open data-sets as educational resources in the Danish public schools, we carefully *analyzed open data-sets of Copenhagen city*, the capital of Denmark that has more than 290 open data-sets from different sources, accessible from the national Open Data portal of Denmark. These data-sets are available in different data types e.g. graphical data, statistical data and live data and in different data formats, e.g. CSV, PDF, JSON etc.

---

[1] http://www.opendata.dk/.

We *identified four impact domains (educational domains), i.e. environment, demographic, geographical and statistical data domains* that can easily facilitate teaching being a part of basic school subjects, (science, social science, geography and mathematics), in public schools. Some *open source data visualization tools were also analyzed* for their possible adoption to visualize Open Data. We also *surveyed ten Danish public schools* to understand teacher and student perspectives in Open Data usage in schools. All this work is discussed in [6]. Teachers were very positive in facilitating teaching with actual information, but they required ready to use data-sets and visualizations as part of teaching assignments. In addition, it was mentioned that the available open source tools for visualization are not in Danish, which was also considered a hurdle for the presentation of Open Data at school level in Denmark. Teachers requested an overview of what data-sets are available; and pointed to the fact that it requires both time and skills of teachers to present the right information to the students. Hence, development of an *Open Data interface* that enables students and teachers to select data-sets within educational themes, visualize them in the form of simple graphs, compare with other areas, and design activities to explore more data as part of respective subjects, *could solve above-discoursed issues.*

For the development of the Open Data interface for schools and to identify teacher and student requirements, we use RE, which is a process to investigate, define, document and maintain the requirements for the best desired solution. RE is not principally about just documenting requirements; instead, it focuses on understanding a business problem, and providing a solution for it [16,17]. RE discipline has expanded over the last decade, and the process includes not only traditional techniques such as interviews, surveys and workshops [12] or viewpoint oriented RE [11], but has also steered several new techniques and models, e.g. GBRAM [13], i* [14], and KAOS [15]. There can be two different views on RE [18,19], problem-oriented and solution oriented RE. Problem-oriented RE, focuses more on investigating and documenting a problem domain. The requirements engineer identifies the different factors (reasons) for the problem, the relations between these factors, why this is seen as problem, and who experience these problems. Goal Oriented RE (GORE) [20] is a very popular and widely used technique within problem-oriented RE. Goals are considered as high-level objectives of the system, business or organization that identify the reasons for the development of a system, and help to make decisions at different levels within an enterprise. Related work [21] gives a general description of the GORE, where as GBRAM and KAOS use the GORE techniques. Solution-oriented RE, on the other hand, uses the traditional techniques for software engineering, i.e. object-oriented analysis [22] and structured analysis [23]. The requirements specification for a solution represents the system from the software engineers perspective [24], e.g. system specification, system functions, quality attributes of these functions; and defines the alternatives for the best solution of the problem. Hence, the generic RE process consists of the following functions:

- Requirements Elicitation
- Requirements Analysis

– Requirements Specification
– Requirements Validation

Within, the RE domain, research is made in almost every field of business such as transport, education, health-care, etc., but no work is done within the development of requirements models for Open Data usage in schools.

We use RE with EA [25,26]. EA can have a significant impact on the requirements engineering process [7]. EA is the complete, consistent and coherent set of methods, rules, models and tools, which guide the design, migration, implementation and governance of business processes, organizational structures, information systems and the technical infrastructure of an organization according to a vision [8,27]. EA is the practice of analyzing, designing, planning and implementing enterprise analysis, to successfully execute on business strategies.

In our study, to derive the enterprise architecture models, the requirements were identified through interviews with Danish public school teachers, pilot tests and observations with students. Using EAORE, we explore and investigate requirements of Open Data interface for schools. For the representation of EA issues we use a selected set of elements of EA representation language Archi-Mate [30] shown in Fig. 1. Whereas for modelling, we used the Archi modelling toolkit [31]. To design the EA models in EAORE approach, we used four-layer enterprise architecture frame as shown in Fig. 2. Models are discussed in the next section. The developed frame is based on the above mentioned five steps of research method.

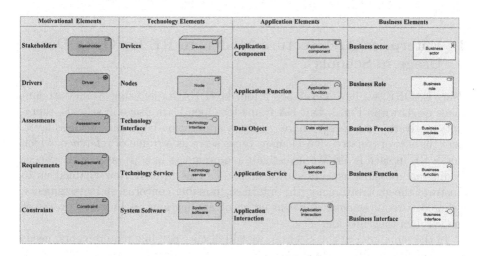

Fig. 1. Selected set of elements from ArchiMate

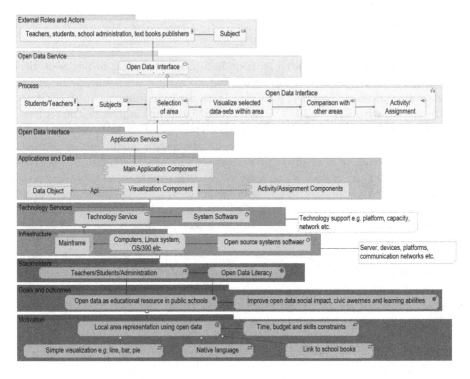

Fig. 2. Layered view of EA for Open Data usage in schools.

3   Enterprise Architecture Models in RE for Open Data Usage in Schools

Using EAORE, we have developed a four-layer EA frame using ArchiMate language as shown in Fig. 2. Our EA frame for Open Data usage in schools, represents motivational layers, technology layer, application layer and business layer. Here the sets of (related) EA element types serve as a frame of reference, which guides RE in each layer. We investigate requirements in each layer with respect to different possible aspects shown in Fig. 2. This layered view enabled us to illustrate the motivation for the interface, possible concerns and assessments, technology requirements, and the usage of applications in business processes and services they provide.

In the remainder of this Section, we will discuss possible requirements, needs and goals for each layer shown in Fig. 2.

3.1   Motivation Layer

On the motivational layer, we have explored the stakeholders, their needs, concerns and assessments, and how they interact with the system (Open Data interface),

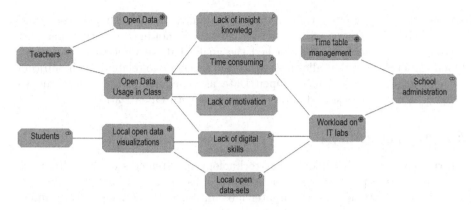

Fig. 3. Stakeholder, concerns and assessments.

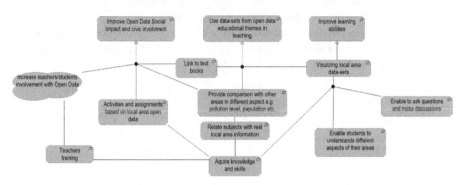

Fig. 4. Motivational level model.

what are the motivational aspects, (e.g. why teachers use Open Data), and domain knowledge. The resulting model is shown in Fig. 3.

Figure 4 represents the RE issues for the above mentioned needs and concerns. In our case, we have identified four main stakeholders, namely, teachers, students and school administration (as internal stakeholders), and textbook publishers as external stakeholders. Teachers are concerned with different data types, their graphs, cleaning of data-sets and transformations of data into other formats. Students need simple interactive graphs in their own native language. Teachers are reluctant to spend long time on data-sets searching. These identified concerns from the students and teachers, can lead to assessments. For instance, there exist many open data-sets with useful information, which are not being exploited. These data-sets can easily be used as open educational resources that can relate actual information to the study subjects to develop learning skills discussed in previous sections. This would lead to the high level goal, "increase Open Data social impact and youth engagement with Open Data". Teachers and students are not able to work directly with Open Data as they need simple presentations of open data-sets in their own native language. This can be a problem, as teachers are hesitant to spend long time in identifying and visualizing the data-sets; and the available open source software for visualization is not in their native language. Through goal refinement, we reached the goals that we want to introduce an Open Data interface that allows students and teachers, to relate to their subjects with actual information using Open Data as an educational resource and to improve civic awareness and youth engagement with Open Data.

3.2 Technology Layer

On this layer, we will explore what technology requirements are seen from the user and system perspectives. For instance, it is important that students and teachers have easy access to computer labs, internet, etc. For Open Data interface, open data-sets need to be divided further into smaller data-sets, containing the local area information. These data-sets are in different formats, e.g. CSV files, PDF files or other formats. A data management interface is required, to store these data-sets before visualizing. Open source operating systems and visualization software are required to visualize the local open data-sets. Figure 5 represents a technology layer model for Open Data usage in schools.

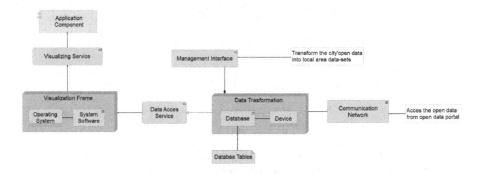

Fig. 5. Technology layer requirements model.

3.3 Application Layer

Figure 6 represents an application layer EA model for Open Data usage in schools. The application layer focuses more on application components, e.g. application specifications. This includes language, appearance, and being ease of use. The RE for this layer leads us to the development of one main component with navigation to three sub-components, i.e., data object, visualization component, and activity component. Teachers need local area open data-sets in the form of simple visualizations, (line, pie, bar), in native (Danish) language, to relate their subjects with actual information. The application should be easy to use without any programming expertise, and with explained features.

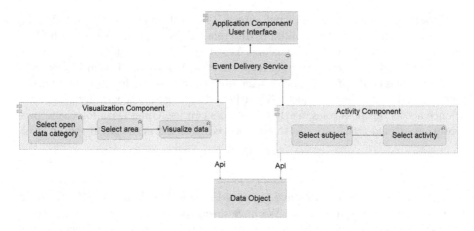

Fig. 6. Application view.

3.4 Business Layer

The business layer leads towards the solution, i.e. an Open Data interface for the schools that enables teachers and students to take benefit from the data-sets. Figure 7 represents a usage view (model) for Open Data interface and Fig. 8 represents business model for Open Data interface. In the business layer, textbook

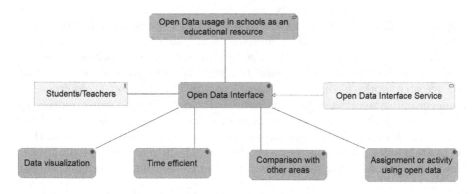

Fig. 7. Open Data Interface usage view.

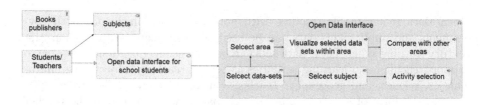

Fig. 8. Open Data interface for Open Data usage in schools.

publishers are identified as external actors. They will play a central role for the active use of this interface; by linking different subjects themes with Open Data interface for activities and explanations, e.g., in geographic subjects, they can link the interface for the presentation of respective local areas; or in science class, real local examples could provide information about pollution, noise or other environmental conditions. Such subjects as mathematics, science, geography and social science act as business roles, as these subjects can use Open Data for visual presentation of local areas aspects, to facilitate educational activities at school level.

3.5   Evaluation

In the above sub-sections, we have presented models based on EAORE approach for Open Data usage in schools. We have discussed the four layers, which form the base for our frame, and identified requirements in different aspects within these layers. Our EAORE approach for Open Data usage in schools is flexible and could be used by the neighboring countries to extend the potentials of Open Data at school level as an educational resource. Using EAORE, we cover motivational, application, technical and business aspects that enables us to make a transparent alignment between all these aspects. Using this approach, we derive systematic requirements at different layers that are aligned with each other in the form of models. These models will help us to compare how the need for Open Data usage will be met in an efficient, sustainable, and adaptable manner. Using EAORE approach, we can easily trace and change requirements at different stages of development of Open Data interface. Using this approach, we can also save time, e.g. we can identify requirements at different layers and change or validate them easily at any level using less time to compare to descriptions in text documents. The approach is easy to adopt and in future when we extended our research work (having more cases), we will also envision a requirements management system based on this approach. Currently this paper represents only a case specific model; we will elaborate EA models and develop analysis mechanism for more formal EA analysis in future work. It has to be noted that there are many relationships between elements of different layers of the frame. However, we showed only some of them in order to keep the discussion as simple as possible.

4   Concluding Remarks and Future Work

Open Data is a valuable resource with potential opportunities for both governments and public. This data can be used as a raw material to develop 21st century learning skills. These data-sets can be used as an educational resource to support teaching and learning activities as part of teaching subjects, e.g. mathematics, science, and geography. Teachers can relate their subject with Open Data in the form of simple graphs. In this paper, we investigated the teacher and student needs and requirements to stimulate the use of Open Data as an educational resource in Danish public schools. We used the EAORE approach and developed *EA oriented RE for Open Data usage in Schools*. The use of EA models helped to identify the requirements regarding different aspects i.e. motivational, technology, application and solution aspects. Our EAORE approach has a number of potential advantages, e.g. time saving, easiness of traceability and flexibility of modeling as discussed in Sect. 3.

In the future, we will elaborate this approach after having more cases and use it for requirements management system development. To validate the solution i.e. Open Data interface, we will first develop prototypes to test different parts of the Open Data interface in schools. This phase will help to explore and identify new problems, based on the proposed solutions. Based on these new problems, revised prototypes will lead us towards the final development of the interface. The interface will not only provide interesting information about local areas, but will also help to develop learning and digital skills, and bring more awareness, among the younger generation of school students about their communities and cities.

References

1. Kitchin, R.: The Data Revolution: Big Data, Open Data, Data infrastructures and Their Consequences. Sage, Ireland (2014). https://doi.org/10.4135/9781473909472
2. Cordasco, G., et al.: Engaging citizens with a social platform for open data. In: Proceedings of the 18th Annual International Conference on Digital Government Research, pp. 242–249. ACM, NewYork, USA (2017). https://doi.org/10.1145/3085228.3085302
3. Anokwa, Y., Hartung, C., Brunette, W., Borriello, G., Lerer, A.: Open source data collection in the developing world. Computer **42**(10), 97–99 (2009). https://doi.org/10.1109/MC.2009.328
4. Kassen, M.: A promising phenomenon of open data: a case study of the Chicago open data project. Gov. Inf. Q. **30**(4), 508–513 (2013). https://doi.org/10.1016/j.giq.2013.05.012
5. Janssen, M., Charalabidis, Y., Zuiderwijk, A.: Benefits, adoption barriers and myths of open data and open government. Inf. Syst. Manag. **29**(4), 258–268 (2012). https://doi.org/10.1080/10580530.2012.716740
6. Saddiqa, M., et al.: Open data visualization in Danish schools: a case study. In: Proceeding of 27th International Conference in Central Europe on Computer Graphics, Visualization and Computer Vision. World Society for Computer Graphics, Pilsen, Czech Republic (2019)
7. Marosin, D., van Zee, M., Ghanavati, S.: Formalizing and modeling enterprise architecture (EA) principles with goal-oriented requirements language (GRL). In: Nurcan, S., Soffer, P., Bajec, M., Eder, J. (eds.) CAiSE 2016. LNCS, vol. 9694, pp. 205–220. Springer, Cham (2016). https://doi.org/10.1007/978-3-319-39696-5_13
8. Iacob, M.E., Meertens, L.O., Jonkers, H., Quartel, D.A., Nieuwenhuis, L.J., Van Sinderen, M.J.: From enterprise architecture to business models and back. Softw. Syst. Model. **13**(3), 1059–1083 (2014). https://doi.org/10.1007/s10270-012-0304-6
9. Atenas, J., Havemann, L., Priego, E.: Open data as open educational resources: towards transversal skills and global citizenship. Open Praxis **7**(4), 377–389 (2015). https://doi.org/10.5944/openpraxis.7.4.233

10. Renuka, T., Chitra, C., Pranesha, T.S., Shivakumar, M.: Open data usage by undergraduate students. In: 5th IEEE International Conference on MOOCs, Innovation and Technology in Education (MITE), pp. 46–51. IEEE, India (2017). https://doi.org/10.1109/MITE.2017.00014
11. Kotonya, G., Sommerville, I.: Requirements engineering with view points. Softw. Eng. J. **11**(1), 5–18 (1996). https://doi.org/10.1049/sej.1996.0002
12. Pohl, K.: Requirements Engineering: Fundamentals, Principles, and Techniques. Springer Publishing Company, Incorporated, Heidelberg (2010)
13. Kavakli, E.: Goal-oriented requirements engineering: a unifying framework. Requir. Eng. **6**(4), 237–251 (2002). https://doi.org/10.1007/PL00010362
14. Eric, S.K., Giorgini, P., Maiden, N., Mylopoulos, J.: Social Modeling for Requirements Engineering. MIT Press, England (2011)
15. Heaven, W., Finkelstein, A.: UML profile to support requirements engineering with KAOS. IEEE Proc. Softw. **151**(1), 10–27 (2004). https://doi.org/10.1049/ip-sen: 20040297
16. Bray, I.K.: An Introduction to Requirements Engineering. Pearson Education, UK (2002)
17. Jackson, M.: Software Requirements and Specifications: A Lexicon of Practice, Principles and Prejudices. Addison-Wesley, Harlow, England (1995)
18. Wieringa, R.J.: Requirements engineering: problem analysis and solution specification (extended abstract). In: Koch, N., Fraternali, P., Wirsing, M. (eds.) ICWE 2004. LNCS, vol. 3140, pp. 13–16. Springer, Heidelberg (2004). https://doi.org/10. 1007/978-3-540-27834-4_3
19. Aurum, A., Jeffery, R., Wohlin, C., Handzic, M. (eds.): Managing Software Engineering Knowledge. Springer Science & Business Media, Heidelberg (2013). https://doi.org/10.1007/978-3-662-05129-0
20. Van Lamsweerde, A.: Goal-oriented requirements engineering: a guided tour. In: Proceedings of 5th IEEE International Symposium on Requirements Engineering, pp. 249–262. IEEE, Toronto, Canada (2001). https://doi.org/10.1109/ISRE.2001. 948567
21. Van Lamsweerde, A.: Requirements Engineering: From System Goals to UML Models to Software, vol. 10. Wiley, Chichester (2009)
22. Lethbridge, T.C., Laganiere, R.: Object-Oriented Software Engineering. McGraw-Hill, New York (2005)
23. Dick, J., Hull, E., Jackson, K.: Requirements Engineering. Springer, Switzerland (2017)
24. Nuseibeh, B.: Weaving together requirements and architectures. Computer **34**(3), 115–119 (2001). https://doi.org/10.1109/2.910904
25. Engelsman, W., Quartel, D., Jonkers, H., van Sinderen, M.: Extending enterprise architecture modelling with business goals and requirements. Enterp. Inf. Syst. **5**(1), 9–36 (2011). https://doi.org/10.1080/17517575.2010.491871
26. Lankhorst, M.M., Proper, H.A., Jonkers, H.: The anatomy of the ArchiMate language. Int. J. Inf. Syst. Model. Des. (IJISMD) **1**(1), 1–32 (2010). https://doi.org/ 10.4018/jismd.2010092301
27. Jonkers, H., Lankhorst, M., Van Buuren, R., Hoppenbrouwers, S., Bonsangue, M., Van Der Torre, L.: Concepts for modeling enterprise architectures. Int. J. Coop. Inf. Syst. **13**(03), 257–287 (2004). https://doi.org/10.1142/S0218843004000985
28. Alper, B., Riche, N. H., Chevalier, F., Boy, J., Sezgin, M.: Visualization literacy at elementary school. In: Proceedings of the 2017 CHI Conference on Human Factors in Computing Systems, pp. 5485–5497. ACM, USA (2017). https://doi.org/10. 1145/3025453.3025877

29. Teaching Children and Young People to Transform Cities Through Community and Data-Driven Methods, Community Drive. https://www.communitydrive.aau.dk/
30. ArchiMate® 3.0.1 Specification, an Open Group Standard. https://pubs.opengroup.org/architecture/archimate3-doc/
31. Archi – Open Source ArchiMate Modelling. https://www.archimatetool.com/
32. Education: Open Data in Schools. https://www.europeandataportal.eu/en/highlights/open-data-schools

Deriving Key Performance Indicators from Business Process Model

Václav Řepa[✉][iD]

Faculty of Informatics and Statistics, Department of Information Technologies,
University of Economics, Prague, Czech Republic
repa@vse.cz
http://www.vse.cz

Abstract. During the last several decades Key Performance Indicators (KPIs) became the standard approach to the monitoring and management of the enterprise performance. At the same time, Business Process Management (BPM) brought the revolutionary alternative to the traditional way of the management of an enterprise. As BPM dramatically changes the managerial perspective and consequently the view of the enterprise performance this perspective should also significantly change the approach to KPIs. Instead of establishing the KPIs for the particular places of the organization they should be derived from its business processes. In this paper we introduce the idea of deriving KPIs from the business process definitions based on our methodology MMABP in order to contribute to the theory of Key Performance Indicators as well as their practical application.

Keywords: Key Performance Indicators · Business process model · MMABP · Process states and steps · Service-orientation

1 Introduction

Key Performance Indicators (KPI) represent widely popular approach to the monitoring and management of the enterprise performance. Since 1990ties Business Process Management (BPM) represents the revolutionary alternative to the traditional way of the management of an enterprise. BPM brought to the management, traditionally driven by the organizational structure, completely new perspective – business process as a primary point of view of the performance of an enterprise. From this point of view all other important aspects of the enterprise management, including even the organizational structure and its related aspects like competences and responsibilities, play the role of the infrastructure for the processes. Figure 1 describes the main factors of the process-driven management of an organization. It shows the organization (the white area) placed in its environment (the grey area), a socioeconomic system. As the general importance of the organization

This paper has been processed with the institutional support of the Faculty of Informatics and Statistics, University of Economics in Prague.

M. Pańkowska and K. Sandkuhl (Eds.): BIR 2019, LNBIP 365, pp. 148–162, 2019.
https://doi.org/10.1007/978-3-030-31143-8_11

always comes from its meaning for other actors in the system its primary function has to be always targeted at the goals from its environment, not inside the organization. Primary function represents the values which the organization provides other system actors with. Primary function originates from what the organization does, from its business processes. To fulfill the primary function the organization has the information and organization systems as basic infrastructures. Information and organization systems represent the secondary function supporting the primary function of the organization. Information technologies allowing the performance of both infrastructural systems then represent tertiary function. But at the same time the information technologies work as a trigger of changes in business processes. This double role of IT in the organizational development characterizes the essence and main purpose of the process-driven management; technology development allows us "doing things in a different way" [10] which should be understood as simplifying the processes towards their natural substance. Following the idea of primary function directly oriented on the customer all business processes have to be designed so that each process clearly belongs to one of two main categories: *key processes* which directly fulfill the primary function and representing all other needed infrastructural functions and activities. This division of processes represents the important value of the process-driven management. It is a sophisticated way of exploiting the effect of specialization as a primary tool for increasing the effectiveness and efficiency. In the traditionally managed organizations the specialization is exploited via the organizational hierarchy which breaks key processes to fragments according to the organization functions, specializations. Organizational structure then fixates each key business process as a particular sequence of tasks which can be changed only with the change of the organizational structure. In this way the effect of specialization can exploited only at the cost of the complete loss of flexibility. Business goals can be achieved only the way predefined by the organizational structure. Process-driven management offers the way of exploiting the effect of specialization without the loss of the ability to immediately change any process if needed. In this approach directly the processes are specialized which makes specialization independent of the organizational structure. Process-driven management thus represents really revolutionary change in the managerial approaches, they are traditionally based on the organizational structure as a root of the enterprise's behavior. This change of perspective causes many significant changes in other important aspects of the organization's life as it is excellently explained in related literature, namely in [10]. At first it requires to organize the competences and responsibilities according to the need of processes instead of the organizational functions which naturally leads to the decomposition of competences traditionally accumulated in the hierarchical managerial positions. This change naturally increases the need for the personal responsibility and competency in all employees which consequently requires also the change of their basic attitudes. Therefore, the process-driven management is actually the way of implementation of the ideas of visionaries like Deming [7] and Porter [16]. As BPM dramatically changes the managerial perspective and consequently the view of the enterprise performance this perspective could also significantly contribute to the theory of Key Performance Indicators as well as their practical application. Instead of establishing the KPIs for the particular places of the organization they should be derived from its business processes. In this paper we introduce the idea of deriving KPIs from the business process definitions based on our Methodology for Modelling and Analysis of Business Processes (MMABP) as a complement to this methodology in the field of implementation of the process-based management system. In the following section we briefly introduce the Key Performance Indicators and their relation to business processes. In the third section we outline the essence of our methodology MMABP focusing mainly on its features important for the topic of this paper. In the fourth section we propose the procedure for the derivation of "soft" KPIs from process interfaces. In the Discussion section we then discuss important consequences of the proposed approach and in the Conclusions section we summarize main ideas from the paper and outline some general conclusions.

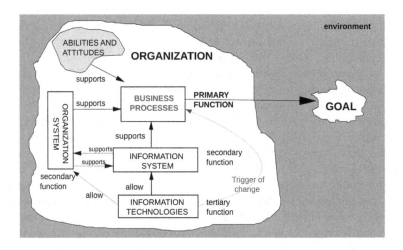

Fig. 1. Main components in the process-driven organization [3].

2   Key Performance Indicators

Key Performance Indicators (KPIs) as an approach are rooted already in the work of Taylor [25] from the beginning of the 20th century and also in the work of the evangelists of the quality-oriented management Deming [7] and Porter [16]. They are also closely related to the development of information technologies and informatics in general [1,6]. In this field, there exist many different approaches nevertheless for all them the common meaning of this keyword can be found. According to the Strategy Management Group the "Key Performance Indicators (KPIs) are the critical (key) indicators of progress toward an intended result. KPIs provide a focus for strategic and operational improvement, create an analytical basis for decision making and help focus attention on what matters most." [22]. Existing approaches to the classification of KPIs differ mainly in details, they have well visible common basis and relation to other significant managerial methods especially the famous Balanced Scorecard from Kaplan and Norton [12]. Strategy Management Group (SMG) brings the general classification of KPI in the context of their use for the management of an enterprise to *Strategic Measures* usually structured in detail according to the Balanced Scorecard perspectives (Customer/Stakeholder, Financial, Internal Processes and Organizational Capacity measures), *Operational Measures, Project Measures, Risk Measures, Employee* and *Other Measures*. Other widely used classifications of KPIs can be found for instance in [28] and [18]. Different conceptions of KPI vary in different details nevertheless they share the same general contents and the strong relation of KPIs to the Balanced Scorecard conception [12].

From another point of view KPIs are classified as *lagging* and *leading*. A *lagging* indicator typically measures an output, a result. It measures something that has already happened, a fact. A *leading* indicator typically measures an input, or a catalyst. It is a predictor of the desired result. Leading indicators actually measure the real business drivers that need to be managed by the managers. KPIs should be oriented on fulfilling Performance Objectives (PO), consequently they should be derived from POs which are regarded as a source and essential purpose for using the KPIs. In general, the two first dimensions (Financial and Customer) are lagging Strategic Key Performance Objectives and the two other ones are leading Performance Objectives [28]. Derivation of KPIs from the definitions of business processes as a leading idea for the proposals presented in this paper undoubtedly leads to the suppression of lagging indicators in behalf of the leading ones. Many traditional lagging indicators loose the sense in the process-driven organization and at the same time this approach opens the space for more sophisticated leading indicators as it significantly changes the notion of business drivers.

Association of KPIs with business processes is an attractive topic and a lot of various approaches to it can be found in the literature. [31] offers a comprehensive overview of the literature about business process performance measurement. Most approaches take KPIs traditionally and regard processes just as a way of fulfilling them. Only a little of them focus on specific KPIs coming from business process orientation of management and just some of these aim to the derivation of KPIs from processes. For instance [4] focuses on specific performance indicators for the complete monitoring of business process execution, [32] maps the relationships between the business process management and service-orientation in the context of KPIs and [5] even introduces so-called Process Performance Indicators (PPIs) that should be considered in the SLA. In our opinion, there is no one existing approach using KPIs for the internal quality of the whole system of business processes. This can be regarded as an original contribution of our approach.

Pretty exhaustive overview of the problem of KPIs from the business process perspective can be found in [8]. The authors classify KPIs from the four basic dimensions of the business process performance as: *time, cost, quality* and *flexibility* - oriented. This classification allows more sophisticated approach to KPIs and also their association with related techniques for the quantitative business process analysis like the techniques related to the Balanced Scorecard [12], namely the Activity-Based Costing technique (ABC) [13], flow analysis and process simulation techniques and others. For instance, [8] offers the technique of *Flow Analysis* for the estimation of the process time using the essential types of algorithmic structures (exclusivity, parallelism and repetition). The same approach can be used also for the estimation of the process costs. Nevertheless, these techniques are well usable for the indicators from "hard" dimensions (time and cost) unlike the indicators in the remaining "soft" dimensions (quality and flexibility) whose quantification usually leads to the use of intuition, subjective estimations etc. The approach of deriving indicators from business processes presented in this paper is focused especially on the quantification of those aspects of the business process system which are usually regarded to belong to the "soft" dimensions of the enterprise's performance: quality and flexibility.

3   Background Methodology

The approach to the modeling of business processes presented in this paper is firmly grounded in our Methodology for Modelling and Analysis of Business Processes (MMABP) [3]. In spite of its name MMABP is a methodology for the complex modeling of "business system", not only its business processes. Nevertheless, the MMABP's conception of "business system" is influenced mainly with the ideas of process-driven management. By "business system" we generally understand the system of human activities leading to creating the values. MMABP models aim to cover the business system itself as well as its basic infrastructure, its information system. The complete MMABP business system model consists of the set of inter-related models of two basic kinds (see Fig. 2). Model of the business system consists of the model of being (ontological model) and the model of behavior (intentional model).

Being (so-called Real World ontology) is modeled with two basic diagrams from the Unified Modelling Language (UML) [27]: **Class Diagram** represents the *system view of being*. By this diagram we model objects and their mutual relationships. **State Chart** represents the particular view of being as a *temporal model of the single object*. By this diagram we model the object's life cycle.

Behavior in the business system is also modeled with two kinds of diagrams: *Model of the process system* represents the system view of intentional behavior: business processes and their mutual collaboration. MMABP uses for this model the **Process Map** diagram based on the methodology of Eriksson and Penker [9]. *Model of the process flow* represents the particular view of behavior as a temporal model of the single business process. MMABP uses for this model the **BPMN** diagram [15].

Figure 2 outlines basic relationships between the ontological (business objects) and intentional (business processes) dimensions of models. Objects from the Class Diagram manifest themselves in the process model as products, inputs, outputs, actors, and other kinds of process aspects. Relationships among objects from the Class Diagram then represent the essential business rules and restrictions (i.e. modality of the business system) which the processes have to respect and fulfill. Looking from the opposite side one can see the business processes from the process diagrams as the ways of fulfilling the modality of the business system in terms of achieving individual business goals. On the detailed level, the life cycles of objects (State Charts) can be seen as definitions of essential causality related to the individual object, while detailed process models (BPMN models) as intentional combinations of the lives of related objects. Business object models (i.e. contextual Class Diagram and related State Charts describing life cycles of selected objects) thus contain the information about events and their general context in terms of the causality of the business system. Models of business processes complete the information about events and their intentional context; intentionality in the business system. More details about MMABP particular consistency rules for tuning business system models can be found in [20]. From the point of view of this paper the most important part of MMABP are process models and related aspects following from the need for the consistency with other models. As the main philosophical source of MMABP are the process-driven management ideas the methodology is especially elaborated in the field of business processes with the primary respect to those ideas. Details of these features of MMABP which are especially important from the point of view of the proposals introduced in this paper are discussed in the following sub-section.

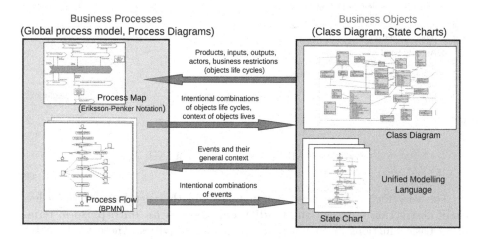

Fig. 2. MMABP business system models and their essential relationships [3].

3.1 Process States and Process Steps as Basic Points for Internal Indicators of the Enterprise's Performance

MMABP defines four levels of abstraction of a process (see Fig. 3). We can find different approaches to levels of process abstractions in a number of standards and methods [17,18,29,30]. MMABP has its own synthesizing method build on [23] in which the individual approaches we analyzed and synthesized into four level approach on which MMABP now builds on. Abstraction levels 1 and 2 belong to the Global model of processes while levels 3 and 4 belong to the Model of the processes run. In other words, in MMABP there are two abstraction levels of the system view of processes and two abstraction levels of the temporal view of a process. Each abstraction level is related to the aspect of the business system which MMABP regards as essential: standardization of enterprise functionality (level 1), individualization of enterprise processes (level 2), individual collaboration of processes (level 3), and general causality of the business (level 4). From the point of view of potential KPIs each level of process abstraction represents the special kind of KPIs:

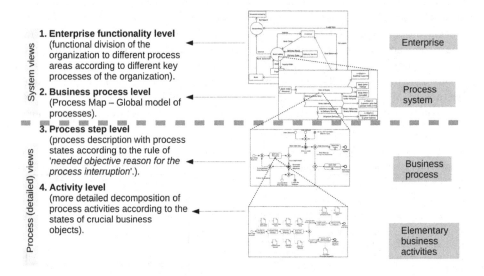

Fig. 3. MMABP process abstraction levels [3].

The very high - *Enterprise functionality* and the very low - *Activity* levels of abstraction represent the **traditional view of an enterprise** in terms of its basic functions and elementary enterprise activities. These levels match also the traditional approach to KPIs: expressing the performance of individual parts of the enterprise decomposed according to the organizational structure as an amount of financial or substantive units. The traditional simple technique of Activity-Based Costing (ABC) [13] cumulated from the lowest level of abstraction can be effectively used there for instance.

The two middle levels of abstraction – *Process Map* and *Process Steps* levels represent the **internal organization of the work in the enterprise**. Process Map describes existing logical business processes and their mutual associations which represent their collaboration on the service basis. Detailed definition of the process steps flow in the BPMN then describes the collaboration from the perspective of the given process. Each process step represents one process task starting with the event and resulting either in the waiting for the following event or in the end of the process. The points of waiting for the event which allows the further process run are called *Process States*.

In MMABP the definition of the process at the level of process steps and consequential description of process states (alias waiting for events) is essential. It follows from the so-called **principle of negative feed-back**. In the legendary article [19], which is regarded as essential for cybernetics, the authors expressed the idea which substantially influenced the later development of cybernetics: "all purposeful behavior may be considered to require negative feed-back". The concept of negative feed-back is explained there as follows: "...the behavior of an object is controlled by the margin of error at which the object stands at a given time with reference to a relatively specific goal. The feed-back is then negative, that is, the signals from the goal are used to restrict outputs which would otherwise go beyond the goal". According to the basic work in the field of process-driven management [10] goal is a fundamental attribute of a business process which is regularly respected in matured methodologies like in [9] for instance. Business process thus has to be regarded as an intentional process,

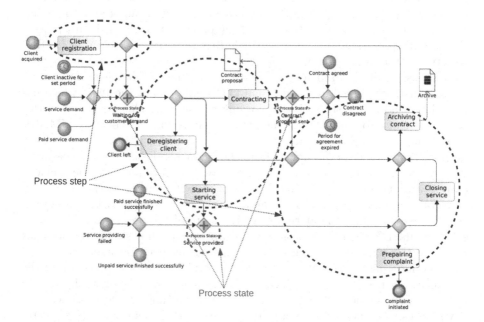

Fig. 4. Example of process states and steps: client management process.

the process of purposeful behavior of an interested object following some goal. For instance the behavior of the process manager is undoubtedly an intentional behavior which follows the goal of the process. Therefore MMABP requires that **every business process definition contains the negative feed-back** which ensures restriction of its outputs in order to keep them in the margins of its goal. In business processes the feed-back is represented by the input which is causally connected with some process output. The information from the input should influence the following behavior of the process in terms of keeping it within the margins of its goal. This means that 'intermediate' inputs to the process (i.e. none-starting inputs to the process coming between its starting and end points) are critically important parts of the business process distinguishing it from other, non-intentional (i.e. non-business), processes. When working with processes we have to take into the account even the time dimension; every input to the process has to be synchronized with the process run. Thus, in each part of the process where some input which influences the following process run is expected the process state has to be placed. The process state represents such points in the process structure where nothing can be done before the input to the process occurs, i.e. the point of waiting for the input. Process state thus represents the essential need to synchronize the process run with expected events. This need follows from the fact that the event is always an objective external influence and thus it must be respected. From the physical point of view such respect means synchronization – waiting for the event. Intentionality or purposefulness is also very important topic for the ideas Business Process Management Automation in general, particularly robotics and similar fields. Figure 4 shows the example of the business process definition at the process steps level. It can be seen there that at this level the process is a structure of the process steps divided with process states. Each process step is either a single task or a (usually selection (XOR)) structure of the tasks. The principle of negative feed-back discussed in previous paragraphs manifests itself in the fact that each internal process state has to be immediately followed by the decision (XOR gate) about the event which has caused the end of the state. Just according to the particular attributes of this event the next particular step of the process can be chosen. This way MMABP implements the required negativeness of the feed-back – the restriction of the future actions based on the signals from the feed-back. From the business point of view process state represents waiting for events as a response to the previous process activity. From the technical point of view it represents synchronization with collaborating processes/actors and also the process memory because of the need for remembering the attributes of the state of the process until the next event occurs. BPMN, unlike most of other process modeling standards, does not recognize the concept of process state. This insufficiency is closely connected with the ignoring of essential difference between the business process and the system of business processes which is discussed in more detail in the following Discussion section. Based on the technical meaning of the process state, MMABP uses for the modeling of process states in BPMN so-called "AND gateway" as a point of the synchronization of the process run with the expected

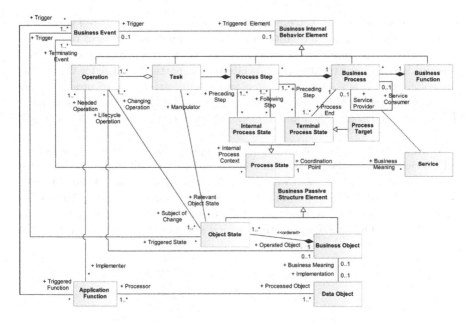

Fig. 5. Process steps, states and services in MMABP meta-model [3].

event(s) (see Fig. 4). *Process Step* represents the set of activities where there is **no objective reason for the decomposition to the detailed level**. Such decomposition can be motivated only by subjective factors like the qualification of actors (which can cause the need for the decomposition to the set of activities respecting the existing qualification of particular actors), existing technology (including even the given structure of the IS functionality, for instance), existing organizational structure if necessary (which disallows the grouping of activities across the boundaries of particular organizational units), and others. Therefore MMABP defines for such deeper decomposition one more level of detail: Activity (Task) level (see Figs. 3 and 5).

4   Deriving KPIs from Inter-process Services

In the following text we focus on the indicators which express the attributes of process states and process steps as we believe that especially this level of detail can significantly contribute to the current state in the field of KPIs. Process states represent **points of communication** of the process with other processes or actors. From the perspective of the performance of the enterprise the process state represents the **handover of the responsibility** for the given task what is in general an **essence of collaboration**. MMABP defines for the process states the standard general attributes based on the generalized theory of service-orientation. Each collaboration point is regarded as a service which one process/actor another process/actor provides with. For each collaboration point the general Service Level Agreement (SLA) prescript can be created containing standardly also the general quality- and time-oriented indicators of the service. At the time of the run of the particular process (ie. the process instance) this prescript is then implemented (instantiated) as a particular SLA for the particular collaboration act. Particular time and quality attributes of process states and awaited events are then used as a basic source for the indicators used in the SLA prescriptions. Details about the role of services in MMABP can be found in [21].

Mutual essential relations among the concepts of Process State, Process Step and Service are described in the full context at Fig. 5 which shows the MMABP meta-model based on the meta-model of Archimate notation for the TOGAF Enterprise Architecture framework [2,24,26]. The meta-model also shows basic relations to the ontological dimension of the business system models, particularly to the Business Object life cycle states which also play an important role in the enterprise performance measuring.

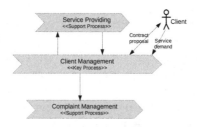

Fig. 6. Example of Process Map: Client Management Process System

Below the **procedure for the derivation of KPIs from inter-process communication** is described with use of the example of Client Management Process System (see Figs. 4 and 6):

Step 1: *Create the SLA* for each communication point of two processes. In the example at Fig. 6 there are two communication points between the key process *Client Management* and support processes *Service Providing* and *Complaint Management*. Also the communication with *Client* is visible there as a bi-directional negotiation about the *Contract proposal* and one-way *Service demand*. The details of each communication point can be seen at Fig. 4 as a context of particular process states (awaited events and consequential reactions of the process). The result of this step will be three SLAs for the *Service* management, *Complaint* management and for the communication with *Client*.

Step 2: In each SLA *specify the service* and its standard parameters of time, cost and quality. For instance, SLA with the *Service Providing* process should contain the specification of both types of the client *Service* (paid and unpaid) and their quality parameters, time of the service delivery and the cost of the service (all values for each defined service level).

Step 3: *Specify the detailed leading KPIs* based on the optimal values of SLA parameters separately for each communication point.

Step 4: *Calculate the global leading KPIs* from the detailed ones according to their process contexts using the key process(es) in each functional area as a contextual pivot.

For instance, the KPIs derived from the SLA between the *Client Management* process and the *Service Providing* process measure the inter-processes collaboration, execution of one service for the *Client*. From the client's point of view the overall quality of company's services is rather represented by the communication with the *Client Management* process which covers all services during the whole life cycle of the client. It is because the key process represents the primary function of the organization and consequently the needed context of all supporting services. Therefore it should be used as a pivot for the cumulation of KPIs. This way the hard KPIs (time, cost) derived from the Service Level Agreements representing particular cooperation points are used as a basis for the calculation of the overall KPIs for the whole process system (i.e. enterprise) which represent the optimal value of the enterprise's performance (i.e. the best possible for the given structure of processes). In the opposite way, the deviations of the actual values from the optimal ones can be analyzed by their decomposition according to the structure of the process system in order to find out the bottleneck or the problem point in the communication structure of processes.

The difference between the process steps and process activities (*Tasks* at Fig. 5) levels actually maps the difference between the objectively optimal structure of the process and the actually necessary structure which respects also the specifics and necessities of the current state. This difference can be used for the estimation of the enterprise performance in comparison to the theoretically optimal (best possible) performance. This difference can then be used as a **leading KPO for the future development of the process system** which represents its flexibility.

5   Discussion

Father of the enterprise quality management William Deming expressed in his famous critical book "Out of the crisis" from 1982 [7] the fourteen points for management expressing this way the basic rules for the management which can lead the enterprise to the high-quality performance. Some of these rules has been later directly fulfilled by the idea of process-driven management, particularly: *Point 1: "Create constancy of purpose towards improvement"*, *Point 3: "Cease dependence on inspection"*, *Point 7: "Institute leadership"*, *Point 9: "Break down barriers between departments"*, and point 14: *"The transformation is everyone's job"*. Most of remaining points are at least closely related to the process-driven management as its consequences or basic conditions: *Point 2: "Adopt the new philosophy"*, *Point 5: "Improve constantly and forever"*, *Point 8: "Drive out fear"*, *Point 10: "Eliminate slogans"*, *Point 11: "Eliminate the management by objectives"* and *Point 13: "Institute education and self-improvement"*. Deming is especially critical to the typical approach of the traditional managers which is based on the direct control, inspections, stating the goals and continuous measurement of their achievement. KPIs are traditionally regarded as a tool right for this kind of management. Most of current typical and general KPIs are oriented on the simply quantifiable aspects of the enterprise's performance usually expressed as short-term goals for the purpose of measuring their deviations against the plan. As it follows from the first paragraph of this section, process-driven management significantly moves the managerial practices towards the ideas of W.Deming. From the point of view of the use of KPIs this approach fulfills especially the point 3 (Cease dependence on inspection) particularly by breaking down barriers between departments (point 9) introducing the system of "internal customers" as a basic meaning of the collaboration of processes built on the basis of Service Level Agreements (SLA). In this way the competences of the enterprise's performance actors (employees) are naturally decomposed down to the optimal level driven exclusively by the needs of business processes (in the roles of internal customers) which completely eliminates the need for the management by objectives (Deming's point 11).

The common and widely popular mistake in the field of business process management is the lack of the respect to the essential difference between the business process and the system of business processes. One of the most visible consequence of this misunderstanding is even the fact that the commonly used standard for the business process modeling BPMN [15] do not offer the diagram for modeling so-called Process Map although such diagram is a regular part of many older and matured standards, for instance [9,17]. Instead of the clear distinguishing between a single process and the system of processes BPMN just offers to describe the casual communication with other processes and actors as a part of the definition of the process flow. BPMN thus can be regarded just as a "language" for the definition of the process flow, not for the complex business process system modeling. Looking at the communication with other processes only from the perspective of the particular process disallows perceiving the inter-process relationships as services which can be exactly described in the SLA manner, their attributes analyzed, measured, and everything finally managed using the service-oriented style.

6 Conclusions

In this paper we propose the approach to the derivation of KPIs from the description of business processes focused mainly on the inter-process communication. We believe that right this focus can harmonize the theory as well as the practice of using KPIs with the idea of process-driven organizations. Existing approaches to the derivation of KPIs from business processes are mainly based on the traditional notion of the processes in the enterprise which is not in accordance with the ideas of process-driven management presented in the essential resources [10,11,16]. This fact is understandable regarding the state-of-the-art in the field of business process modeling discussed in the last paragraph of the preceding section. Ignoring of the importance of the inter-process communication as a standalone aspect of the process management leads to inability to manage the process system on the basis of the services which is a direct way to the use of indicators of the internal quality of the process system. A comprehensive overview of existing business performance measurement frameworks can be found in [14]. In all integrated measurement frameworks the business processes play one of essential roles. At the same time, in all those approaches the business processes are subordinated to the organizational structure which contradicts with the essence of the process-driven management. Respecting the main principles of process-driven organization, especially the freeing from the organizational structure and other infrastructural aspects, generally recommended also by Deming [7], can open the space for using KPIs for the internal quality of the process system. In the light of the essential qualities of this style of management it can be supposed that the traditional approach to the management of enterprise via KPIs will be consequently reduced just on the objectively measurable indicators which replace the traditional intuitive estimations and trial-based settings of KPObjectives.

References

1. Austin, R.D.: Measuring and Managing Performance in Organizations. Dorset House Publishing, New York (1996)
2. The Open Group: ArchiMate 3.0 Specification. Van Haren. 2016. ISBN 94-01-80047-2
3. Business System Modeling Specification. http://opensoul.panrepa.org/metamodel.html
4. Calabro, A., Lonetti, F. and Marchetti, E.: Monitoring of business process execution based on performance indicators. In 2015 41st Euromicro Conference on Software Engineering and Advanced Applications, pp. 255–58. IEEE, Madeira (2015). https://doi.org/10.1109/SEAA.2015.73
5. Cho, M., et al.: A new framework for defining realistic SLAs: an evidence-based approach. In: Carmona, J., Engels, G., Kumar, A. (eds.) BPM 2017. LNBIP, vol. 297, pp. 19–35. Springer, Cham (2017). https://doi.org/10.1007/978-3-319-65015-9_2
6. Davenport, T.H. (ed.): Enterprise Analytics: Optimize Performance, Process, and Decisions Through Big Data. FT Press, Upper Saddle River (2013)
7. Deming, W.E.: Out of the Crisis. MIT Press, Cambridge (2000)
8. Dumas, M., La Rosa, M., Mendling, J., Reijers, H.A.: Fundamentals of Business Process Management. Springer, Heidelberg (2013)
9. Eriksson, H.E., Penker, M.: Business Modeling with UML: Business Patterns at Work. Wiley, Hoboken (2000)
10. Hammer, M., Champy, J.: Reengineering the Corporation: A Manifesto for Business Revolution. Nicholas Brealey Publishing, London (1993)
11. Hammer, M.: The process audit. Harv. Bus. Rev. **85**(4), 111–123 (2007)
12. Kaplan, R.S., Norton, D.P.: The Balanced Scorecard: Translating Strategy into Action. Harvard Business School Press, Boston (1996)
13. Kaplan, R.S., Anderson, S.R.: Time-Driven Activity-Based Costing: A Simpler and More Powerful Path to Higher Profits, 3rd edn. Harvard Business School Press, Boston (2009)

14. Neely, A.D. (ed.): Business Performance Measurement: Theory and Practice. Cambridge University Press, Cambridge (2002)
15. Object Management Group: Business Process Model and Notation (BPMN) Specification Version 2.0.2. http://www.omg.org/spec/BPMN/
16. Porter, M.E.: Competitive Advantage: Creating and Sustaining Superior Performance, 1st edn. Free Press, New York (1998)
17. von Rosing, M., von Scheel, H., Scheer, A.W.: The Complete Business Process Handbook: Body of Knowledge from Process Modeling to BPM. Elsevier Science, San Francisco (2015)
18. Rosenberg, A.: SAP Modeling Handbook - Modeling Standards. https://wiki.scn.sap.com/wiki/display/ModHandbook/
19. Rosenblueth, A., Wiener, N., Bigelow, J.: Behavior, Purpose and Teleology. Philos. Sci. **10**(1), 18–24 (1943)
20. Repa, V.: Business system as an equilibrium of intention and causality. In E+M Ekonomie a Management, vol. 20, no. 4, 14 December 2017. https://doi.org/10.15240/tul/001/2017-4-015
21. Repa, V.: Role of the concept of services in business process management. In: Pokorny, J., et al. (eds.) Information Systems Development, pp. 623–634. Springer, New York (2011). https://doi.org/10.1007/978-1-4419-9790-6_50
22. Strategy Management Group: What is a Key Performance Indicator? https://kpi.org/KPI-Basics
23. Svatoš, O., Řepa, V.: Working with process abstraction levels. In: Řepa, V., Bruckner, T. (eds.) BIR 2016. LNBIP, vol. 261, pp. 65–79. Springer, Cham (2016). https://doi.org/10.1007/978-3-319-45321-7_5
24. Svatos, O.: Business process modeling method for archimate. In: IDIMT-2017 Digitalization in Management, Society and Economy. Poděbrady, 06 September 2017 - 08 September 2017. Trauner Verlag Universität, Linz (2017). ISBN 978-3-99062-119-6
25. Taylor, F.W.: The Principles of Scientific Management. Enna Products Corp., Bellingham (2007)
26. The Open Group: TOGAF Version 9.1. Van Haren (2011). ISBN 90-87536-79-8
27. UML Superstructure Specification, v2.0 document 05–07-04, Object Management Group (2004)
28. Welvago: Define the right KPI starting from Key Performance Objectives. https://www.wevalgo.com/know-how/define-right-kpi
29. Process Classification Framework APQC. https://www.apqc.org/pcf
30. The Supply Chain Operations Reference model (SCOR). http://www.apics.org/sites/apics-supply-chain-council/frameworks/score
31. Van Looy, A., Shafagatova, A.: Business process performance measurement: a structured literature review of indicators, measures and metrics. SpringerPlus **5**(1), 1797 (2016). https://doi.org/10.1186/s40064-016-3498-1
32. Wetzstein, B.: KPI-related monitoring, analysis, and adaptation of business processes (2016). https://doi.org/10.18419/opus-8956

The Unexpected Benefits of Paying for Information: The Effects of Payment on Information Source Choices and Epistemic Thinking

Daphne R. Raban[1]([⊠]) ⓘ, Sarit Barzilai[2] ⓘ, and Lina Portnoy[1] ⓘ

[1] School of Business Administration, University of Haifa, Haifa, Israel
draban@univ.haifa.ac.il, portnoy.lina@gmail.com
[2] Faculty of Education, University of Haifa, Haifa, Israel
sarit.barzilai@edu.haifa.ac.il

Abstract. People often need to select, evaluate, and integrate information from diverse online sources to support decision-making processes in everyday life. Information is a product which is often available for free, but which people are willing to pay for. Free access to information can presumably facilitate greater use of information sources, thereby leading to improved learning and knowledge. But does it? Is "more of a good thing" actually better? This study examined how paying for information affects information source choices and information consumers' epistemic perspectives regarding the status and justification of knowledge. 106 university students participated in an experiment presenting an online information store in which participants acquired information products in order to reach a decision concerning a controversial health topic. Participants were assigned to two pricing conditions; one with paid information based on an incentive-compatible bidding mechanism (payment condition) and the other with information offered at a zero price (free condition). Results indicated that in the payment condition, participants accessed fewer information sources but that these sources were more diverse and balanced in their positions. Differences in epistemic perspectives emerged between the two conditions, suggesting payment requirements affected epistemic perspectives. Specifically, in the payment condition, evaluativism was higher and absolutism was lower than in the free condition. This is the first study to indicate a potential relation between the consumption characteristics of information products and the epistemic thinking of information users. The study has theoretical and practical implications, connecting the fields of information economics and personal epistemology.

Keywords: Free information · Paid information · Information consumption · Epistemic thinking

M. Pańkowska and K. Sandkuhl (Eds.): BIR 2019, LNBIP 365, pp. 163–176, 2019.
https://doi.org/10.1007/978-3-030-31143-8_12

1   Introduction

We all enjoy free access to information online because information is the raw material for learning, generating knowledge, and producing information. It stands to reason that free access to information facilitates greater and better use of information, thereby leading to improved learning and knowledge. But does it? Is "more of a good thing" actually better? One of the basic premises of economics is that scarcity increases demand and value. How does the so-called 'homo economicus' deal with the abundance of information? This paper explored the effects of abundance by examining how paying for information affects information source choices and information consumers' epistemic perspectives regarding the status and justification of knowledge. Thus, we examined value with a dual lens by linking between research on the economic value of information and psychological research on people's epistemic values. We explored the effects of payment using an innovative online laboratory experiment.

Information is widely available at no direct charge because of its cost structure [12]. Rather, it is often paid for by third parties such as advertisers. The availability of seemingly-free information to consumers results in setting a "free mentality" towards digital goods [23]. An exceptional preference for free products has been demonstrated using a behavioral approach [35]. People tend to expect and prefer free-of-charge information.

The de-facto abundance of free information available to consumers has led to academic assertions such as there being a weak link, if any, between quality, quantity, and pricing or value of information [15]. However, abundance may be linked to concepts such as information overload [9] or congestion [37], meaning that "all-you-can-eat" may be, at times, detrimental to the ability to process information and generate knowledge from it. This suggests that limiting access to information may enhance the ability to use it well. In this study, we made a first attempt to empirically test the effect of payment for information on information source use and on epistemic thinking. We investigated how imposing a mind-set of economic scarcity influences of the epistemic approach to and the demand for information goods.

Epistemic thinking, or epistemic cognition, involves thinking that is related to knowledge and knowing and to the achievement of epistemic aims, such as acquiring true beliefs or understanding [8, 13]. Research on epistemic thinking has demonstrated that people have implicit assumptions regarding the certainty, complexity, sources, and justification and knowledge which come into play in everyday reasoning [15]. Previous studies found that people's epistemic perspectives, i.e., their views regarding the nature of knowledge and knowing, influence the ways in which they evaluate and integrate multiple information sources [1, 4, 6]. Researchers have typically assumed that epistemic perspectives develop gradually through social and educational experiences [38]. In this study, we examined whether the economic value of information might also affect epistemic perspectives.

2   Theoretical Background

2.1   The Economic Value of Information

Information as a Unique Product

Information is an intangible product with a marginal cost of zero or close to zero. Despite its unusual character, information is considered an economic good, for which people are willing to pay [7, 36]. Unlike other products, the amount of information or its marginal cost do not attest to its value. Information is an experience good whose full value and qualities are revealed only after its purchase and use. Generally, many new products are experience goods, but information is an experience good every time it is consumed [36].

The Subjective Economic Value of Information

The economic value of information is dynamic and is perceived differently by people at different times and situations [36]. This value may change with time and is not necessarily rational. Therefore, the economic value of information is mainly subjective, perceived [28].

The perceived value may be affected by the individual characteristics of a person (such as knowledge and experience), the characteristics of the environment and the social situation (such as level of interaction, social feedback, relations of authority and social perceptions), and/or the characteristics of the information itself (such as format, accuracy, timing, source of the information and its availability) [27, 28]. In the present study, we assessed subjective value using the measure of Willingness-to-Pay (WTP) for an information product [30].

Willingness-to-Pay for Products and the 'Free' Effect.

Observed behaviour online as well as laboratory experiments have shown that people are willing to pay for information products to some extent [30]. Prior research has used WTP (Willingness-to-Pay) as a measure of subjective value rather than as an indicator of actual pricing [32]. In such cases, change in, or relative value of WTP are more relevant than the absolute size of WTP. In the present study as well, WTP is not taken at face value. It is used in two ways: 1. to assess the relation between WTP and the experience value of information; 2. as a primer for an economic framing of the experimental group in contrast to the group exposed to free information.

Because information is an experience good, information value should be explored both before and after it is consumed. However, only few studies have investigated this theoretical framework [28, 33]. Subjective value is defined as the value perceived and attributed to the information by the user *before* purchasing and/or using it. Experience value is defined as the value of the information that is revealed to the user *after use* [28].

It can be argued that the value of information after use will be low or non-existent because the decisions based on the information have already been made and it is no longer relevant. While this value may indeed be lower that the pre-use value due to its lower practical relevance, it may become a crucial factor in shaping future decisions and acquisitions and become a part of the user's thinking pattern in future events requiring information evaluation. Therefore, there is theoretical importance in researching the connection between the subjective value (before use) and the experience value (after use) [27, 28]. Specifically, it is possible that if people are required to pay for information, the subjective value of information will increase and this may result in lower experience value. Hence, we hypothesized that:

H1: Requiring payment for information products will reduce subsequent experience-based willingness to pay for these products.

Nowadays, people are both consumers and producers of information. A large amount of online information is accessible to consumers for free and without human intermediation, at any time and any place, so that consumers are in a constant state of information overload [36]. This situation is created when the amount of information required for processing is higher than the information processing abilities of a person at a given time. We expected that implementing a payment mechanism will cause users to become more selective in their information choices and acquire fewer items that when the items are available at no charge.

In addition, a series of experiments in the field of behavioural economics, in which the participants were offered chocolates for different prices, has found that the price of zero has a special value for the consumers leading to preference reversal, that is, preferring an inferior product offered for free over a better-quality offered for low payment [35]. Such behaviour leads to the following hypothesis:

H2: More information sources will be chosen when the information is offered for free than when participants are required to pay for them.

Because we expected that payment will reduce the number of information sources that are selected, we also conjectured that participants will be more selective and discerning in their information source choices. This is because scarcity leads to a greater focus on product selection [34]. Hence, we expected that participants who are required to pay for information sources will be more attentive to information quality. More specifically, we expected that they may select information sources that are more trustworthy (i.e., produced by authors with greater expertise and benevolence), that are more relevant to their task, and that represent multiple positions rather than just a single position regarding the issue at stake. Hence, we hypothesized that:

H3: Requiring payment for information will result in selecting a higher proportion of trustworthy, relevant, and multiple-position information sources.

2.2   Epistemic Thinking

Epistemic Perspectives Regarding the Nature of Knowledge and Knowing
According to the developmental model of Kuhn and her colleagues [21, 22], there are three main epistemic perspectives regarding the nature of knowledge and knowing: According to the *absolutist* perspective, knowledge is certain and objective. It is based on facts and there exists only one right account. According to the *multiplist* perspective, knowledge is subjective, based on personal opinions and experience, and uncertain. Everyone is entitled to their own opinion, therefore all opinions are equal. According to the *evaluativist* perspective, knowledge is comprised of judgements and interpretations that involve both subjective and objective dimensions (e.g., data are interpreted within

particular viewpoints). Multiple right accounts may exist; however, some may be more right than others. Knowledge is essentially uncertain, but it is possible to improve the degree of certainty. Kuhn and Weinstock argue that epistemic thinking is a theory-in-action manifested in interpretation and judgement of information and in decision making in everyday lives [22]. The epistemic perspectives described by Kuhn and her colleagues have been found to affect the ways in which people evaluate and integrate information sources [1, 2, 4, 6]. Specifically, evaluativism has been associated with better integration and argumentation processes.

Change in Epistemic Perspectives

As mentioned, researchers have traditionally attributed epistemic development to educational and social experience [38]. Developmental studies have shown that epistemic perspectives are slow to change and that only a minority of the adult population adopts evaluativist perspectives. In recent years, several educational intervention studies have demonstrated that instruction that develops students' argumentation and evaluation competencies can lead to growth in students' epistemic perspectives, presumably by advancing students' awareness of the value of weighing multiple accounts [2, 16, 17]. These studies have assumed that epistemic perspectives are not easy to change, and that change requires actively fostering appreciation of the value and means of engaging with contrasting viewpoints.

In contrast, studies that have focused on epistemic beliefs, that is, specific beliefs about the nature of knowledge and knowing, such as beliefs regarding the certainty of knowledge, have found that these beliefs can be quite malleable and may shift even following brief exposure to conflicting information. For example, Porsch and Bromme [26] documented a shift in epistemic beliefs following a brief "epistemic sensitization" text that described knowledge regarding a particular topic as controversial. Participants who read the text that highlighted the controversial nature of knowledge tended to increase their beliefs that knowledge in this topic is complex, imprecise, and dynamic. Other studies have documented that exposure to conflicting information sources can also lead to an immediate shift in epistemic beliefs toward stronger beliefs that knowledge is developing, uncertain, and complex [10, 11, 19, 20].

It is currently unclear if epistemic perspectives can be as malleable as epistemic beliefs. Epistemic perspectives are multi-dimensional and therefore might be potentially more difficult to change than epistemic beliefs [2, 5]. Nonetheless, in one recent study, Zavala and Kuhn [39] found that asking students to write an argumentative dialog between advocates of two candidates for mayor of a fictional city resulted in lower adoption of absolutism and greater adoption of evaluativism compared to writing an essay about the merits of the candidates. This study provides initial evidence that epistemic perspectives may be more dynamic than has been previously assumed and can be sensitive to the ways in which people interact with the information available to them.

In light of prior research that suggested the malleability of epistemic beliefs and perspectives, we wished to examine if paying for conflicting information sources may affect epistemic perspectives. As mentioned in Sect. 3.1, we hypothesized that requiring participants to pay for information sources will lead them to become more selective and discerning information consumers. Specifically, requiring participants to pay for conflicting information sources might lead them to think more carefully and critically about the conflicting claims presented by these information sources, and to become more aware of the uncertain nature of knowledge. This could potentially result in greater agreement with evaluativist views that knowledge is uncertain yet can be critically evaluated. Hence, we tentatively hypothesized that:

H4: Paying for information sources will affect topic-specific epistemic perspectives and lead to higher endorsement of evaluativism.

3 Method

A controlled laboratory experiment was designed in an online environment, using a platform named FlexiPrice [29, 30]. The experiment consisted of a decision-making problem, online questionnaires, and an information store offering a list of information products.

106 Hebrew-speaking university students recruited by advertising on campus and on social media participated in the online experiment (79.2% female; 68% BA students; $M_{age} = 26.93, SD = 5.66$).

Participants were presented with a controversial topic: the influence of dairy consumption on the cardiovascular system. A scenario was introduced in which a close friend who is concerned with his health needs assistance in deciding whether he should consume dairy products. The scenario was meant to motivate participants to acquire information on the topic. After answering preliminary questionnaires, participants were presented with a virtual information store, containing a variety of information sources. Participants were asked to read information on the topic, as many information sources as they like, in order to make an informed decision regarding the influence of dairy products on the cardiovascular system and provide their friend a recommendation based on what they have read.

Participants were randomly assigned to one of two conditions:

1. Free condition: In this condition, participants were given access to the information sources with no payment required. Participants had an option of giving voluntary payment post factum, after the information was revealed.

2. Payment condition: In this condition, participants were asked to choose information sources they wish to read after placing a price bid (WTP), using virtual money presented in a virtual wallet. The WTP bid was applied as described elsewhere [31]. Participants in this group also had an option of giving additional voluntary payment post factum.

The information store included 19 online information sources on the topic of dairy products consumption and cardiovascular health in the Hebrew language. The information sources were authentic web pages that were captured on the Internet and presented in a way that mimicked regular browsing. The information sources were written by authors with high expertise (e.g., medical professionals), medium expertise (e.g., health journalists), and low expertise (e.g., laypersons). The publishers displayed high benevolence (e.g., information provided by public health organizations) or low benevolence (e.g., information provided by organizations with commercial interests).

The content of the information sources had high relevance (content related to the connection between dairy product consumption and cardiovascular health), medium relevance (content related either to dairy consumption or the vascular system but not both), and low relevance (content related to other issues such as bone density). Author positions were in favour of dairy consumption, against dairy consumption, or two-sided. Thus, the information store reflected the authentic diversity of information sources that people may encounter when reading online about a controversial health topic.

3.1 Measures

Epistemic perspectives (absolutism, multiplism, and evaluativism) were measured via a validated epistemic thinking assessment based on Kuhn's model and referring to beliefs about conflicting knowledge claims regarding the topic of dairy product consumption [5]. The questionnaire consisted of 10 questions, each containing three statements, representing the three epistemic perspectives. The internal consistency reliability of the scales was absolutism, $a = .82$, multiplism, $a = .82$, and evaluativism, $a = .71$. The score for each of the epistemic perspectives ranged from 1 to 10 and was based on the mean of the 10 relevant items.

Subjective value of information was measured by price bids made in order to access information sources, reflecting willingness- to-pay (WTP) for information. WTP was measured once by the first price offer for each chosen information source which reflects the person's authentic WTP; and once by the mean of the offers made for that source, in case there was more than one offer. Participants in the free condition were offered the same information products without charge.

Experience value of information was measured by the amount of supplementary payment, which was not mandatory and available for both groups.

Information source selection was measured by the number of sources selected for purchase in the payment condition and the number of sources selected for access in the free condition.

Three control variables were taken into account: personal topic relevance, prior topic knowledge, and position on the topic. According to prior research, these might have an impact on the findings [3]. The participants completed two questionnaires measuring the control variables. Prior position on the topic was measured by two questions which were strongly correlated $(r = .49, p < .001)$ and therefore averaged into one variable of prior position. Prior knowledge was measured by two open questions regarding dairy consumption. The first question was: "How does consumption of dairy products influence health? State as many influences as are known to you." The second question was: "What is the relation between consumption of dairy products and cardiovascular diseases?" The number of idea units provided by each participant in response to these questions were counted. Each idea unit had to be relevant to the topic and contain new information. The number of idea units in the two prior knowledge questions was significantly correlated $(r_s = .38, p < .001)$, and therefore averaged into one variable. Personal topic relevance was measured using five items adapted from Hartwell and Kaplan's [14] self-relevance measure.

4 Results

In order to examine the equivalence of the conditions, differences in the control variables (topic relevance, prior position, and prior topic knowledge) between the free and payment conditions were tested using independent sample T-tests. No significant differences were found between the two conditions.

Hypothesis **H1** stated that requiring payment for information products will reduce subsequent experience-based willingness to pay for these products. Because the experienced-based WTP (voluntary payment following reading) variable was not normally distributed we employed a Mann-Whitney U test to compare the two conditions. Mean experienced-based WTP was found to be higher in the free condition than in the payment condition as expected, $M = 77.82, SD = 113.80$ vs. $M = 18.53$, $SD = 47.20, Z = -3.26, p < .001$. Hence, **H1** was supported.

The information source selection variable was not distributed normally hence the Mann-Whitney U test was used to compare the number of information sources that were selected in the payment and free groups. The results, $Z = -2.06, p < .05$, indicated a statistically significant difference between the payment and free conditions in the number of selected information sources. Participants in the free condition chose to read a significantly higher number ($M = 8.79, SD = 5.55$) of information sources than participants in the payment condition ($M = 6.72, SD = 3.65$). Thus, **H2** was supported.

Because the number of information sources differed across conditions, to compare the characteristic of the selected information sources, we calculated the ratio between the number of selected information sources of each type and the total number of selected information sources, for each participant. Mann-Whitney U tests were performed, because the variables were not normally distributed. The findings revealed several differences between conditions in the types of selected information sources:

1. Level of expertise: Participants in the payment condition selected a significantly higher proportion of information sources with a medium level of expertise compared to participants in the free condition ($Z = -2.79, p = .005$). Differences between conditions in high and low expertise information sources were not significant.
2. Topic relevance: Participants in the payment condition selected a significantly lower proportion of information sources with high relevance than participants in the free condition ($Z = -3.65, p < .0.01$). In contrast, participants in the payment condition ($Z = -2.98, p = .003$) selected a significantly higher number of information sources with medium or low relevance to the topic.
3. Two-sided position: Participants in the payment condition selected ($Z = -2.09, p = .037$) a significantly larger proportion of information sources that presented a two-sided or neutral position regarding dairy consumption compared to participants in free condition. In contrast, participants in the free condition selected a greater proportion of information sources that had a pro position title ($Z = -2.21, p = .027$).

No further statistically significant differences were found. Thus, we concluded that **H3** was partially supported.

A mixed ANOVA was performed with epistemic perspective (absolutism, multiplism and evaluativism) as a within-subjects variable and condition (payment or free) as a between-subjects variable. The results indicated a statistically significant main effect of epistemic perspective, $F(2, 103) = 147.81, p < .001, \eta_p^2 = .74$. Pairwise comparisons showed that absolutism and evaluativism were significantly higher than multiplism $(p < .001)$. The difference between absolutism and evaluativism was not significant. The main effect of condition was also non-significant, $F(2, 103) = .013$, $p = 0.908, \eta_p^2 = .00$. However, the interaction effect of epistemic perspective and condition was significant, $F(2, 103) = 17.96, p < .001, \eta_p^2 = .26$. To interpret the significant interaction effect, independent-samples t-tests, with Bonferroni correction of $p = 0.17$, were conducted to examine differences between the free and payment conditions for each epistemic perspective. Absolutism was significantly higher in the free condition than in the payment condition, $t(104) = 3.67, p < .001, d = .71$. In contrast, evaluativism was significantly higher in the payment condition than in the free condition, $t(104) = 4.88, p < .001, d = .94$. This led us to conclude that H4 was supported, that is, that payment had an effect on the epistemic perspectives.

5 Discussion

The purpose of the present investigation was to examine the effect of paying for information on experience value of information, information source selection, and epistemic perspectives. To examine the hypotheses, the participants took part in an online experiment, in which they selected and purchased information sources regarding a controversial topic, in two pricing conditions; one with information sources offered for payment based on a WTP bid, and one with information sources offered at a zero price. Participants were required to value the information products presented to them through willingness-to-pay (WTP) for them before (subjective value) and/or after (experience value) receiving the information.

Our first hypothesis dealt with the point of measurement of the perceived value of information. The results show that perceived value is significantly higher before purchase and use than after the actual experience of using information. The effect is stronger when payment was required in advance, as the experience-based value is lower in this condition as compared to the free condition – people who already paid a certain amount to obtain access provided lower post-use WTP values than people who received the information without pre-use charge in the free condition. While from a business perspective we may be tempted to recommend advance payment in order to maximize profit, our recommendation is to consider application of post-use payment for information. While people will pay less post use, they are likely to feel more satisfied when the remittance is commensurate with their actual experience of the content purchased. This may provide a solution to the non-excludability of information while taking advantage of its non-rivalrous nature, enabling broader application of payment compared to the current norm. Although only some (39% in payment condition and 63% in free condition) of the participants chose to provide post use payment, building user interfaces that enable this option may contribute to instilling such a norm online, making this behaviour more prevalent.

Information becomes valuable when people use it and increases in value when it can be compared and combined with additional information [24]. In the present study, the information presented was taken from Internet platforms which people are used to accessing without charge. Despite the general 'free mentality' of consumers and the expectancy for receiving information goods for free on the Internet, which reduces WTP for online information [23], the results show that people are willing to pay for information products. The present study supports the claim that information has an economic value, for which people are willing to pay [7, 36], both before and after receiving the information. Participants offered to pay different amounts of money for the same information products, supporting the claim that the value of information is perceived differently by different people [28, 36].

Even though the participants were given a generous amount of play money for buying the information (1,500 NIS), they still limited themselves in consuming information products. Although budget was plentiful and virtual, participants behaved as if they are experiencing scarcity, in line with our second hypothesis. The higher number of information selections in the free condition shows that the price of zero enhances the demand for the product, in agreement with Shampanier, Mazar & Ariely [35], who found that zero is a special price in the eyes of consumers and it is treated qualitatively different from other numbers. Another possible explanation for participants of the payment condition selecting fewer information sources is feeling of loss aversion when paying for information, which was identified as a factor which might influence WTP [18]. In the free condition, participants did not experience loss aversion while selecting information sources, since they were not required to pay for them.

Participants in the payment condition selected a significantly greater proportion of medium expertise information sources and more two-sided information sources compared to the participants in the free condition. Surprisingly, they also selected less sources of high relevance, possibly because they preferred to determine relevance for themselves or to gain a broader understanding of the topic (see below in discussion of H4). In contrast, participants in the free condition selected more high relevance and pro-position information sources. Because participants' initial position regarding the topic leaned to favouring dairy consumption, the behaviour of the participants in the free condition suggested a confirmation bias pattern [25]. Requiring payment appeared to reduce confirmation bias and lead to selection of more diverse and balanced information sources, in partial agreement with our third hypothesis.

In line with the fourth hypothesis, we found differences in epistemic perspectives between the free and payment conditions. In the payment condition, endorsement of absolutism was lower and endorsement of evaluativism was higher compared to the free condition. We conjecture that requiring payment made participants more selective and discerning in their information consumption. It might have made them examine the conflicting knowledge claims more attentively and to exercise greater critical judgement in their selections. Paying more attention to the conflicting claims made by the information sources could have increased awareness of the uncertain and controversial nature of knowledge and thus might have resulted in decrease in absolutism and increase in evaluativism.

Other interactions that await future research are the links between epistemic perspectives and the preference for expertise-based sources, two-sided sources and source relevance.

6 Research Limitations and Further Research

The present study was based on a laboratory experiment, which has some artificial characteristics that affect the ecological validity of the study. Although there was an effort to simulate a regular online search, the number of presented information sources was limited and there was a time limit for going through the content. In addition, the money that was used by participants in order to purchase information was virtual. If real money would have been used, the results might have been different. There is also a limitation in external validity, due to the participants' characteristics: The participants were mostly female students of one university that majored in certain fields. Therefore, the findings cannot be generalized for all the adult population. Future studies may sample students from other academic institutes and/or other disciplines as well as other non-student populations.

The information sources that were presented in the experiment dealt with only one controversial topic. The results may differ with another topic, since people tend to have different views on different topics and in different situations.

Regarding the comparison between payment and free conditions, the experiment setup in the current research did not include a comparison between choices of free information and fee-based information by the same person, as there was in other experiments with other products, such as the one conducted by Shampanier, Mazar & Ariely [35]. Future experiments should examine the way people value and consume information when presented with a choice.

The present study assessed epistemic perspectives only after the economic activity. We suggest that subsequent studies would examine the epistemic perspectives both before and after the experiment in order to gain an indication for the extent of epistemic change.

7 Summary and Research Implications

The present study illuminates novel connections between research on epistemic thinking and research on the economic value of information. The relation between users' epistemic perspectives and the economic value of information has not been addressed in previous studies. The findings suggest that information pricing scenarios can affect information consumers' epistemic views regarding the nature, certainty and justification of knowledge, reducing absolutist views and increasing evaluativist ones. Pricing condition was also found to have an effect on the ways people select information sources. These findings may have theoretical importance because they indicate that economic value can have an impact on epistemic values. More research should be conducted with comparisons of pre and post epistemic perspectives as well as comparisons to other topics, in order to examine the extent of change in epistemic perspectives and whether this change extends to different situations and topics.

Practical implications may also arise for producers and consumers of information. Information is a strategic business asset. The subjective value of information should become a central factor in the information economy. The present study supports the claim that the price of zero is viewed differently in the eyes of consumers and effects their way of thinking when they decide to consume information. The relations between subjective and experience values should be further explored. Experience value has importance in understanding motivations for consuming and using information in subsequent events requiring information-based decision making. Much additional work is needed to understand the formation of experience value and the complexities of zero prices in information market places.

References

1. Barzilai, S., Eshet-Alkalai, Y.: The role of epistemic perspectives in comprehension of multiple author viewpoints. Learn. Instr. **36**, 86–103 (2015). https://doi.org/10.1016/j.learninstruc.2014.12.003
2. Barzilai, S., Ka'adan, I.: Learning to integrate divergent information sources: the interplay of epistemic cognition and epistemic metacognition. Metacognition and Learning **12**, 193–232 (2017). https://doi.org/10.1007/s11409-016-9165-7
3. Barzilai, S., Strømsø, H.I.: Individual differences in multiple document comprehension. In: Braasch, J. (ed.) Handbook of Multiple Source Use, pp. 99–116 (2018)
4. Barzilai, S., Tzadok, E., Eshet-Alaklai, Y.: When Experts Disagree: Sourcing Practices While Reading Conflicting Online Information Sources, pp. 721–728. International Society of the Learning Sciences, Boulder (2014)
5. Barzilai, S., Weinstock, M.: Measuring epistemic thinking within and across topics: a scenario-based approach. Contemp. Educ. Psychol. **42**, 141–158 (2015). https://doi.org/10.1016/j.cedpsych.2015.06.006
6. Barzilai, S., Zohar, A.: Epistemic thinking in action: evaluating and integrating online sources. Cogn. Instr. **30**, 39–85 (2012). https://doi.org/10.1080/07370008.2011.636495
7. Bates, B.J.: Information as an economic good: a re-evaluation of theoretical approaches. In: Ruben, B.D., Lievrouw, L.A. (eds.) Mediation, Information, and Communication, pp. 379–394. Transaction Publishers, New Brunswick (1990)
8. Chinn, C.A., Rinehart, R.W.: Epistemic cognition and philosophy: developing a new framework for epistemic cognition. In: Greene, J.A., Sandoval, W.A., Bråten, I. (eds.) Handbook of Epistemic Cognition, pp. 460–478. Routledge (2016)
9. Eppler, M.J., Mengis, J.: The concept of information overload: a review of literature from organization science, accounting, marketing, MIS, and related disciplines. Inf. Soc. **20**, 325–344 (2004). https://doi.org/10.1080/01972240490507974
10. Ferguson, L.E., Bråten, I.: Student profiles of knowledge and epistemic beliefs: changes and relations to multiple-text comprehension. Learn. Instr. **25**, 49–61 (2013). https://doi.org/10.1016/j.learninstruc.2012.11.003
11. Ferguson, L.E., Bråten, I., Strømsø, H.I., Anmarkrud, Ø.: Epistemic beliefs and comprehension in the context of reading multiple documents: examining the role of conflict. Int. J. Educ. Res. **62**, 100–114 (2013). https://doi.org/10.1016/j.ijer.2013.07.001

12. Goldfarb, A., Tucker, C.: Digital economics. J. Econ. Lit. **57**, 3–43 (2018). https://doi.org/10.1257/jel.20171452
13. Greene, J.A., Sandoval, W.A., Bråten, I.: Handbook of Epistemic Cognition. Routledge, New York (2016)
14. Hartwell, M., Kaplan, A.: Students' personal connection with science: investigating the multidimensional phenomenological structure of self-relevance. J. Exp. Educ. **86**, 86–104 (2018). https://doi.org/10.1080/00220973.2017.1381581
15. Hilbert, M.: How to measure "How Much Information"? Theoretical, methodological, and statistical challenges for the social sciences introduction. Int. J. Commun. **6**, 1042–1055 (2012)
16. Hofer, B.K., Pintrich, P.R.: The development of epistemological theories: beliefs about knowledge and knowing and their relation to learning. Rev. Educ. Res. **67**, 88–140 (1997). https://doi.org/10.3102/00346543067001088
17. Iordanou, K.: Developing epistemological understanding in scientific and social domains through argumentation. Zeitschrift für Pädagogische Psychologie **30**, 109–119 (2016). https://doi.org/10.1024/1010-0652/a000172
18. Kahneman, D., Knetsch, J.L., Thaler, R.H.: The endowment effect, loss aversion, and status quo bias. J. Econ. Perspect. **5**, 193–206 (1991). https://doi.org/10.1257/jep.5.1.193
19. Kienhues, D., Bromme, R., Stahl, E.: Changing epistemological beliefs: the unexpected impact of a short-term intervention. Br. J. Educ. Psychol. **78**, 545–565 (2008). https://doi.org/10.1348/000709907X268589
20. Kienhues, D., Stadtler, M., Bromme, R.: Dealing with conflicting or consistent medical information on the web: when expert information breeds laypersons' doubts about experts. Learn. Instr. **21**, 193–204 (2011). https://doi.org/10.1016/j.learninstruc.2010.02.004
21. Kuhn, D.: The Skills of Argument. Cambridge University Press, Cambridge (1991)
22. Kuhn, D., Weinstock, M.: What is epistemological thinking and why does it matter? In: Hofer, B.K., Pintrich, P.R. (eds.) Personal Epistemology: The psychology of beliefs about knowledge and knowing, pp. 121–144. Lawrence Erlbaum Associates Publishers, Mahwah (2002)
23. Lin, T.-C., Hsu, J.S.-C., Chen, H.-C.: Customer willingness to pay for online music: the role of free mentality. J. Electron. Commer. Res. **14**, 19 (2013)
24. Moody, D., Walsh, P.: Measuring the value of information: an asset valuation approach. In: ECIS, Copenhagen Business School, Frederiksberg, Denmark (1999)
25. Nickerson, R.S.: Confirmation bias: a ubiquitous phenomenon in many guises. Rev. Gen. Psychol. **2**, 175–220 (1998). https://doi.org/10.1037/1089-2680.2.2.175
26. Porsch, T., Bromme, R.: Effects of epistemological sensitization on source choices. Instr. Sci. **39**, 805–819 (2011). https://doi.org/10.1007/s11251-010-9155-0
27. Raban, D.R., Geifman, D.: A theory based information pricing system. In: MCIS 2011 Proceedings (2011)
28. Raban, D.R.: User-centered evaluation of information: a research challenge. Internet Res. **17**, 306–322 (2007). https://doi.org/10.1108/10662240710758948
29. Raban, D.R., Koren, L.: Risk as a predictor of online competitive information acquisition. Open Inf. Sci. **3**, 47–60 (2019). https://doi.org/10.1515/opis-2019-0004
30. Raban, D.R., Mazor, M.: The willingness to pay for information in digital marketplaces. In: Kobyliński, A., Sobczak, A. (eds.) BIR 2013. LNBIP, vol. 158, pp. 267–277. Springer, Heidelberg (2013). https://doi.org/10.1007/978-3-642-40823-6_21
31. Raban, D.R., Rafaeli, S.: The effect of source nature and status on the subjective value of information. J. Am. Soc. Inform. Sci. Technol. **57**, 321–329 (2006). https://doi.org/10.1002/asi.20280

32. Raban, D.R., Rusho, Y.: Value perception of information sources in the context of learning. Open Inf. Sci. **2**, 83–101 (2018). https://doi.org/10.1515/opis-2018-0007

33. Rafaeli, S., Raban, D.R.: Experimental investigation of the subjective value of information in trading. J. Assoc. Inf. Syst. **4**, 119–139 (2003)

34. Schwartz, B.: The Paradox of Choice: Why More is Less. Harper Perennial, New York (2004)

35. Shampanier, K., Mazar, N., Ariely, D.: Zero as a special price: the true value of free products. Market. Sci. **26**, 742–757 (2007). https://doi.org/10.1287/mksc.1060.0254

36. Shapiro, C., Varian, H.R.: Information Rules: A Strategic Guide to the Network Economy. Harvard Business Press, Boston (1998)

37. Anderson, S.P., de Palma, A.: Information congestion. RAND J. Econ. **40**, 688 (2009)

38. Weinstock, M., Zviling-Beiser, H.: Separating academic and social experience as potential factors in epistemological development. Learn. Instr. **19**, 287–298 (2009). https://doi.org/10.1016/j.learninstruc.2008.05.004

39. Zavala, J., Kuhn, D.: Solitary discourse is a productive activity. Psychol. Sci. **28**, 578–586 (2017). https://doi.org/10.1177/0956797616689248

The Snippets Taxonomy in Web Search Engines

Artur Strzelecki$^{(\boxtimes)}$ and Paulina Rutecka

Department of Informatics, University of Economics in Katowice,
40-287 Katowice, Poland
{artur.strzelecki,paulina.rutecka}@ue.katowice.pl

Abstract. In this paper authors analyzed 50 000 keywords results collected from localized Polish Google search engine. We proposed a taxonomy for snippets displayed in search results as regular, rich, news, featured and entity types snippets. We observed some correlations between overlapping snippets in the same keywords. Results show that commercial keywords do not cause results having rich or entity types snippets, whereas keywords resulting with snippets are not commercial nature. We found that significant number of snippets are scholarly articles and rich cards carousel. We conclude our findings with conclusion and research limitations.

Keywords: Rich Snippets · Rich results · Search engines · Google · Bing

1 Introduction

Rich Snippets as a Google search engine element appeared on the Internet in 2012. It was a Google answer for changing how users asked a search engine. We can risk saying that the style of entering queries to the search engine evolved along with the generation. The X generation were the first global Internet users. They have formed queries in simple and password method. They have been trying to understand computers, learn how they work, assuming that the machine to which the question is being asked isn't intelligent. In response to this, webmasters prepare reflecting the form of the entered enquiry in the 1:1 relationship.

As the effect, they made difficult to read and understand content with low substantive value. Perfect fitting was the sole aim of these contents oneself into factors in the ranking of search engines. In 2005–2010 users have used search engines in the same way that they have used other software. They have tried to learn software, read the user manuals to use it efficiently. In accordance with it, the system of notation of enquiries introduced to the search engine arose collected and at present available in the table summing up types of fitting the keyword.

Google constantly optimizes the way the search engine works. The purpose of this is to make a valuable search engine results pages with interesting and highly reliable content. The search engine of Google was launched in 1997 and in the last 22 years, it elaborated mechanism concerning fitting moved closer more and more. It recognized next variants of the enquiry: the variety, synonyms or mistakes of the spelling.

© Springer Nature Switzerland AG 2019
M. Pańkowska and K. Sandkuhl (Eds.): BIR 2019, LNBIP 365, pp. 177–188, 2019.
https://doi.org/10.1007/978-3-030-31143-8_13

The revolution in search engine have started with a changing generation of computer users. The computer is now a companion of any person from Y generation who grew up with global access to the Internet global. A computer has become not just a working tool but a communication tool. It allows to access knowledge and entertainment. The Y generation doesn't try to learn how a computer works. They took it for granted and they do not attach special importance to learning this (except specialist skills).

Queries entered into the search engine have also become more natural and computer have become to being a partner in discussion. Queries become very similar to the question of which person can ask one another, preserving the syntax characteristic for questions, starts with adverbial - who, when, why, how etc.

The insertion of elements AI to search engine allowed for proper recognition of these types of queries and the evolution of the results display system in the search engine. In relation to change of the type of enquiries, increasing the number of vocal enquiries, leading into use the vocal assistant Google, it is possible to state that different Rich Snippets kinds are a natural reply to the demand of the market.

Establishing the research material of what type and the kind based on conducted analysis is a goal of the present article keywords cause the Snippets appearance in the search engine. It will enable further research above the strategy of building the plot up to get this position in search engine and the assessment of the impact of these results to the value of websites from which he is being downloaded content. We propose following research questions:

1. Is search engine evolving into human oriented system?
2. How search engine answers to specific questions?

The aim of this study is to retrieve information, conduct analysis and draw contribution on search engines rich results. Added value of this study is, that based on real search data for 50 k keywords along with displayed snippet results, authors proposed several observations of current rich results appearing in search engine. Rising importance of search features like scholarly articles and direct answer (also known as featured snippet) was noticed.

The paper is organized as follows. Section 2 contains a review of the relevant literature on the topic. Section 3 includes the concept of the snippets taxonomy, while Sect. 4 presents the data and quantitative results. In Sect. 5, the authors highlight the contribution of the research, discuss its limitations and, finally, draw conclusions about the results and propose possible future research avenues.

2 Literature Review

Snippets in search engines can be considered in five areas. The first area is regular snippets generated for regular, organic results. Four years regular snippets were two lines of description presented below the title and url of displaying results [1]. Recently we can observe some tests of increasing its length either on desktop version or on mobile devices [2, 3]. Scientific interest in regular snippet is mainly whether they are enough informative for readers or not enough [4]. Some tests are done on different age groups to see how these regular snippets are perceived [5].

The second area is rich snippets created based on structured data [6]. Search engines like Google, Microsoft (Bing), Yahoo and Yandex founded schema.org and are able to recognize structured data provided in RDFa, Microdata or JSON [7]. Rich snippets based on structured data are added to regular snippets [8]. Search engines show additional data about product availability, price and condition, recipes, reviews, jobs, music, video and others, included in schema.org. Rich snippets appears to become a more important variable, especially when examining bottom-ranked results [9].

Third area is snippets generated in Google News. These snippets are created completely automatically [10]. These snippets are considered by news publishers in different ways. Recently in Spain or Germany Google news was restricted, cause displaying snippets of news releases violates copyrights of news publishers [11]. To solve this possible violation a plan for ancillary copyright is proposed, by creating original snippets [12].

The fourth area is featured snippets. This is one of a recent snippet type. The search engine extracts pieces of information from web pages and presents it in a box, above organic results along with a source url. Google programmatically determines that a page contains a likely answer to the user's question and displays the result as a featured snippet. The other working name for this snippet is a direct answer or answer box. Direct answer supposed to deliver answers for queries, without need to visit the result presented in search engine [13]. This snippet can be presented in several different forms like paragraph [14], table [15] and ordered or unordered list.

The fifth area is entity types. Entity types are known in Google as Knowledge Graph introduced in 2012 year and in Bing are known as Satori introduced in the same year [16]. These entities are constructed object and concepts, including people, places, books, movies, events, arts, science, etc. Creating and maintaining these entity databases is considered as an important responsibility for search engines [17]. Search engines can create objects displayed in search results and also they remove results because of the variety of reasons [18].

3   Snippets Taxonomy

The authors collected data for analysis using Senuto. Senuto is an online service which collects data from Google search engine. Senuto has a database of 20 million keywords. Each keyword is at least once in a month entered to Polish localized Google search engine and a list of top 50 results is returned. Senuto checks what rich and features snippets appear next to your keywords in Google search. A dataset from senator was acquired in May 2018. The dataset contains a list of 50000 keywords and their metrics. The dataset was limited only to keywords which in results shows not only ten blue links, but also have other rich and feature snippets, displayed above and on the right side in Google's search engine results page. Basic metrics for this keyword dataset are: cost per click (cpc), number of words, the average number of monthly searches in a year, features of keyword, average number of monthly searches in each month.

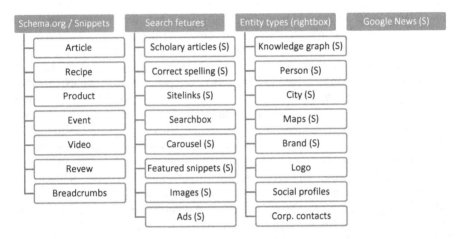

Fig. 1. Snippets taxonomy in Google search engine

Cost per click is estimated price per one click if this keyword would be used in sponsored search results. Number of words defines how long is the keyword. Average number of monthly searches is the number of how many times this keyword was entered into Google search. This number is limited to language. Cost per click and average number of searches is imported to Senuto from Google Planner. Google Planner is Google's tool, which shows metrics for keywords used in sponsored search results.

The most interesting aspect of this keyword dataset is that it contains keyword which cause displaying rich and feature snippets along with search results. Senuto distinguishes between 14 different rich and feature snippets. These 14 snippets are: ads (formerly AdWords), scholarly articles, correct spelling and grammar, Google news, knowledge graph, carousel, person, city, site links, maps, direct answer, right box, brand query and images (Fig. 1).

Google Ads are results displayed in search engine results page which come from an advertising platform [19]. Scholarly articles is a featured snippet which contains around 3 results from Google Scholar together with author and number of citations [20]. Correct spelling and grammar is a snippet which suggests correct spelling and grammar form of provided query [21]. Google News aggregates news articles published in online newspapers and portals. Google News displays automatically results as a snippet together with image for results in a country, where Google News is available [22]. Knowledge Graph is a notion introduced to Google results in 2012. This feature is designed to sort and display known fact, places and persons [23].

The carousel is a graphical form to display similar results in one row above regular results. This placement is also called as knowledge card [24]. Carousel/knowledge card displays results in a structured order. These results are persons or cities. A query containing name and surname of a person which is known or popular artists (e.g. writer or actor) cause results as a set of work by this artist. Similar results looking as a carousel are presented for queries containing the names of cities.

Site links are results displayed only together with the first result mentioned. Site links are extending the first result by providing additional snippets and are only appearing when query is similar or the same as domain name appearing on first place in the ranking. The map is displayed for queries containing the name of known place which has a physical address. Direct answer is feature snippet containing a snippet with extracted answer for the query [25]. The direct answer is a box and usually contains a piece of text in the form of paragraph, table, ordered list or unordered list. Right box is known for displaying knowledge graph or a map [26]. There are types of queries which cause displaying results in right box, e.g. name of the book and author. In this case right box contains name of author, year of publishing and cover of the book. Brand query usually contains brand name and cause displaying in right box additional information about the brand. Images are displayed on result pages as one row, containing several images connected with a query.

4 Data and Results

4.1 Data

The authors summarized the results in following tables. Table 1 presents the frequency of occurrence of snippet depending on the length of the keyword. Most keywords in the analyzed data set are 2 or 3 word-long words. Less popular, but still a large group are 4 or 5 word-long words.

Table 1. Keywords with specific number of words in every types of snippets.

Snippet	Number of words									
	1	2	3	4	5	6	7	8	9	10
Ads	0	9	39	14	3	0	0	0	0	0
Scholarly articles	29	307	9895	3488	1022	327	152	62	29	16
Correct spell. and grammar	4	147	311	53	6	3	1	0	0	0
Google news	0	0	1	0	0	0	0	0	0	0
Carousel	32	10255	17568	5226	1159	373	71	10	0	1
Knowledge graph	9	5131	12284	3312	837	361	97	28	9	4
Person	0	77	2346	504	117	62	16	4	0	0
Site links	6	250	518	199	54	11	3	0	1	0
Maps	0	750	2153	504	54	8	1	0	0	0
City	0	276	1225	315	33	10	0	0	0	0
Direct answer	5	5110	11921	3206	778	328	78	21	4	3
Right box	9	5131	12284	3312	837	361	97	28	9	4
Brand query	4	861	3180	1489	434	171	52	23	12	8
Images	45	5767	11734	3654	884	224	76	24	7	4

Table 2 presents correlations between snippets. Snippets have been divided into two parts. The first part contains most popular snippets. Second part contains snippets occurring less frequently, mostly together with another type of snippet. The second part of snippets is a peculiar group of answers for user's query, which appears in combination with the first set of snippets as a response to particular question containing e.g. person, city, brand query.

Table 2. Correlations between snippets.

	Person	Brand query	Images	City	Site links	Correct spelling and grammar	Google News
Ads	9	2	25	1	1	0	0
Scholarly articles	3117	445	6560	72	91	81	1
Carousel	9	5789	15878	1787	951	444	0
Knowledge graph	0	3631	6829	1562	843	275	0
Maps	0	826	989	253	167	10	0
Direct answer	0	3637	6457	1562	843	275	0
Right box	0	3631	6829	1562	843	275	0

Table 3 presents a summary of the number of snippet instances and percentage of snippet instances. Table also shows average number of monthly searches for keywords that display snippet and median search volume.

Table 3. Summary of impressions and searches for keywords that display snippet.

Snippet	Number of occurrences	% of dataset	Avg. number of monthly searches	Median monthly searches
Carousel	34695	69,39%	248	20
Images	22419	44,84%	112	10
Knowledge graph	22072	44,14%	108	20
Right box	22072	44,14%	183	10
Direct answer	21454	42,91%	183	10
Scholarly articles	15327	30,65%	35	10
Brand query	6234	12,47%	183	10
Maps	3470	6,94%	135	30
Person	3126	6,25%	83	20
City	1859	3,72%	254	50
Site links	1042	2,08%	2765	20
Correct spelling and grammar	525	1,05%	67	10
Ads	65	0,13%	90	20
Google news	1	0,00%	1000	1000

Google Ads. The Google Ads snippet appeared merely 65 times as shown in Table 3. It is only 0,13% of analyzed keywords. The average monthly number of searches for all keywords where the Ads snippet has appeared is 90. The median of the monthly number of searches is 20. All keywords with Ads snippet were questions built out of 2 words (9 results), 3 words (39 results), 4 words (14 results) or 5 words (3 results) in the phrase as confirmed with data in Table 2. Correlations with other snippets were presented in Table 2. Ads snippet was displayed with name 9 times, with a brand query - 2 times, with images - 25 times, with city and site links - 1 time. Google News and correct spelling and grammar were not displayed.

Scholarly Articles. Scholarly article snippets appeared 15327 times as shown in Table 3. For more than 30% of analyzed keywords search results were found in Google Scholar articles index and the snippet suggested by Google led the user to scientific papers. The data in Table 1 shows the vast majority of keywords which have the snippet with scholarly articles as the result to user's query are long tail keywords. Most keywords have 3 words (9895 results), 4 words (3488 results) or 5 words (1022 results) in the phrase. The others have 1 word (29 results), 2 words (307 results), 6 words (327 results), 7 words (152 results), 8 words (62 results), 9 words (29 results), 10 words (16 results).

This means that user's query which causes the appearance of the snippet of the scholarly article are very exact due to the fact that users are looking for specific information. The analysis of individual words indicates that the majority of queries displaying this type of snippets concerns the field of exact and natural sciences ex.: physics, chemistry, medicine, IT. Table 2 presents correlations between keywords with scholarly articles and the other snippets. Scholarly articles were displayed with name (3117 times), brand query (445 times), images (6560 times), city (72 times), site links (91 times), Google news (1 time), correct spelling and grammar (81 times).

Rich Card Carousel. It is one of the most frequently showed snippet during keywords analysis in the research conducted by the authors. It has appeared for 69,39% of keywords that is, for 34695 records what Table 3 shows. Rich card carousel presents answer for user queries most often in a graphic form. In this type of snippets, the query has more than one answer and it is a list of possible answers in a graphic form of a carousel. The data in Table 1 indicates that most keywords that cause carousel snippet are phrases with 2 (10255 results) or 3 words (17568 results). They are rarely words 4 (5226 results), 5 (1159 results) and 6 (373 results) expressive. Keywords with a different number of words very rarely cause the occurrence of carousel snippets. Table 2 shows the correlation with others snippets and in this case. 45.76% (15878 results) of keywords with carousel have images at the same time. This shows the close connection of the carousel with the pictures. In second place in terms of the number of occurrences, there is a correlation between carousels and brand query (5789 results). Carousels also appear together with City (1787 results), Site Links (951 results) and Correct spelling and grammar (444 results).

Knowledge Graph. Knowledge Graph appeared for 44,14% of analyzed keywords (22072 results) independently or along with other snippets depending on the query construction what is show in Table 2. It occurs for such queries, that answer to which may be clearly defined as e.g. first and last name, the name of the city or village. Other snippets appeared with Knowledge Graph are: brand query (3631 results), images (6829 results), city (1562 results), site links (843 results), correct spelling and grammar (275 results). Person snippet does not appear due to the frequent occurrence of a person inside the Knowledge Graph itself.

As shown in Table 1 for this type of snippets, 3 keywords are dominant (12284 results). The occurrence of 2 (5131 results) or 4 (3312 results) word-long words is also popular. Knowledge graph appeared for keywords with any number of words.

Other Snippets. During the research authors also had analyzed other kinds of snippets such as:

- Name - appeared in 3126 analyzed records (6,43%)
- City - appeared in 1859 analyzed records (3,72%)
- Image - appeared in 22419 analyzed records (44,83%)
- Brand word - appeared in 6234 analyzed records (12,47%)
- Maps - appeared in 3470 analyzed records (6,94%) .
- Sitelinks - appeared in 1042 analyzed records (2,08%)

Additional Indicators. There were additional indicators in the set of data analyzed by the authors like CPC, number of words, the average monthly number of searches. These indicators were found to be of minor importance. Type of word and grammatical construction are, however, important.

A different border values in the data like CPC from 0.00 to 44.44, number of words from 1 to 10 or the average monthly number of searches from 10 to 2740000 indicate that there is no impact on the appearance of Snippets depending on these factors.

4.2 Results

The analysis of data clearly shows a dynamic growth and evolution of snippets in Google search engine. The types of snippets depend on the form of the question being asked, the keywords appearing (e.g. games, movies for rich card carousel) or grammatical construction of query (e.g. question form for featured snippets). The observations confirm that the development of the search engine is directed towards voice queries [27] and the user's dialogue with the search engine as an intelligent bot intended to provide specific answers. For most of the keywords, there is more than one type of snippets. The form of the answer given in snippets is short and shall be word or picture based. It encourages the user to read more information about the topic, which confirms the nesting of related headwords and interesting facts in the Knowledge Graph and links to the source page in Rich Answers.

A presentation for over 30% of keywords with answers containing references to scientific publications and target addresses of pages in Rich Answers, which lead to expert pages, confirms that Google in natural, non-advertising search results focuses on the reliability and highest quality of published content. This thesis is confirmed mainly by the results for the medical industry - referring to scientific articles. Google has also introduced an extensive list of medical-related keywords (including chemicals) for which advertising is prohibited. Snippets published on Google are user-friendly on mobile devices and are designed to be useful to users of voice search and chat with the Google Assistant.

5   Conclusion and Discussion

5.1   Discussion

In this paper, we presented an analysis of the set of data that causes Rich Snippets to appear in the search engine. The findings of our study indicate that the Google search engine is being developed in the direction of displaying the query response from the search results page. Google does not discriminate blue links, but makes the valuable site stand out. We collected data for 50000 keywords triggering in search results different types of snippets.

5.2   Contribution

Snippets content come from only reliable websites. The scale of the phenomenon (more than 30% of the keywords contains Snippets in the form of scholarly articles) confirms that Google is to improve its algorithms, trying to get the content of the highest quality distributed to the user from the most reliable source. Academic search behavior can be different from the web search behavior due to different types of contents, search goals and users [28], however placing results from scholarly articles is more and more often.

This paper is a first attempt to analyze the keywords which resulted in rich snippets in Polish localized Google search engine. Collected data reveal, that for 50 k keyword rich snippets appear above organic results. The authors did analyze correlations between overlapping snippets. Correlations show that rich snippets are commercially independent. They usually do not appear for commercial keywords. Rich snippets appear with equal frequency for keywords with low CPC and for keywords with very high CPC. Estimated cost per click is not a defining factor defining the display of any type of Rich Snippet [29]. The keywords analysis shows that the keywords appearing in Google Ads have no influence on snippets appearance. Transactional [30] nature of the query is irrelevant to the appearance of snippets. Most of the keywords with active snippets do not cause displaying ads. Similarly, keywords displaying ads do not have snippets.

Google encourages users to use Rich Snippets by introducing an attractive visual form like in the Rich card carousel case. The image tiled display format, scrolled horizontally, is very mobile-user friendly and allows to present a large amount of information. It concentrates the user's attention, directing by just one click, to websites suggested by Google.

Rich card carousel applies for every query where the answer requires a list ex. titles of games or films, dog breeds or city districts. When the user uses the Google Assistant the result will be returned in the chat bubble or read by the voice assistant.

The Knowledge Graph is also a confirmation of the thesis regarding the credibility of websites used by Google to create Rich Snippet. These snippets in a short and concise way (2–3 sentence) answer for the user question. They also contain many links to subsequent searches that return results with different types of Rich Snippet. Knowledge Graph often appears in the company of a carousel, when it is necessary to present results in the list form.

Our results show that search engine results are more and more adapted to way users are asking questions and the answer is presented directly from results. This kind of solution belongs to human oriented systems.

5.3   Limitation

The limitation of our research was the fact of having a set of data concerning only the Polish language and only within 50,000 keywords. All data concern the Google search engine, which is dominant in Poland, but we realize that some types of Rich snippets can be observed in other search engines. The factors conditioning the appearance of specific types of Rich Snippets may be different in various search engines. Due to the lack of data, we did not analyze why a particular snippet appeared but only its type.

5.4   Future Research

We acknowledge that Google strives to become the most reliable and user-friendly search engine and the snippet richness appears to become a more important variable, especially when examining bottom-ranked results [9]. Further testing will be conducted to investigate the factors affecting the display of results from specific websites in the snippets area. Also, further tests will be interesting for other languages.

References

1. Lewandowski, D.: The retrieval effectiveness of web search engines: considering results descriptions. J. Doc. **64**, 915–937 (2008). https://doi.org/10.1108/00220410810912451
2. Sachse, J.: The influence of snippet length on user behavior in mobile web search: an experimental eye-tracking study. Aslib J. Inf. Manag. (2019). https://doi.org/10.1108/AJIM-07-2018-0182
3. Kim, J., Thomas, P., Sankaranarayana, R., Gedeon, T., Yoon, H.-J.: What snippet size is needed in mobile web search? In: Proceedings of the 2017 Conference on Conference Human Information Interaction and Retrieval - CHIIR 2017, pp. 97–106. ACM, New York (2017). https://doi.org/10.1145/3020165.3020173
4. Elsweiler, D., Kattenbeck, M.: Understanding credibility judgements for web search snippets. Aslib J. Inf. Manag. (2019). https://doi.org/10.1108/AJIM-07-2018-0181
5. Bilal, D., Huang, L.-M.: Readability and word complexity of SERPs snippets and web pages on children's search queries. Aslib J. Inf. Manag. **71**, 241–259 (2019). https://doi.org/10.1108/AJIM-05-2018-0124
6. Hop, W., Lachner, S., Frasincar, F., De Virgilio, R.: Automatic web page annotation with Google *Rich Snippets*. In: Meersman, R., Dillon, T., Herrero, P. (eds.) OTM 2010. LNCS, vol. 6427, pp. 957–974. Springer, Heidelberg (2010). https://doi.org/10.1007/978-3-642-16949-6_21

7. Steiner, T., Hausenblas, M., Troncy, R.: How Google is using linked data today and vision for tomorrow. In: Auer, S., Decker, S., Hauswirth, M. (eds.) Proceedings of Linked Data in the Future Internet at the Future Internet Assembly (FIA 2010), Ghent, pp. 1–10 (2010)

8. Khalili, A., Auer, S.: WYSIWYM authoring of structured content based on Schema.org. In: Lin, X., Manolopoulos, Y., Srivastava, D., Huang, G. (eds.) WISE 2013. LNCS, vol. 8181, pp. 425–438. Springer, Heidelberg (2013). https://doi.org/10.1007/978-3-642-41154-0_32

9. Marcos, M.-C., Gavin, F., Arapakis, I.: Effect of snippets on user experience in web search. In: Proceedings of the XVI International Conference on Human Computer Interaction - Interacción 2015, pp. 47:1–47:8. ACM, New York (2015). https://doi.org/10.1145/2829875.2829916

10. Das, A.S., Datar, M., Garg, A., Rajaram, S.: Google news personalization: scalable online collaborative filtering. In: Proceedings of the 16th International Conference on World Wide Web - WWW 2007, pp. 271–280. ACM, New York (2007). https://doi.org/10.1145/1242572.1242610

11. Calzada, J., Gil, R.: What do news aggregators do? Evidence from Google News in Spain and Germany. Universitat de Barcelona, Barcelona (2016). https://doi.org/10.2139/ssrn.2837553

12. Potthast, M., Chen, W., Hagen, M.: A plan for ancillary copyright: original snippets. In: Albakour, D., Corney, D., Gonzalo, J., Martinez, M., Poblete, B., Vlachos, A. (eds.) Proceedings of the Second International Workshop on Recent Trends in News Information Retrieval at ECIR, Grenoble, France, pp. 3–5 (2018)

13. Miklosik, A.: Search engine marketing strategies: Google answer box-related search visibility factors. In: Carvalho, L., Isaías, P. (eds.) Handbook of Research on Entrepreneurship and Marketing for Global Reach in the Digital Economy, pp. 463–485. IGI Global, Hershey (2019). https://doi.org/10.4018/978-1-5225-6307-5.ch020

14. Zhao, Y., Zhang, J., Xia, X., Le, T.: Evaluation of Google question-answering quality. Libr. Hi Tech. (2018). https://doi.org/10.1108/LHT-10-2017-0218

15. Hancock, B., Lee, H., Yu, C.: Generating titles for web tables. In: Proceedings of the 2019 World Wide Web Conference, WWW 2019, pp. 638–647. ACM, New York (2019). https://doi.org/10.1145/3308558.3313399

16. Uyar, A., Aliyu, F.M.: Evaluating search features of Google Knowledge Graph and Bing Satori. Online Inf. Rev. **39**, 197–213 (2015). https://doi.org/10.1108/OIR-10-2014-0257

17. Juel Vang, K.: Ethics of Google's knowledge graph: some considerations. J. Inf. Commun. Ethics Soc. **11**, 245–260 (2013). https://doi.org/10.1108/JICES-08-2013-0028

18. Strzelecki, A.: Website removal from search engines due to copyright violation. Aslib J. Inf. Manag. **71**, 54–71 (2019). https://doi.org/10.1108/AJIM-05-2018-0108

19. Jansen, B.J., Mullen, T.: Sponsored search: an overview of the concept, history, and technology. Int. J. Electron. Bus. **6**, 114–171 (2008). https://doi.org/10.1504/IJEB.2008.018068

20. Kousha, K., Thelwall, M.: Google Scholar citations and Google Web/URL citations: a multidiscipline exploratory analysis. J. Am. Soc. Inf. Sci. Technol. **58**, 1055–1065 (2007). https://doi.org/10.1002/asi.20584

21. Jacquemont, S., Jacquenet, F., Sebban, M.: Correct your text with Google. In: IEEE/WIC/ACM International Conference on Web Intelligence (WI 2007), pp. 170–176. IEEE (2007). https://doi.org/10.1109/WI.2007.38

22. Liu, J., Dolan, P., Pedersen, E.R.: Personalized news recommendation based on click behavior. In: Proceedings of the 15th International Conference on Intelligent User Interfaces - IUI 2010, pp. 31–40. ACM, New York (2010). https://doi.org/10.1145/1719970.1719976

23. Singhal, A.: Official Google Blog: Introducing the Knowledge Graph: things, not strings (2012)

24. Wang, H., Fang, Z., Ruan, T.: KCF.js: a Javascript library for knowledge cards fusion. In: Proceedings of the 25th International Conference Companion on World Wide Web - WWW 2016 Companion, pp. 267–270. ACM, New York (2016). https://doi.org/10.1145/2872518.2890556

25. Wakefield, C.C.: Achieving position 0: optimising your content to rank in Google's answer box. J. Brand Strateg. **7**, 326–336 (2019)

26. Heersmink, R.: A virtue epistemology of the internet: search engines, intellectual virtues and education. Soc. Epistemol. **32**, 1–12 (2018). https://doi.org/10.1080/02691728.2017.1383530

27. Guy, I.: Searching by talking: analysis of voice queries on mobile web search. In: Proceedings of the 39th International ACM SIGIR Conference on Research and Development in Information Retrieval - SIGIR 2016, pp. 35–44. ACM, New York (2016). https://doi.org/10.1145/2911451.2911525

28. Kim, J., Trippas, J.R., Sanderson, M., Bao, Z., Croft, W.B.: How do computer scientists use Google Scholar? A survey of user interest in elements on SERPs and author profile pages. In: Cabanac, G., Frommholz, I., Mayr, P. (eds.) Proceedings of the 8th Workshop on Bibliometric-Enhanced Information Retrieval, pp. 64–75 (2019)

29. Kritzinger, W.T., Weideman, M.: Parallel search engine optimisation and pay-per-click campaigns: a comparison of cost per acquisition. South African J. Inf. Manag. **19**, 1–13 (2017). https://doi.org/10.4102/sajim.v19i1.820

30. Broder, A.: A taxonomy of web search. ACM SIGIR Forum. **36**, 3–10 (2002). https://doi.org/10.1145/792550.792552

Model-Driven Context Configuration in Business Process Management Systems: An Approach Based on Knowledge Graphs

Mihai Cinpoeru[1], Ana-Maria Ghiran[1], Alisa Harkai[1],
Robert Andrei Buchmann[1(✉)], and Dimitris Karagiannis[2]

[1] Business Informatics Research Centre, Babeş-Bolyai University,
Cluj-Napoca, Romania
{mihai.cinpoeru, anamaria.ghiran, alisa.harkai,
robert.buchmann}@econ.ubbcluj.ro
[2] Knowledge Engineering Research Group, University of Vienna,
Vienna, Austria
dk@dke.univie.ac.at

Abstract. Business Process Management Systems (BPMSs) are inherently model-driven, relying on machine-readable process repositories that are typically standards-based. However, a requirement for semantic agility is emerging as knowledge-driven applications become less blueprint-oriented and more context-aware. The integration of process knowledge with contextual data can be subjected to this agility requirement – i.e., having the process modelling environment customised in terms of (expanding) its knowledge space and in terms of model-data interoperability. Such customisations may capture any of the enterprise perspectives proposed by the Zachman Framework (among which the How, Who and Where facets are in our particular focus) towards the benefit of establishing a hybrid knowledge-data fabric underlying flexible, context-driven BPMSs.

This paper presents a project-based technical solution, based on the interplay of semantic technology and agile modelling methods, for setting up a hybrid knowledge base derived from several heterogeneous sources: diagrammatic models, semantically lifted legacy data and open geospatial data, with reasoning rules on top of this conglomerate. Together, these sources cover the How, Who and Where facets of the Zachman Framework concepts in a Knowledge Graph that drives the front-end Task Management panel of a BPMS. The proposal advocates complementarity and integration of paradigms that rarely converge – i.e., knowledge representation, open data and process-aware information systems.

Keywords: Business process management system ·
Agile modelling method engineering · GeoSPARQL · Knowledge graphs ·
Semantic data fabric

M. Pańkowska and K. Sandkuhl (Eds.): BIR 2019, LNBIP 365, pp. 189–203, 2019.
https://doi.org/10.1007/978-3-030-31143-8_14

1 Introduction

The development of Business Process Management Systems (BPMSs) has traditionally relied on standards-based process descriptions (e.g., BPMN, EPC) and serialisations (e.g., BPEL, XPDL) for storing machine-readable process knowledge. One key BPMS component is the Task Manager, which must expose to the end-user interface functionality supporting each process task, as well as the means for participating in task execution and for progressing along process paths.

The development of the Task Manager meets a challenge deriving from the fact that process modelling standards provide fixed, consensus-based semantics (in a rigid modelling environment), whereas the Task Manager may be subjected to situational or evolving requirements just like any software. Consequently, a conceptual gap opens between (i) *what information is available in the process repository* and (ii) *what information the Task Manager needs to use or expose in the user interface*. The BPMS must compensate for the semantic gap, usually with intermediate tiers involving complementary data schema.

The goal of this paper is to showcase an approach to bridging this gap, based on a semantic data fabric that integrates process model contents and contextual data in a customised modelling environment that supports the front-end Task Manager. BPMS developers are thus empowered to raise requirements for the process modelling environment, which can be agilely adapted to satisfy them. Examples of adaptations will be selected from a project-based case. The proposal can bring diagrammatic semantics closer to what the BPMS needs in terms of process-data integration.

Process models thus become the core of a hybrid "knowledge-data fabric" built with the help of Linked Data techniques and exposed as RESTful services to the BPMS front-end. The hybridised information assets are: (i) diagrammatic process models (agilely extended with domain-specific or contextual aspects); (ii) semantically lifted legacy data; (iii) geospatial Linked Data (cf. the GeoSPARQL standard [1]) representing the geographical context where process tasks should be performed and (iv) a reasoning layer to further derive any properties that are necessary to run the front-end Task Manager. The kind of systems that can be built on such a semantic data fabric are a generalisation of *process-aware information systems*, where the role of the modelling language expands to acting as an agile Knowledge Graph schema (encompassing a process repository). A Design Science approach [2] is therefore adequate to gradually expand both the modelling language and the derived Knowledge Graph according to the Task Manager requirements.

The remainder of the paper is structured as follows: Sect. 2 introduces the problem statement. Section 3 provides a summary of the proposed technical solution and engineering method. Section 4 presents background on the key ingredients. Section 5 introduces an application scenario and provides an overview of the deployment architecture. Section 6 provides insight to implementation details. Section 7 comments on related works. The paper ends with a concluding discussion, including performance evaluation.

2   Motivation and Problem Statement

The proposal was inspired by recent debates in the conceptual modelling community around the umbrella notion of "Next-Generation Enterprise Modelling" - see the talks in the NEMO summer school series [3] on the convergence of the following three ideas:

1. The *assimilation of diagrammatic models in the traditional Knowledge Conversion cycles* introduced by the discipline of Knowledge Management [4];
2. *Agility enabled in modelling languages and tools* – i.e., not only in model contents as typically understood in Agile Modelling [5];
3. *Bridging human-oriented knowledge representation* (i.e., diagrammatic content) and *machine-readable representations* (i.e., RDF Knowledge Graphs [6]) in an open-ended manner, amenable to linking and reasoning across an enterprise data fabric.

The first idea advocates the function that diagrammatic modelling can fulfil within the traditional knowledge conversion cycle known under the acronym *SECI* (Sociali-sation – Externalisation – Combination - Internalisation) [4]. This role has been analysed in detail in [7], where it is argued that, in order to have the flexibility required for knowledge acquisition scenarios, certain layers of agility must be enabled in modelling methods. Modelling standards support consensus, reusability and known requirements from established practices (Business Process Management, Software Engineering), rather than exposing a flexible semantic space - in our case this covers the Where, Who or other facets of the Zachman framework [8] (could be expanded to include others as well).

The second idea comes into play to fulfil the aforementioned agility requirement by establishing methodologies and platforms for Agile Modelling Method Engineering [9], to allow the customisation of modelling languages according to the depth and breadth of information required by applications – in our case, by a BPMS at runtime.

The third ingredient is necessary to make available the semantics of the customised modelling language to model-driven engineering. This ingredient is essentially an interoperability mechanism between agile modelling software and Knowledge Graphs – a proof-of-concept plug-in underlying the hereby discussed technical solution, pre-viously introduced in [10].

The paper at hand presents a proof-of-concept for how these ideas flow one into the other. BPMSs provide an ideal application area to showcase the convergence, as their "model-driven" quality is tied not only to the development of such systems, but also to their daily operation - i.e., interaction with models is not limited to system designers/roundtrip engineers, it is also extended to end-users who must be able to configure the execution context of processes in a model-driven manner. The work is primarily relevant for BPMS engineers, as it showcases the application of a novel engineering method where back-end data sources are replaced with a hybrid knowledge-data fabric that integrates agile process descriptions with execution context elements. It is also relevant for business process managers as it brings their process knowledge closer to the BPMS, bridging the Task Manager-Process Repository gap with the help of semantic technology.

3 Engineering Method and Solution Summary

The governing engineering principle is to benefit from reasoning patterns on a conglomerate of Knowledge Graphs derived from heterogeneous sources that capture certain facets of the Zachman framework [8]: *Where* (legacy data annotation with a semantic geospatial standard such as GeoSPARQL), *Who* (organisational structure captured in models together with, or linked to, instance data) and *How* (diagrammatic process models linked to all of the above).

The core idea is that domain-specificity and modelling agility can give a modelling tool the quality of a "control panel" for how a BPMS behaves, allowing the coordinating user to adjust not only the process flow, but also domain-specific properties, related models, instance properties (some of them assimilated in the modelling language) and links to open data sources that could be relevant during process execution.

The Agile Modelling Method Engineering (AMME) framework [8] and a meta-modelling platform (e.g., ADOxx [11]) are therefore necessary to prototype such a customised BPM tool. The purpose of this customisation is to enable (i) *on-demand domain specificity* and (ii) *a bridge between design-time modelling elements and contextual data needed for run-time operation* of the BPMS.

Regarding the first point, one significant advantage of *domain specific modelling,* as advocated in the multitude of language examples inventoried by [12] is that stakeholders find it easier to understand model constructs and properties that are specific to their business – not only through visual ornamentations, but also in terms of contextual relations that can be set in the model (and exposed to model-driven systems).

Regarding the second point, *instance data may be included in diagrammatic models* if the modelling language is adequately (and agilely) extended to integrate instance-level information. In a traditional BPMS, instance data is typically decoupled from models – i.e., stored and handled separately. However, some data is invariant enough to be included in models and it is not uncommon to have instance descriptions that are relevant to diagrammatic modelling goals (e.g., process simulation). Company maps, requirements models, work environment descriptions, supply chain models with geographical coverage, enterprise architecture models often include diagrammatic elements that represent instances (e.g., concrete business partners, concrete locations, concrete services, As-Is or To-Be components). Multi-level modelling [13] also considers the different layers of specialisation and instantiation that may be present within the same model. Considering all this, *parts of the data model employed at run-time by the BPMS can be pushed into the modelling language and managed through diagrammatic means by the end-user.* This effectively fills some of the conceptual gap between the process description and the BPMS front-end.

For those instances that doesn't make sense to be described with modelling means (e.g., because their properties are volatile), AMME is hereby employed to attach to the modelling concepts adequate bridges between model elements and external data sources. For this purpose, we couple AMME with the Linked Data paradigm to facilitate data linking and publishing techniques relying on the Resource Description Framework (RDF) [6], with the help of the GraphDB semantic data management system [14] which offers support for legacy data lifting (OntoRefine) [15] and geo-reasoning (GeoSPARQL).

This integration is suggested in the left part of Fig. 1 while the software engineering method (called "model-aware software engineering") is summarised as an extension of AMME in the right part of the same figure. Insights on the overall software engineering method, including effort estimations from past iterations and projects have been discussed in [16] - we only summarise the method steps in Fig. 1 (right):

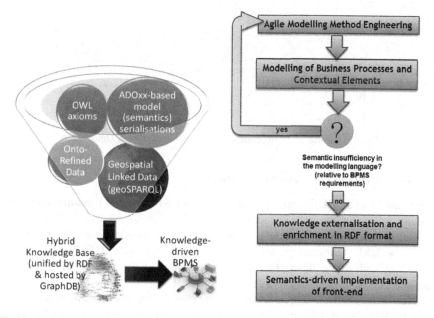

Fig. 1. Solution summary (left) and the "model-aware software engineering" method (right)

4 Enablers

4.1 Knowledge Graphs and Semantic Data

The hybrid knowledge-data fabric is designed as a "rigid core" (based on the modelling language vocabulary) complemented by a "flexible boundary" (agile customisations of the modelling language and links between models and external resources that support the process execution).

GraphDB [14] is an enterprise ready Semantic Graph Database that supports Knowledge Graph management and reasoning. Recent versions of GraphDB come with features such as OntoRefine [15] - which transforms legacy data structures into RDF statements. An example is given in Fig. 2, for lifting home addresses of employees from a tabular datasheet. GraphDB also supports GeoSPARQL, a geographic lightweight ontology with several geo-comparison functions defined by the Open GeoSpatial Consortium – e.g., for calculating distances or overlapping between geospatial representations. In our prototype these become a key reasoning mechanism to compare task locations (e.g., where a task must be performed) with real locations of key available resources (parkings, hotels) retrieved from external geographical data.

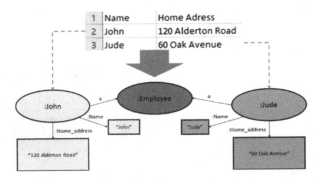

Fig. 2. Lifting table structures to graph structures with OntoRefine

4.2 Dereferencing Diagrammatic Elements

Each resource in an RDF graph is identified by a URI (Uniform Resource Identifier), typically following the HTTP address scheme. *URI dereferencing* is a server-side mechanism for retrieving subgraphs connected to such a node - it treats the resource URI as a URL (Uniform Resource Locator) by accepting HTTP requests and responding with some description of that resource, in the format desired by the requester. As we have shown in a previous publication [17] this can be achieved by a RESTful Web Service acting as a navigation endpoint for any element in a diagrammatic model. The dereferencing response should include links to directly related resources, according to the visual connectors present in models (the referenced paper experimented this on BPMN). In the case of our proposed BPMS, such a service supports client-level navigation across the process model and across customised links between process elements and context elements – either from related models or external Linked Data.

5 Motivating Application Case and Deployment Architecture

The business scenario for our proof-of-concept involves a clothing company that procures supply materials, creates clothes in a factory and transports them to the selling points or customers - between the production or administrative tasks, transportation tasks are fulfilled by a courier department. There is a need of coordination between the couriers and other departments – e.g., tailors, warehouse, sellers/customers – not in terms of scheduling (which is not in our scope), but in terms of tracking the relations between the process steps and their contextual requirements (Who and Where should accomplish a certain task, what are their dependencies on other tasks). For example, the drivers need to know where they can park the car when taking products to a store or to a warehouse. This can be accomplished by geocomparing the process requirements (the coordinates where the task must be accomplished) to external open data (the geo-coordinates of all parking lots in a city).

The targeted use cases are shown in Fig. 3, distinguishing between employees (task performers), admins (monitoring execution progress) and modellers (defining processes and their requirements with agile modelling means).

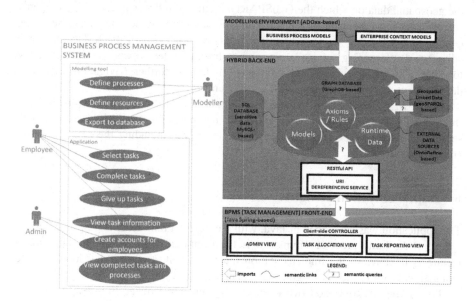

Fig. 3. Use cases and deployment architecture

Figure 3 also presents on the right side an overview of the deployment architecture across three tiers:

A. *The modelling environment* consists of a modelling tool whose language is tailored to allow not only the description of processes, but also of relevant context elements - instances with stable characteristics (employees, organisational structures, contact data), geospatial data or semantic links to external resources where comple-mentary runtime information is available. ADOxx [11] was employed to fulfil the desideratum formulated in the Introduction - of having the modelling language sub-ordinated to BPMS requirements (rather than vice versa, as commonly understood in model-driven or process-aware systems). An RDFiser plug-in exports models of arbitrary types (subordinated to the graph-based meta-metamodel of ADOxx) to RDF structures that will become the core of the knowledge-data fabric in the back-end of the BPMS. The RDFiser employs a set of diagram-to-graph transformation patterns ini-tially introduced in [18] (later reused in other projects for streamlining semantics of requirements models [19, 20]). It is based on a dual layer RDF schema – one layer to distinguish between different types of diagrammatic constituents (node, connector, container etc.); the other to distinguish between the concepts/relations/properties prescribed by the modelling language vocabulary - thus bridging the semantic gap between the modelling environment and the front-end Task Manager.

B. The hybrid back-end is designed around the pivotal role of a graph database that stores the RDFised models, relevant reasoning axioms/rules and links to data that remain external due to factors such as: (i) *security* – Linked Databases raise specific access control challenges [21] which are not in our scope, thus we separate this concern by keeping user credentials in a separated traditional (SQL) database; (ii) *externality* – the geospatial data on which the GeoSPARQL standard relies is intended to be openly shared across the Semantic Web. A RESTful back-end service manages the graph content and delivers it on-demand to the front-end. One part of the service acts as a "diagram dereferencing service", exposing to front-end developers any diagram node together with all its visual and non-visual links for further navigation and agile development of convenient front-end components.

C. The BPMS front-end is built on a traditional MVC pattern – however the M layer (traditionally delegated to an object-relational mapping library) is replaced here with service calls to the RESTful interface of the back-end, including the diagram dereferencing service.

6   Implementation Insights

The application was developed in Java, with the Spring Framework and Spring Boot to speed up the build process. Thymeleaf is the front-end template engine - the architecture is flexible, so the implementation must match it, as future developments are planned, conforming to a Design Science engineering cycle.

For the reported iteration two types of diagrams are isolated in order to focus of running examples: (i) *Business Process Model*, which is a simplified flavour of BPMN with customised notation and a domain-specific taxonomy of tasks and (ii) *Resource Model*, where enterprise resources involved in the execution of processes are described either as abstract "capabilities" (e.g., individual roles, business roles) or depictions of instances that can provide those capabilities (e.g., employees that can fulfil those roles, business partners, concrete organisations where the instances are affiliated through organigram relations).

Process tasks can be linked to resources – if linked to a capability, this should be interpreted as a requirement (e.g., a textile provider is required to supply textile for the clothing production); if linked to an instance, this should be interpreted as an As-Is situation (e.g., a concrete employee/partner was assigned to a particular task). Thus, hyperlinks shift the interpretation on the process model between the "blueprint" and the "execution" levels.

Figure 4 suggests the possibility to switch between the two levels when assigning task responsibilities (instance employees can also be connected to their organisational hierarchy). Similar mappings can link tasks to geographical areas with a slightly different interpretation of the same pattern – the requirement would be the location/destination for the execution of a task, whereas the "resource" instances would be any "point of interest supporting the task accomplishment" – e.g., a parking lot where the courier must reserve free places (it could also be a hotel, a gas station etc., all domain-specific specialisations of a "Point of Interest" concept).

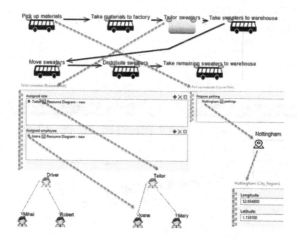

Fig. 4. Linking process tasks to requirements or instances

All instance elements that are present in models are enriched with a schema of annotation fields that hold stable data about them – phone number, e-mail address for persons/organisations, geocoordinates for points of interest. Alternatively, instance data may also be loosely coupled to model elements: a "sameAs" field can establish semantic links to external resources which may exist in legacy data sources (e.g., human resources database, linked geodata locations).

Figure 5 shows a fragment of a model that is subjected to linking and reasoning: A model fragment was converted to an RDF graph structure and linked to external data that was semantically lifted through the OntoRefine adapter of the GraphDB server – e.g., a table of parking lots with various characteristics. GeoSPARQL annotations, SPARQL rules and OWL axioms provide reasoning over models and data, producing results needed in the BPMS front-end. The nodes derived from the modelling language have been aligned with the GeoSPARQL vocabulary (the *geo:Feature* concept). Examples in Fig. 6 show an OWL property chain axiom generating a direct *:atCoordinates* relation between these "geofeatures" and their coordinates. Then an INSERT rule builds the : *recommendedParking* relation between the task and the parkings that are within some range from where the task must be accomplished. This is further chained (via OWL) with the employee assignment, to generate a direct relation *:parkingForUser* – a property that will become, in the BPMS front-end, a parking lot recommendation for that particular user. In other words, parts of the BPMS logic are delegated to the knowledge base. Note that OWL is not employed here to build a fully-fledged ontology, but as a reasoning mechanism tailored to enrich the modelling language (axioms therefore will have to be adapted to possible language evolutions).

The hereby presented example uses a simple case of geocomparison – the INSERT rule computes geof:distance between two points. The GeoSPARQL standard provides a rich taxonomy of geometries, including linestrings and polygonal areas, each with specific geocomparison operations (e.g., if an area overlaps with another, or contains another etc.), as well as computations and topological relations based on traditional geospatial models.

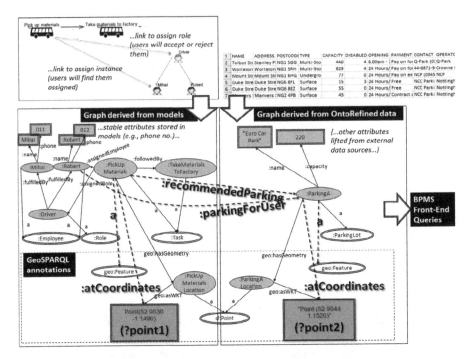

Fig. 5. Sample from the hybrid knowledge-data fabric

Spatial inference on models+data	Axiomatic (OWL) inference on model+data
...generates parking recommendations for courier process tasks...	...aligns model information with GeoSPARQL and generates parking recommendations for users...
INSERT {?task :recommendedParking ?parking} WHERE { ?task :atCoordinates ?point1; a :Task. ?parking :atCoordinates ?point2; a :Parking. BIND((geof:distance(?point1, ?point2, uom:metre)) as ?distance) FILTER (?distance < 500) }	geo:Feature owl:unionOf (:Task :ParkingLot). :atCoordinates owl:propertyChainAxiom (geo:hasGeometry geo:asWKT). :parkingForUser owl:propertyChainAxiom ([owl:inverseOf :assignedEmployee] :recommendedParking)

Fig. 6. Inference rule examples

Figure 7 shows the front-end page of a logged user and the status of assigned tasks. For each task, the recommended parking lots are retrieved and attached to the corresponding tasks. The clock symbol indicates that the task is still pending (someone else needs to finish the previous task), whereas the symbols for "Pick up materials" shows that the task is active but was rejected by the user. If a task is not directly assigned and it is pending, an employee cannot take a task until the ones that precede it are finished (example: "Take materials to factory" waits for "Pick up materials"). This driver sees only the driving tasks (other drivers don't see the ones this one has as active, only the available ones and the ones assigned to them).

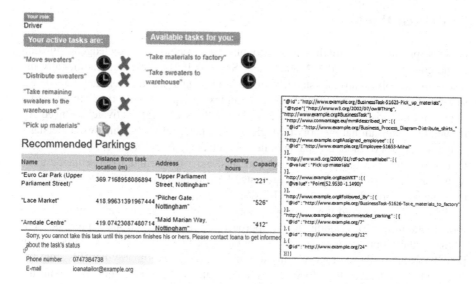

Fig. 7. Task selection page (left) and JSON-LD task description delivered by back-end (right)

When a task is completed, the application logs its completion and checks if it has any visual connectors outgoing, assigned or assignable to the same or other user. The employees do not have access to the overall process structure, only to the process fragments that are relevant for them, or to the contact data for those after which they need to wait (or to contact them, as suggested in Fig. 7). This filtering is again accomplished through the semantic queries on the process graph and its links, and in some cases on the task URI dereferencing service, getting back graph fragments in JSON-LD format - see a sample on the right side of Fig. 7.

Table 1 shows performance measures for key interactions during the BPMS run-time operation. The time is measured for 4 factors: Request (time taken to send to the back-end the request with the parameters), Response (time needed to get the response back), DOM (time needed to load the browser's Document Object Model), and Total time to reload the page with the new data. TSP represents the Task Selection Page in Fig. 7.

Table 1. Performance evaluation

Operation performance (ms)	Req	Res	DOM	Tot.
Login (and get TSP)	368	3	564	935
Take task (and reload TSP)	208	2	461	953[a]
Get data about pending task (redirect to contact page)	54	2	452	510
Complete task (and reload TSP)	195	3	571	1192[b]

[a]The redirect operation took an extra 281 ms
[b]The redirect operation took an extra 423 ms

7 Related Works

Business process modelling has been recognised as a method of knowledge acquisition in the context of Knowledge Management Systems [22] – however traditionally the discussion revolves around standard modelling languages to facilitate knowledge sharing. This has been extended to more complex enterprise "blueprints" in the wider scope of Enterprise Modelling [23, 24]. The authors of [25] motivate the need for managing organisational memory through multiple perspectives – which we understand as multiple types of models capable of flexibly attaching elements of enterprise context to a core of process blueprints. To support this, our work brings forth semantic technology as means of bridging human-oriented knowledge representation with machine-readable structures that must feed a BPMS.

Studies have covered how process model elements can be annotated by terms of a formal ontology [26], leading to an approach of "semantic business process modelling". Other approaches to semantic annotation of processes have been proposed in [27–29]. None of these proposals aim to build a BPMS that directly benefits from the extended semantics, as they focus on process evaluations (e.g., compliance) with the help of reasoning. Targeting formal verification of process tasks, the paper [30] considers the semantics of the execution context and raises the question how to attach it to tasks. Our paper can be considered a technical proposal of doing this through a mix of Linked Data techniques and Agile Modelling.

We advocate AMME as a key enabler for additive semantics included directly in the modelling language, rather than as annotations to some standards-based models. New types of models can be linked to the core process models in meaningful ways – i.e., those links are machine-readable and distinguished by their semantics so that the BPMS front-end can navigate and retrieve what is necessary at any point during the process execution (not only from related models, but also from model-data links pertaining to the execution context). This agile notion of a modelling method reflects ideas from domain-specific language engineering [31, 32] or situational method engineering [33] and relies on metamodelling platforms for iterative and requirements-driven fast prototyping of modelling tools – e.g., ADOxx [11] MetaEdit + [32].

Besides reflecting a particular take on model-driven engineering, our proposal can also be considered the output of a digital transformation method in the sense discussed by [34] (the extended process models can reach the scope of enterprise architecture across several Zachman framework facets as shown in [19]); or, as means of bridging the gap between stakeholders and developers in the sense surveyed by [35] - where a lack in traceability-oriented work is highlighted. Through our proposal of reducing the middleware between the BPMS front-end and the modelling environment, semantic traceability between model elements and the front-end features driven by those elements is enabled. The work of [36] also bridges requirements modelling with business process modelling through the lens of "capability" as the core modelling concept. The same capability concept is extended with context awareness in [37] on a conceptual level, however without considering possible use in a BPMS at runtime.

8 Concluding Evaluation

This paper showcases a project-based Design Science artefact whose engineering cycle is a novel software engineering approach that bridges the semantic gap between process models and model-driven BPMS features that rely on contextual data for process execution. We conclude with a SWOT analysis to structure an assessment on the current progress of this technical proposition:

Strengths: The paper proposes a knowledge-driven approach to BPMS engineering, where the term "knowledge" covers a conceptual fabric that integrates diagrammatic models, instance (legacy) data and reasoning. Models are not employed in the traditional standards-driven roundtrip engineering cycles, but as part of a knowledge conversion cycle giving a novel interpretation to the SECI cycle.

Weaknesses: Further evaluations with respect to the development method's productivity are required across development projects – however access to comparable projects is an obstacle and requires further longitudinal study. Some simplified evaluations on the software engineering method's productivity have been provided in [16]. One usability weakness is related to streamlining the modelling tool and the graph database server, due to how the current version of the RDFiser is implemented – i.e., it requires a manual upload of RDFised models (which is cumbersome on frequent changes). In an ideal case the modelling tool would use the graph database as its main model storage, and share it with the BPMS.

Opportunities: The above observation is also aimed at inspiring the development of RDF-based metamodelling platforms (currently unavailable to the best of our knowledge). Furthermore, the proposal can be applied to standard modelling languages and could be further generalised to enterprise modelling (4EM, Archimate).

Threats: The proposal's reusability and generality relies on the adoption of its ingredients and enablers, most of them emerging from experimental contexts of limited popularity. However, since graph databases are a fast growing segment of the database industry and fast prototyping of agile modelling tools is now enabled by several open platforms and methodologies, new opportunities for open knowledge hybridisation can be investigated.

Acknowledgment. This work was supported by the Romanian National Research Authority through UEFISCDI, under grant agreement PN-III-P2-2.1-PED-2016-1140. Technical aspects of the model-driven implementation are detailed in the master dissertation of M. Cinpoeru, *A "Hybrid Knowledge"-based Approach to Business Process Management Systems*, while the modeling tool engineering is covered in the dissertation of A. Harkai, *Proof of Concept for a Technology-Specific Modelling Language*, at University Babeş-Bolyai.

References

1. Open GeoSpatial Consortium, GeoSPARQL – the official page. http://www.opengeospatial. org/standards/geosparql. Accessed 29 Jan 2019

2. Wieringa, R.J.: Design Science Methodology for Information Systems and Software Engineering. Springer, Heidelberg (2014). https://doi.org/10.1007/978-3-662-43839-8

3. OMiLAB, NEMO Summer School – the official page. http://nemo.omilab.org. Accessed 28 Jan 2019

4. Nonaka, I., von Krogh, G.: Perspective—tacit knowledge and knowledge conversion: controversy and advancement in organizational knowledge creation theory. Organ. Sci. **20**(3), 635–652 (2009)

5. Ambler, S.: Agile Modeling: Effective Practices for eXtreme Programming and the Unified Process, 1st edn. Wiley, New Jersey (2002)

6. W3C, RDF - Semantic Web Standards. http://www.w3.org/RDF/. Accessed 14 Mar 2019

7. Karagiannis, D., Buchmann, R.A, Walch, M.: How can diagrammatic conceptual modelling support knowledge management? In: Proceedings of the 25th European Conference on Information Systems (ECIS), AIS 2017, pp. 1568–1583 (2017)

8. Zachman, J.A.: A framework for information systems architecture. IBM Syst. J. **26**(3), 276–292 (1987)

9. Karagiannis, D.: Conceptual modelling methods: the amme agile engineering approach. In: Silaghi, G.C., Buchmann, R.A., Boja, C. (eds.) IE 2016. LNBIP, vol. 273, pp. 3–19. Springer, Cham (2018). https://doi.org/10.1007/978-3-319-73459-0_1

10. Karagiannis, D., Buchmann, R.A.: A proposal for deploying hybrid knowledge bases: the ADOxx-to-GraphDB interoperability case. In: Proceedings of the 51st Hawaii Conference on System Sciences (HICSS), University of Hawaii, pp. 4055–4064 (2018)

11. BOC, AdoXX official website. https://www.adoxx.org/live/home. Accessed 30 Jan 2019

12. Karagiannis, D., Mayr, H., Mylopoulos, J. (eds.): Domain-Specific Conceptual Modeling. Springer, Cham (2016). https://doi.org/10.1007/978-3-319-39417-6

13. Gonzalez-Perez, C., Henderson-Sellers, B.: A foundation for multi-level modelling. In: CEUR Workshop Proceedings, pp. 43–52 (2014)

14. Ontotext, GraphDB – the official website. http://graphdb.ontotext.com/. Accessed 29 Jan 2019

15. Ontotext, OntoRefine – the official page. http://graphdb.ontotext.com/documentation/free/loading-data-using-ontorefine.html. Accessed 29 Jan 2019

16. Buchmann, R., Cinpoeru, M., Harkai, A., Karagiannis, D.: Model-aware software engineering: a knowledge-based approach to model-driven software engineering. In: Proceedings of the 13th International Conference on Evaluation of Novel Approaches to Software Engineering (ENASE), pp. 233–240. SCITE Press (2018)

17. Cinpoeru, M.: Dereferencing service for navigating enterprise knowledge structures from diagrammatic representations. In: Abramowicz, W. (ed.) BIS 2017. LNBIP, vol. 303, pp. 85–96. Springer, Cham (2017). https://doi.org/10.1007/978-3-319-69023-0_9

18. Karagiannis, D., Buchmann, R.: Linked open models: extending linked open data with conceptual model information. Inf. Syst. **56**, 174–197 (2016)

19. Buchmann, R., Karagiannis, D.: Modelling mobile app requirements for semantic traceability. Requirements Eng. **22**(1), 41–75 (2017)

20. Buchmann, R., Karagiannis, D.: Enriching linked data with semantics from domain-specific diagrammatic models. Bus. Inf. Syst. Eng. **58**(5), 341–353 (2016)

21. Costabello, L., Villata, S., Rodriguez Rocha, O., Gandon, F.: Access control for HTTP operations on linked data. In: Cimiano, P., Corcho, O., Presutti, V., Hollink, L., Rudolph, S. (eds.) ESWC 2013. LNCS, vol. 7882, pp. 185–199. Springer, Heidelberg (2013). https://doi.org/10.1007/978-3-642-38288-8_13

22. Maier, R.: Knowledge Management Systems, 3rd edn. Springer, Heidelberg (2007). https://doi.org/10.1007/978-3-540-71408-8

23. Loucopoulos, P., Kavakli, V.: Enterprise knowledge management and conceptual modelling. In: Goos, G., Hartmanis, J., van Leeuwen, J., Chen, P.P., Akoka, J., Kangassalu, H., Thalheim, B. (eds.) Conceptual Modeling. LNCS, vol. 1565, pp. 123–143. Springer, Heidelberg (1999). https://doi.org/10.1007/3-540-48854-5_11

24. Frank, U.: Multi-perspective enterprise models as a conceptual foundation for knowledge management. In: Proceedings of the 33rd Annual Hawaii International Conference on System Sciences (HICSS). IEEE (2000)

25. Kingston, J., Macintosh, A.: Knowledge management through multi-perspective modelling: representing and distributing organizational memory. Knowl.-Based Syst. 13(2–3), 121–131 (2000)

26. Thomas, O., Fellmann, M.: Semantic process modeling – design and implementation of an ontology-based representation of business processes. Bus. Inf. Syst. Eng. 1(6), 438–451 (2009)

27. Smolnik, S., Teuteberg, F., Thomas, O.: Semantic Technologies for Business and Information Systems Engineering. IGI Global, Hershey (2012)

28. Corea, C., Delfmann, P.: Detecting compliance with business rules in ontology-based process modeling. In: Proceedings der 13. Internationalen Tagung Wirtschaftsinformatik (WI) 2017, pp. 226–240 (2017)

29. Fill, H.: SeMFIS: a flexible engineering platform for semantic annotations of conceptual models. Seman. Web 8(5), 747–763 (2017)

30. Kaindl, H., Hoch, R., Popp, R.: Semantic task specification in business process context. In: 11th International Conference on Research Challenges in Information Science (RCIS), pp. 286–291. IEEE (2017)

31. Frank, U.: Domain-specific modeling languages: requirements analysis and design guidelines. In: Reinhartz-Berger, I., Sturm, A., Clark, T., Cohen, S., Bettin, J. (eds.) Domain Engineering, pp. 133–157. Springer, Heidelberg (2013). https://doi.org/10.1007/978-3-642-36654-3_6

32. Kelly, S., Lyytinen, K., Rossi, M.: MetaEdit + a fully configurable multi-user and multi-tool CASE and CAME environment. In: Constantopoulos, P., Mylopoulos, J., Vassiliou, Y. (eds.) CAiSE 1996. LNCS, vol. 1080, pp. 1–21. Springer, Heidelberg (1996). https://doi.org/10.1007/3-540-61292-0_1

33. Kumar, K., Welke, R.: Methodology engineering: a proposal for situation-specific methodology construction. In: Cotterman, W.W., Senn, J.A. (eds.) Challenges and Strategies for Research in Systems Development, pp. 257–269. Wiley, Chichester (1992)

34. Hafsi, M., Assar, S.: What enterprise architecture can bring for digital transformation: an exploratory study. In: 2016 IEEE 18th Conference on Business Informatics (CBI), pp. 83–89. IEEE (2016)

35. Assar, S.: Model driven requirements engineering: mapping the field and beyond. In: 4th International Model-Driven Requirements Engineering Workshop (MoDRE), pp. 1–6. IEEE 2014)

36. Pastor, O.: A capability-driven development approach for requirements and business process modeling. In: Link, S., Trujillo, Juan C. (eds.) ER 2016. LNCS, vol. 9975, pp. 3–8. Springer, Cham (2016). https://doi.org/10.1007/978-3-319-47717-6_1

37. Henkel, M., Stratigaki, C., Stirna, J., Loucopoulos, P., Zorgios, Y., Migiakis, A.: Extending capabilities with context awareness. In: Krogstie, J., Mouratidis, H., Su, J. (eds.) CAiSE 2016. LNBIP, vol. 249, pp. 40–51. Springer, Cham (2016). https://doi.org/10.1007/978-3-319-39564-7_4

Can I Help You? – The Acceptance of Intelligent Personal Assistants

Richard Lackes, Markus Siepermann[⊠] [iD], and Georg Vetter

Technische Universität Dortmund, Dortmund, Germany
{richard.lackes,markus.siepermann,
georg.vetter}@tu-dortmund.de

Abstract. Intelligent personal assistants (IPA) experience increasing popularity. They are designed to make everyday life easier. But for that purpose they monitor their users. This study investigates how the perceived advantages and disadvantages of using an IPA affect its acceptance. In addition, trust in the IPA and trust in the manufacturer are considered as further influencing factors. The results show that the advantages have a higher impact on acceptance than the disadvantages. The influence of trust in the manufacturer affects both the trust in the IPA and the perceived advantages. Trust in the IPA in turn influences the perceived advantages and disadvantages, and acceptance. In order to increase the perceived advantages, manufacturers should increase the range of functions, particularly in the area of house control, and thus increase the acceptance of IPAs. Another positive effect on acceptance is the reduction of perceived disadvantages by building trust in the IPA and the manufacturer.

Keywords: Intelligent personal assistant · Acceptance · Smart speaker

1 Introduction

The popularity of intelligent personal assistants (IPA) has increased dramatically since 2015 [1] and will continue to increase in the future. Gartner [2] forecasts that 3.3% of households worldwide will have at least one IPA in their household. Cision [3] expects an annual market growth of IPAs of 32.8% from 2016 to 2024. Examples of IPAs are Google Home, Amazon Echo with Alexa, Apple's Siri or Microsoft's Cortana. This is software that is usually implemented in a device that has a loudspeaker and microphones. IPAs are therefore often called smart speakers.

The functionality of IPAs ranges from simple daily functions to complex tasks. The simple functions include saving reminders, ordering products or obtaining information. The rather complex functions of IPAs include integration into the smart home, i.e. communication with other electronic devices [4]. Therefore, IPAs differ in their functional scope, but the ability to understand what the user wants and to put information into context is the same for all IPAs [5].

IPAs are controlled via voice. In order for the IPA to perform a task, the user must say a code word. The IPA then attempts to execute all voice commands after the code word. The acoustic signals given by the user after the code word are recorded by the IPA and sent to a server via the Internet. This server has the ability to analyse audio

© Springer Nature Switzerland AG 2019
M. Pańkowska and K. Sandkuhl (Eds.): BIR 2019, LNBIP 365, pp. 204–218, 2019.
https://doi.org/10.1007/978-3-030-31143-8_15

files. The server then creates the answer of the IPA. The answer of the IPA can either consist of the output of information or of the execution of tasks such as buying something or controlling another device. In addition to the analysis of pure language, approaches are developed that can also recognize emotions based on the user's facial expressions [6] or monitor the user's vital signs automatically and continuously. However, this study will focus exclusively on voice-controlled IPAs.

One aim of voice control is to make IPAs more humane. In this way, the user can ask the IPA questions just like a real person. Further developments of IPAs are increasingly trying to imitate human response behaviour, like for example telling jokes. The quality of the NLP is also rising steadily and conversation with an IPA comes very close to conversation with a real person [7]. IPAs can now even answer follow-up questions which refer to a previous question. Through the human-like communication, the conversation with the IPA should also become socially more pleasant [7] and the user should thus build up an emotional connection to the IPA [7]. Hence, IPAs are often referred to as "digital buddies" [7]. Once the user has established a binding, he then uses the IPA more often [7].

In addition to the functions and applications of IPAs listed here, there are also disadvantages regarding the use of IPAs. For example, in a morning show at the CW6 station in San Diego, a reporter triggered mass orders for dollhouses. The reporter interviewed a girl named Alexa. At the end of the interview, the reporter said "I love the little girl, saying 'Alexa ordered me a dollhouse.'" As a result the Amazon Echos of the viewer then ordered dollhouses [8]. This example is part of a series of incidents where IPAs acted on instructions of unauthorized people. But the biggest disadvantages concern privacy and data security. For example, the IPA receives all talks in its surrounding via its microphones. Even if the IPA only responds to questions and instructions after the code word, it still analyses every conversation in its environment. By using IPAs, the user's data is stored centrally. Therefore, the misuse or theft of this data is another risk and disadvantage of using IPAs.

Due to the advantages and disadvantages presented, the acceptance of IPAs is not guaranteed. In order to clarify this, the factors influencing the acceptance of IPAs should be determined and their influence measured. The following research question is to be answered in this way.

RQ: Which factors drive the acceptance of intelligent personal assistants?

2   Literature Review

The literature for the investigation of the acceptance of IPAs can be differentiated according to the influencing factors considered. The previous focus was on the social relationship to the IPA [7], trust in the IPA [9], or enjoyment in using IPAs [10].

The influence of the social relationship to the IPA on continuous use was investigated by Han und Yang [7]. They designed a structural equation model (SEM) based on the Para-Social-Relationship Theory. The aim of the study was to investigate whether there is a social relationship between the IPA and the user and whether this relationship influences satisfaction with the IPA. A total of 304 participants were interviewed. As a result, Han und Yang showed that security/privacy risk and interpersonal attraction (task attraction, social attraction and physical attraction) have a significant influence on para-social-relationship, which in turn, in addition to task attraction, was influential in satisfaction. Finally, there was a significant positive correlation between the satisfaction with IPA and the intention to use IPA.

Siddike und Kohda [9] developed a framework of trust determinants to examine the use of IPAs more closely. Through an extensive literature review they found out that reliability, attractiveness, and emotional attachments are important factors influencing the trustworthiness of IPAs. They also found that innovativeness moderates the intention to use IPAs.

In addition to the risk of using an IPA, the work of Kowalczuk [10] distinguishes from other works by integrating perceived enjoyment. He investigated the behavioural intention to use smart speaker via an SEM. For the development of the SEM he analysed 2,186 customer reviews and 899 tweets and combined these results with models from the literature. The resulting model was tested by interviewing 293 people in an online survey. The influence of risk and perceived enjoyment on behavioural intentions to use smart speakers could be confirmed next to the influence of perceived usefulness and perceived ease of use. The influence of technology optimism, system diversity, and system quality on perceived usefulness was also confirmed. The perceived enjoyment had the strongest influence on the behavioural intention to use smart speaker.

One of the first publications on the influence of the benefits of using IPAs on acceptance comes from Orehovački et al. [11]. They examined the antecedents of adoption of an IPA in an educational setting. The Google Assistant was used as a representative for this. After using the IPA, the indicators for the constructs effectiveness, controllability, reliability, accuracy, ease of use, usefulness, satisfaction, and loyalty were measured using a questionnaire. A total of 309 students were interviewed. Whether the IPA is perceived as an advantageous application depends on whether it improves the participants' performance, helps the user to process a task in a particular way or is perceived as easy to communicate with. If students see the benefits of using the IPA, they are likely to use it continuously.

Studies on IPAs as a combination of loudspeaker and speech assistant are scarce [11], but there are further studies dedicated to the acceptance of IPAs in mobile devices. For example, IPAs were already used on smartphones before smart speakers were ready for the market.

Sano et al. [12] investigated the continuous use of IPAs such as Siri on mobile devices. For this purpose, they developed a prospective user engagement prediction model. The authors define engagement as whether a user likes IPA and whether he wants to use it continuously. For this purpose, large-scale user logs of 348,295 users of an IPA were analysed. Through the analysis of usage patterns, 338 attributes were identified as influencing factors on engagement. The attributes could be categorized into utterance frequency features, response frequency features, and time interval features. Jiang et al. [13] investigated the quality of IPAs such as Siri or Cortana on mobile devices. The aim was to develop a method for the automatic evaluation of user satisfaction. A total of 60 participants of a local IT-company took part in the study. The participants had to submit standardised requests to the assistant. The results showed that the quality of speech recognition and intent classification influences the user experience. Kiseleva et al. [14] also examined IPAs on mobile devices. They observed the factors influencing satisfaction with the IPA in various scenarios. These scenarios were controlling a device, web search, and structured search dialog. Satisfaction with the IPA differed between the different scenarios. The task completion, the amount of effort spent, and the ability of the IPA to understand the context of the conversation were identified as factors influencing the satisfaction.

The studies on the acceptance of IPAs on smartphones can only be transferred to smart speakers to a limited extent. Unfortunately, the few studies that examined smart speakers ignored some influencing factors. Thus, only trust in the smart speaker as an influencing factor is considered and not additionally the trust in the manufacturer. Furthermore, although the expected advantages are measured as a separate construct, literature is still lacking of the analysis of disadvantages when using IPAs.

3 Research Model

For the analysis of the acceptance of a new technology, models such as the Technology Acceptance Model (TAM) [15, 16] or its successors are frequently used [17], because they usually provide good results in explaining the factors influencing acceptance [18, 19]. Even if the TAM is criticized for its simplicity [20], it provides a sound basis for the development of a suitable research model.

The TAM core states that the attitude to an innovation (such as an IPA) (1st type of acceptance) influences the behavioural intention to use it (2nd type) which in turn influences the actual use (3rd type). For the purposes of this study, the third type of acceptance is not measured because the technologies under consideration are still in their infancy and most people have not had contact with these technologies. Therefore, the model is limited to the first two types of acceptance. This is hardly a limitation, since the intention to use an innovation has often proven to be a very good predictor of its use [21, 22]. In line with TAM, we therefore hypothesise:

H1: A positive attitude towards the smart system positively influences the intention to use it.

Several factors influence the attitude towards an IPA. In the first place, the attitude is shaped by the positive characteristics of the IPAs and how people assess them [15, 16]. TAM postulates that the ease of use of an innovation influences the way how users perceive its usefulness. Perceived ease of use and usefulness in turn both have an impact on the users' attitude towards the innovation [15, 16, 19]. Usefulness depicts the characteristics of the innovation and how advantageous people perceive them [22]. Perceived ease of use measures the usability of the innovation, i.e. how it is to use it [23]. Nowadays, the usability is a prerequisite for the economic success of an innovation [23]. If the usability is low, an innovation will hardly be used [23] so that it serves as a kind of hygiene factor [24]. In addition, assessing the usability of an innovation that cannot be tested by people is quite difficult and may distort the results of the investigation. Therefore, we refrain from measuring the perceived ease of use.

However, even if consumers have no experience with an IPA, its usefulness can be judged on the basis of expected advantages and disadvantages which can be assessed as they can be described easily.

The main advantage of IPAs is their simple voice-controlled user interface (indicator PA1) that makes the interaction with the underlying system extremely easy [25]. Further, IPAs serve different purposes. They can report the weather forecast (PA2) [7]. They remind people of appointments [26] or things to do (PA3) [25]. They can make bookings and place orders (PA4) [27], and they can help to control different devices in the household like light, TV, radio, heating etc. (PA5) [7]. Therefore, we hypothesise:

H2a: Perceived advantages positively influence the attitude towards the IPA.
H2b: Perceived advantages positively influence the intention to use the IPA.

In contrast to other papers, this research model does not consist of separate constructs for each benefit but uses them as measures for the now formative construct *Perceived Advantages*. The main advantage is that respondents are not asked several times for the same aspect so that the resulting questionnaire can be kept short. The disadvantages of the IPAs are modelled in the same way. While TAM and its successor models focus on a system's benefits and the environmental conditions for its use [15, 16, 19, 22], several extensions have proven the importance of perceived disadvantages and risks on attitude and intention to use an innovation [28, 29].

Besides a general aversion against talking with a machine (indicator PD3) [30] and the fear that the IPA does not do what it should (PD2) [11], the data security risk may play an important role. The continuous recording of all conversations by the IPA may be seen as disadvantageous (PD5). The protection of this data is therefore very important (PD1). In addition, the data can be used to save detailed user profiles (PD6) making users and their behaviour transparent to the service provider (PD4) [7]. A misuse of the data and the profiles may harm attitude towards IPAs. We hypothesise:

H3a: Perceived disadvantages negatively influence the attitude towards the IPA.
H3b: Perceived disadvantages negatively influence the intention to use the IPA.

Trust is an important antecedent for the interaction of people and therefore for the behaviour of a person towards another person or an artefact [31, 32]. It is a multidimensional concept [33–35]. Menon et al. [36] regard trust as the belief of the trusting person in attributes of the trustee while Fung and Lee [37] understand trust as the trustor's willingness to believe the trustee. In other words, trust is *"the willingness of a party to be vulnerable to the action of another party [...] irrespective of the ability to monitor or control the other party"* [33]. Thus, trust exhibits two facets: The involved parties and the control mechanisms [38]. In general, two parties are involved: The trustor and the trustee [38–40].

In the case of IPAs, the trustor is the user of an IPA. Concerning the trustee, two different parties can be distinguished: The IPA itself and the manufacturer who runs the IPA's services on his servers. The user interacts with the IPA. He confides in the functions of the IPA and its reliability to do what it is intended to do. This is to some extent a technical perspective concerning the capability and performance of the IPA. However, the user also has to trust the manufacturer as all the data that is collected during the interaction with the IPA is sent to the manufacturer, analysed and stored on the vendor's server. Thus, the user has to believe in the benevolence of the manufacturer [34]. Without that belief, the user will hardly trust the IPA and regard the IPA as useful. Therefore, trusts influences how benefits [28, 29] and risks [40] are perceived. It is also conceivable that the mistrust of people against an IPA or their manufacturer reduces people's attitude towards this innovation. As a result, the following hypothesises can be formulated for trust in the IPA (H4a - H4c) and for trust in the manufacturer (H4d – H4g):

H4a: *The trust in the IPA positively influences the user's attitude towards the IPA.*

H4b: *The trust in the IPA positively influences the perceived advantages.*

H4c: *The greater the trust in the IPA is, the less severe are the disadvantages perceived. (The trust in the IPA negatively influences the perceived disadvantages.)*

H4d: *The trust in the manufacturer positively influences the perceived advantages.*

H4e: *The greater the trust in the vendor is, the less severe are the disadvantages perceived. (The trust in the vendor negatively influences the perceived disadvantages.)*

H4f: *The trust in the manufacturer positively influences the user's attitude towards the IPA.*

H4g: *The trust in the manufacturer positively influences the user's trust in the IPA.*

The resulting specified research model is depicted in Fig. 1 together with the results of the analysis.

4   Analysis

To answer the research question, a questionnaire with 31 questions was designed for the presented structural equation model. The survey took place in November 2018. Not every question of the questionnaire had to be answered. Questions could also be skipped. The questionnaire included 5 demographic questions. 213 persons took part in the online survey. 84 responses had to be eliminated as they had more than 15% missing values [41]. 51.41% of the remaining 129 respondents were female. 70.63% have already used an IPA, but only 33.57% have their own IPA. 5.52% of respondents were younger than 20 years, 55.86% between 20 and 29 years, 12.41% between 30 and 39 years, 25.52% between 40 and 79 years and 0.69% older than 80 years. In terms of monthly net income, 27.78% earned less than 500€, 32.54% between 500€ and 1,500€, 24.6% between 1,500€ and 3,000€, 10.32% between 3,000€ and 4,000€, and 4.76% more than 4,000€.

4.1   Measurement Model

According to Jarvis et al. [42], measurement models can be differentiated into formative and reflective measurement models. Therefore, the above described constructs of the research model can be divided into four reflective constructs (*Intention to Use,*

Attitude, Trust in IPA, Trust in Manufacturer) and two formative constructs (*Perceived Advantages, Perceived Disadvantages*). For the analysis SmartPLS 3 [43] was used. Since SmartPLS 3 is based on the partial-least-squares algorithm, both formative and reflective constructs can be analysed in one model. For the analysis we used case wise replacement and 5,000 samples. Formative and reflective constructs are evaluated differently. Therefore, in the following, the evaluation is performed separately first for reflective and then for formative constructs.

When testing the reflective measured constructs, the convergence criterion, the discriminant validity, the indicator reliability and the predictive validity must be examined [41, 44]. The evaluation of the convergence criterion is based on the analysis of the three measures Cronbach's Alpha, the average variance extracted (AVE) and the composite reliability [45, 46]. Cronbach's Alpha describes the internal consistency of a construct [44, 47, 48]. This consistency should exceed 0.7 [48, 49 requires a limit of 0.6]. The AVE of a construct must be higher than 0.5 [50] in order to explain more than half the variance of its indicators [44]. The composite reliability of a construct indicates how accurately the indicators measure the construct and must exceed the limit of 0.7 [44, 46, 48]. The discriminant validity is used to check whether the constructs are sufficiently different from each other, which has to be tested using the Fornell-Larcker criterion and the cross loadings. The Fornell-Larcker criterion is met when the square root of the AVE of a construct is greater than the correlations of that construct to all other constructs [41, 44, 50]. When checking cross loadings, the loadings of each indicator to its corresponding construct must be larger than the loadings to the other constructs [44]. The loadings are to be analysed beside the p-value also for the indicator reliability. The loading of an indicator represents the relationship between the indicator and its construct and should be greater than 0.7 [44, 45]. The p-value represents the significance level of an indicator [46]. For a minimum significance level, the p-value must be less than 0.1. Further threshold values for higher significance are 0.05 and 0.01 [44]. The predictive validity of a reflective construct shows whether the data points of the construct's indicators are well predicted. For this, the Stone-Geisser's Q^2 (1-SSE/SSO community) must be greater than zero [41]. Indicators that do not meet these criteria must be eliminated from the model.

The examination of the formative constructs is based on the analysis of the three measures: discriminant validity, significance of the indicators and multicollinearity. To ensure discriminant validity, the relationship between the formative construct and all other constructs must not exceed 0.9 [46]. The significance of an indicator is again tested using the p-value, which must be below the known thresholds (0.1, 0.05, 0.01). In addition, the weights of indicators of formative constructs must be greater than 0.1 [41, 46] or less than −0.1 [51]. To be able to distinguish the influence of the individual indicators on the construct, there must be no multicollinearity [52]. Multicollinearity is calculated using the variance inflation factor (VIF = $1/(1-R^2)$) for each indicator [51]. Multicollinearity can be assumed with a VIF of 5 or more [44]. If indicators of formative specified constructs do not meet these requirements, they must not be eliminated, as this would mean a change in the definition of the construct. Formative indicators can only be eliminated due to multicollinearity [42, 53].

Table 1. Results of the research model and shares of answers

Construct	Ind.	Loadings/ weights	AVE/VIF	CR	CA	Share of answers				
						1 (low)	2	3	4	5 (high)
Intention to use (reflective)	I1	0.92***	0.73	0.92	0.88	45.0%	30.0%	13.3%	9.2%	2.5%
	I2	0.81***				36.0%	24.0%	10.7%	7.3%	22.0%
	I3	0.92***				60.0%	24.2%	9.2%	5.0%	1.7%
	I4	0.77***				63.6%	16.5%	11.6%	4.1%	4.1%
Attitude (reflective)	A1	0.87***	0.81	0.93	0.88	7.1%	11.2%	15.9%	32.4%	33.5%
	A2	0.91***				7.1%	16.0%	24.9%	33.7%	18.3%
	A3	0.92***				8.3%	16.7%	20.8%	31.0%	23.2%
Perceived Advantages (formative)	PA1	0.00^{ns}	2.74			7.0%	7.0%	8.9%	35.7%	41.4%
	PA2	0.31***	2.63			3.8%	6.4%	14.6%	33.8%	41.4%
	PA3	0.25*	2.49			7.1%	6.4%	14.1%	35.9%	36.5%
	PA4	0.30**	1.77			35.3%	30.8%	14.1%	12.8%	7.1%
	PA5	0.34***	2.24			16.1%	12.3%	11.6%	25.8%	34.2%
Perceived Disadvantages (formative)	PD1	0.31**	1.39			2.0%	10.7%	25.3%	31.3%	30.7%
	PD2	0.09^{ns}	1.94			1.3%	15.7%	13.1%	34.6%	35.3%
	PD3	0.51***	1.76			31.2%	14.3%	20.1%	18.8%	15.6%
	PD4	0.14^{ns}	2.26			5.3%	15.1%	17.1%	30.3%	32.2%
	PD5	0.04^{ns}	1.58			4.6%	16.6%	7.3%	34.4%	37.1%
	PD6	0.36***	1.24			0.7%	6.5%	24.6%	31.9%	36.2%
Trust in IPA (reflective)	TI1	0.80***	0.65	0.88	0.82	13.3%	25.9%	41.5%	15.6%	3.7%
	TI2	0.82***				15.8%	28.6%	43.6%	9.0%	3.0%
	TI3	0.82***				17.8%	32.6%	37.8%	10.4%	1.5%
	TI4	0.78***				11.2%	20.9%	26.1%	26.1%	15.7%
Trust in Manufacturer (reflective)	TM1	0.87***	0.67	0.89	0.84	13.6%	17.9%	48.6%	14.3%	5.7%
	TM2	0.78***				14.3%	27.1%	41.4%	16.5%	0.8%
	TM3	0.82***				14.7%	33.3%	24.6%	18.8%	5.8%
	TM4	0.80***				23.0%	40.7%	29.6%	6.7%	0.0%

Significance of indicators; ns = not significant; $*p < 0.10$; $**p < 0.05$; $***p < 0.01$

First, the reflective constructs (*Intention to Use, Attitude, Trust in IPA* and *Trust in Manufacturer*) are to be examined. The indicator reliability is below the 1% significance level for all reflective constructs (see Table 1). The convergence criterion is also met, since the AVE for each construct is greater than 0.5, the composite reliability (CR) is above 0.7, and Cronbach's alpha (CA) is above the critical value of 0.7. With regard to discriminant validity, Table 2 shows that the highest correlation between the constructs is below the root of the respective AVE. Thus, the Fornell-Larcker criterion is fulfilled. In Table 3 it can be seen that all loadings of the indicators are highest in the corresponding construct. Thus, the reflective constructs differ sufficiently from each other. The predictive validity is also fulfilled for each construct. Thus, a prediction of the constructs by their indicators is obtained.

Table 2. Fornell-Larcker criterion

Construct	Highest correlation to other constructs	$\sqrt{AVE}$
Intention to use	0.636	0.856
Attitude	0.806	0.900
Trust in IPA	0.604	0.804
Trust in manufacturer	0.604	0.818

Table 3. Cross loadings

Indicator	Intention to use	Attitude	Trust in IPA	Trust in manufacturer
I1	**0.919**	0.580	0.363	0.256
I2	**0.807**	0.523	0.283	0.323
I3	**0.917**	0.505	0.379	0.257
I4	**0.771**	0.389	0.314	0.115
A1	0.569	**0.872**	0.438	0.252
A2	0.462	**0.909**	0.472	0.258
A3	0.556	**0.919**	0.531	0.290
TI1	0.211	0.389	**0.803**	0.374
TI2	0.234	0.320	**0.821**	0.428
TI3	0.168	0.500	**0.818**	0.398
TI4	0.537	0.475	**0.775**	0.655
TM1	0.291	0.335	0.649	**0.865**
TM2	0.206	0.245	0.477	**0.783**
TM3	0.276	0.273	0.371	**0.824**
TM4	0.129	0.056	0.435	**0.797**

For formative constructs, a few indicators are not significant due to their p-value or weight (see Table 1). One (PA1) of five indicators of the construct *Perceived Advantages* has an insufficient weight. The weight of two (PD2 and PD5) of six indicators of the construct *Perceived Disadvantages* are also too low. All these indicators with insufficient weight (PA1, PD2 and PD5) are non-significant as well. In addition to these indicators, one more indicator (PD4) of the construct *Perceived Disadvantages* is not significant. Except for one indicator (PA3) with a significance level of 10% and two indicators (PA4 and PD1) with significance level of 5%, all other indicators are significant at the 1%-level. Since there is no evidence of multicollinearity (VIF < 5), all indicators are sufficiently different and no indicator must be eliminated. The highest correlation between constructs exists between *Perceived Advantages* and *Attitude* with 0.806. Since this is below 0.9, the discriminant validity has to be assumed.

4.2   Structural Model

For the analysis of the structural model, the hypotheses are tested. In addition to the already known key measures of significance and multicollinearity, the coefficient of determination (R^2) is also examined. The coefficient of determination resulting from the regression analysis can be either 'substantial' ($R^2 \geq 0.67$), 'moderate' ($R^2 \geq 0.33$) or 'weak' ($R^2 \geq 0.19$) [41]. Multicollinearity is also not permissible at the structural model level [46, 49]. The calculation and the thresholds are the same as described in the previous section. Finally, the significance and path coefficients have to be examined. To determine the significance of a hypothesis, the same thresholds are used as before (0.1, 0.05, and 0.01). In addition, the path coefficients of the connections between the constructs must be greater than 0.1 or less than −0.1 [45 claims a limit of 0.2, 51].

The R^2 is moderate for our target construct *Intention to Use* ($R^2 = 0.450$). *Attitude* ($R^2 = 0.665$) and *Perceived Disadvantages* ($R^2 = 0.502$) and *Trust in IPA* ($R^2 = 0.365$) achieve as well a moderate level, but *Attitude* just missed the threshold for a substantial explanatory power. *Perceived Advantages* ($R^2 = 0.317$) achieves a weak level. The VIF indicates that there is no multicollinearity [46, 49]. Figure 1 shows the hypotheses with their path coefficients, significance, and effect sizes f^2. For each construct, the R^2 and the predictive relevance Q^2 is provided.

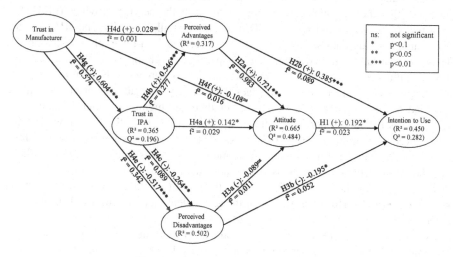

Fig. 1. Results of the research model

5 Discussion

5.1 Conclusion

The results of our study are very satisfying. Only three (H3a, H4f and H4d) out of twelve hypotheses could not be confirmed. Concerning the research question, several driving and inhibiting factors could be found. The most important of the advantages studied was the control of the home (music, light, TV) (PA5) followed by the possibility of obtaining information via the IPA (PA2). While the advantages of both, the control of the home (60%) and the possibility to obtain information about the IPA (45.2%), were partially and fully approved by a large number of respondents, the possibility of booking and ordering via the IPA was ambiguous. Although this possibility has an influence, most respondents (35.3% disagree; 30.8% rather disagree) did not consider this function of the IPA to be advantageous. The possibility of being reminded of things by the IPA (PA3) had a significant influence and was also considered advantageous by most respondents (35.9% partially agree; 36.5% fully agree). The control of the IPA via speech (PA1) had no influence. In contrast, a total of 77.1% partially and fully agreed that voice control of the IPA was advantageous. One possible explanation is that voice control is already regarded as a basic component of these assistants and is therefore considered to be advantageous, but has no effect.

Concerning the disadvantages, the strongest influence is the aversion to talking to a machine (PD3). However, the opinions of the interviewees differ greatly. Although 31.2% do not agree that speaking with a machine is disadvantageous, the remaining 68.8% are relatively evenly distributed between "rather disagree" and "fully agree" (between 14.3% and 20.1%). This shows that communication is perceived very diversely, but a large proportion of respondents have no problem with talking to a machine. This is followed by user concerns about data security. An important disadvantage is that the user's data is evaluated and used elsewhere (PD6) and that there is a high risk that the personal data is not secure with the service provider (PD1). For example, 62% (PD1) and 68.1% (PD6) agreed partially or fully that IPAs do not necessarily provide data security. Privacy is perceived as a relatively weak problem. Thus, the fear that the user will become transparent through the use of the IPA has only a weak influence (PD4). The fact that privacy is not perceived as an important disadvantage is also underlined by the fact that the fear that all conversations will be recorded has no influence (PD5). This contradicts the literature, which identifies privacy risk as the most important influencing factor [54]. In both cases, however, the interviewees with more than 60% (62.5% for PD4 and 71.5% for PD5) partially or fully agree that they become transparent and are monitored. A possible explanation could be that the respondents are already used to expose their data and are desensitised to their data privacy. Also, the fear that IPAs will do things that are not intended by the user has no influence (PD2). However, 69.9% of the respondents said that they at least partially agreed with this fear (34.6% agree in part and 35.3% fully agree).

Regarding the constructs Trust in IPA and Trust in Manufacturer, all indicators are important. In summary, the descriptive statistics in Table 1 show that IPAs are considered medium to less reliable and trustworthy, as are their manufacturers. Overall, the model confirmed established hypotheses of the TAM and subsequent models.

5.2 Implications

The results allow several recommendations for action for companies. The attitude towards IPA is mainly influenced by the perceived advantages. Since the perceived advantages are similar to the perceived usefulness, this confirms already existing literature [15]. If the functions of the IPA are regarded as advantageous, people are also more positive towards the IPA (*Attitude*) and their intentions to use increase. In order to promote the acceptance of IPAs, companies should increasingly communicate the advantages of the functions to their customers and develop these functions further. Particular attention should be paid to the control of the house or apartment. New applications could also be developed in which the IPA can be used as a control system. In contrast to trust in the IPA, trust in the manufacturer has no influence on the perceived advantages. Thus, it is particularly important to increase the customer's trust in the product so that the positive effect of the perceived advantages on the intention to use can be fully exploited. Interestingly, the perceived disadvantages have no influence on the attitude and show only a weakly significant influence on the intention to use. Since the descriptive statistics clearly show that respondents perceive disadvantages of IPAs, the low influence on intention to use may perhaps be justified by the low damage that respondents fear from the disadvantages. Even if disadvantages only play a minor role, they can be reduced by trusting both the product and the manufacturer. Since data security and privacy appear to be central disadvantages, companies should dispel their customers' concerns by building trust.

5.3 Limitations and Future Work

The presented study is not without limitations. The number of respondents is low with 129 participants. In order to be able to make more meaningful conclusions, this study should be repeated with more respondents. Most of the respondents were between 20 and 29 years old. People from other age groups may think differently about using an IPA. The intention of older people to use an IPA may decrease considerably, as they may not be as enthusiastic about technology or find it less intuitive to use. Thus, the perceived advantages could be much less significant and perhaps even the perceived disadvantages could become the focus of attention. In future studies, a better balanced sample concerning age would be helpful to create more meaningful results. There may also be a cultural bias in the study, as mainly German respondents were interviewed. For example, the technology affinity in other countries may be different, which may distort the results of this study. Hence, the study should be carried out in several other countries.

References

1. Forrester Research: Ownership of smart home devices and smart speakers in the United States from 2015 to 2022 (in million households/units in use). Statista. https://www.statista.com/statistics/794624/us-smart-home-devices-smart-speaker-ownership-forecast/
2. Gartner: Gartner Says Worldwide Spending on VPA-Enabled Wireless Speakers Will Top $2 Billion by 2020 (2016)
3. Transparency Market Research: Growing Focus on Strengthening Customer Relations Spurs Adoption of Intelligent Virtual Assistant Technology, Says TMR. Albany, NY (2016)
4. Augusto, J.C., Nugent, C.D.: Smart homes can be smarter. In: Augusto, J.C., Nugent, C.D. (eds.) Designing Smart Homes. LNCS (LNAI), vol. 4008, pp. 1–15. Springer, Heidelberg (2006). https://doi.org/10.1007/11788485_1
5. Reis, A., Paulino, D., Paredes, H., Barroso, J.: Using intelligent personal assistants to strengthen the elderlies' social bonds. In: Antona, M., Stephanidis, C. (eds.) UAHCI 2017. LNCS, vol. 10279, pp. 593–602. Springer, Cham (2017). https://doi.org/10.1007/978-3-319-58700-4_48
6. Knight, W.: Amazon Working on Making Alexa Recognize Your Emotions. With Google and Apple preparing voice devices for the home, Amazon is teaching Alexa to listen for emotions. https://www.technologyreview.com/s/601654/amazon-working-on-making-alexa-recognize-your-emotions/
7. Han, S., Yang, H.: Understanding adoption of intelligent personal assistants. Ind. Manag. Data Syst. **118**, 618–636 (2018)
8. Liptak, A.: Amazon's Alexa started ordering people dollhouses after hearing its name on TV. https://www.theverge.com/2017/1/7/14200210/amazon-alexa-tech-news-anchor-order-dollhouse

9. Siddike, M.A.K., Kohda, Y.: Towards a framework of trust determinants in people and cognitive assistants interactions. In: Bui, T. (ed.) Proceedings of the 51st Hawaii International Conference on System Sciences, Hawaii International Conference on System Sciences (2018)

10. Kowalczuk, P.: Consumer acceptance of smart speakers: a mixed methods approach. J. Res. Interact. Market. **12**, 418–431 (2018)

11. Orehovački, T., Etinger, D., Babić, S.: The antecedents of intelligent personal assistants adoption. In: Nunes, I.L. (ed.) AHFE 2018. AISC, vol. 781, pp. 76–87. Springer, Cham (2019). https://doi.org/10.1007/978-3-319-94334-3_10

12. Sano, S., Kaji, N., Sassano, M. (eds.): Prediction of prospective user engagement with intelligent assistants (2016)

13. Jiang, J., et al.: Automatic online evaluation of intelligent assistants. In: Gangemi, A., Leonardi, S., Panconesi, A. (eds.) Proceedings of the 24th International Conference on World Wide Web - WWW 2015, pp. 506–516. ACM Press, New York (2015)

14. Kiseleva, J., et al.: Understanding user satisfaction with intelligent assistants. In: Kelly, D., Capra, R., Belkin, N., Teevan, J., Vakkari, P. (eds.) Proceedings of the 2016 ACM on Conference on Human Information Interaction and Retrieval - CHIIR 2016, pp. 121–130. ACM Press, New York (2016)

15. Davis, F.D.: A technology acceptance model for empirically testing new end-user information systems: theory and results. Massachusetts Institute of Technology (1986)

16. Davis, F.D.: Perceived usefulness, perceived ease of use, and user acceptance of information technology. MIS Q. **13**, 319–340 (1989)

17. Chau, P.Y.K., Hu, P.J.: Examining a model of information technology acceptance by individual professionals: an exploratory study. J. Manag. Inf. Syst. **18**, 191–229 (2002)

18. Mathieson, K.: Predicting user intentions: comparing the technology acceptance model with the theory of planned behavior. Inf. Syst. Res. **2**, 173–191 (1991)

19. Venkatesh, V., Davis, F.D.: A theoretical extension of the technology acceptance model: four longitudinal field studies. Manage. Sci. **46**, 186–204 (2000)

20. Lee, Y., Kozar, K.A., Larsen, K.R.T.: The technology acceptance model: past, present, and future. Commun. Assoc. Inf. Syst. **12**, 752–780 (2003)

21. Armitage, C.J., Conner, M.: Efficacy of the theory of planned behaviour: a meta-analytic review. Br. J. Soc. Psychol. **40**, 471–499 (2001)

22. Venkatesh, V., Morris, M.G., Davis, G.B., Davis, F.D.: User acceptance of information technology: toward a unified view. Manag. Inf. Syst. Q. **27**, 425–478 (2003)

23. Venkatesh, V., Ramesh, V., Massey, A.P.: Understanding usability in mobile commerce. Commun. ACM **46**, 53–56 (2003)

24. Herzberg, F.: One More Time: How Do You Motivate Employees. Harvard Business Review, Boston (1968)

25. Hoy, M.B.: Alexa, Siri, Cortana, and more: an introduction to voice assistants. Med. Ref. Serv. Q. **37**, 81–88 (2018)

26. López, G., Quesada, L., Guerrero, L.A.: Alexa vs. Siri vs. Cortana vs. Google assistant: a comparison of speech-based natural user interfaces. In: Nunes, I.L. (ed.) Advances in Human Factors and Systems Interaction, 592, pp. 241–250. Springer, Cham (2018). https://doi.org/10.1007/978-3-319-60366-7_23

27. Yang, H., Lee, H.: Understanding user behavior of virtual personal assistant devices. Inf. Syst. E-Bus. Manag. **24**, 665 (2018)

28. Chen, C.-F., Xu, X., Arpan, L.: Between the technology acceptance model and sustainable energy technology acceptance model: investigating smart meter acceptance in the United States. Energy Res. Soc. Sci. **25**, 93–104 (2017)

29. Park, C.-K., Kim, H.-J., Kim, Y.-S.: A study of factors enhancing smart grid consumer engagement. Energy Policy **72**, 211–218 (2014)
30. Noyes, J.A.N.: Talking and writing—how natural in human–machine interaction? Int. J. Hum Comput Stud. **55**, 503–519 (2001)
31. Gefen, D., Karahanna, E., Straub, D.W.: Trust and TAM in online shopping: an integrated model. MIS Q. **27**, 51–90 (2003)
32. Reichheld, F.F., Schefter, P.: E-loyalty: your secret weapon on the web. Harvard Bus. Rev. **78**, 105–113 (2000)
33. Mayer, R.C., Davis, J.H., Schoorman, F.D.: An integrative model of organizational trust. Acad. Manag. Rev. (AMR) **20**, 709–734 (1995)
34. McKnight, D.H., Choudhury, V., Kacmar, C.: Developing and validating trust measures for e-commerce: an integrative typology. Inf. Syst. Res. **13**, 334–359 (2002)
35. Rousseau, D.M., Sitkin, S.B., Burt, R.S., Camerer, C.: Not so different after all: a cross-discipline view of trust. Acad. Manag. Rev. (AMR) **23**, 393–404 (1998)
36. Menon, N.M., Konana, P., Browne, G.J., Balasubramanian, S.: Understanding trustworthiness beliefs in electronic brokerage usage. In: Proceedings of the 20th International Conference on Information Systems, pp. 552–555 (1999)
37. Fung, R., Lee, M.: EC-trust (trust in electronic commerce): exploring the antecedent factors. In: Proceedings of the 5th Americas Conference on Information Systems, pp. 517–519 (1999)
38. Tan, Y.-H., Thoen, W.: An outline of a trust model for electronic commerce. Appl. Artif. Intell. **14**, 849–862 (2000)
39. Chopra, K., Wallace, W.A.: Trust in electronic environments. In: Proceedings of the 36th Annual Hawaii International Conference on System Sciences, pp. 1–10. IEEE (2003)
40. Krasnova, H., Spiekermann, S., Koroleva, K., Hildebrand, T.: Online social networks: why we disclose. J. Inf. Technol. **25**, 109–125 (2010)
41. Chin, W.W.: The partial least squares approach to structural equation modeling. In: Modern Methods for Business Research, vol. 295, pp. 295–336 (1998)
42. Jarvis, C.B., MacKenzie, S.B., Podsakoff, P.M.: A critical review of construct indicators and measurement model misspecification in marketing and consumer research. J. Consum. Res. **30**, 199–218 (2003)
43. Ringle, C.M., Wende, S., Becker, J.-M.: SmartPLS 3. SmartPLS GmbH, Boenningstedt (2015)
44. Hair, J.F., Hult, G.T.M., Ringle, C., Sarstedt, M.: A Primer on Partial Least Squares Structural Equation Modeling (PLS-SEM). Sage Publications, Thousand Oaks (2016)
45. Chin, W.W.: Commentary: issues and opinion on structural equation modeling. MIS Q. **22**, 7–16 (1998)
46. Huber, F., Herrmann, A., Meyer, F., Vogel, J., Vollhardt, K.: Kausalmodellierung mit Partial Least Squares. Gabler, Wiesbaden (2007)
47. Cronbach, L.J.: Coefficient alpha and the internal structure of tests. Psychometrika **16**, 297–334 (1951)
48. Nunnally, J.C., Bernstein, I.H., Berge, J.M.T.: Psychometric Theory. MacGrac-Hill, New York (1994)
49. Hair, J.F., Black, W.C., Babin, B.J., Anderson, R.E.: Multivariate Data Analysis. Pearson Education, Upper Saddle River (2006)
50. Fornell, C., Larcker, D.F.: Evaluating structural equation models with unobservable variables and measurement error. J. Mark. Res. **18**, 39–50 (1981)
51. Sarstedt, M., Ringle, C.M., Smith, D., Reams, R., Hair, J.F.: Partial least squares structural equation modeling (PLS-SEM): a useful tool for family business researchers. J. Fam. Bus. Strategy **5**, 105–115 (2014)

52. Diamantopoulos, A., Riefler, P., Roth, K.P.: Advancing formative measurement models. J. Bus. Res. **61**, 1203–1218 (2008)
53. Bollen, K., Lennox, R.: Conventional wisdom on measurement: a structural equation perspective. Psychol. Bull. **110**, 305–314 (1991)
54. Balta-Ozkan, N., Davidson, R., Bicket, M., Whitmarsh, L.: Social barriers to the adoption of smart homes. Energy Policy **63**, 363–374 (2013)

Understanding the Habits: Inertia in Flipped Classroom

Christin Voigt$^{(\boxtimes)}$, Kristin Vogelsang$^{(\boxtimes)}$, Kirsten Liere-Netheler$^{(\boxtimes)}$, Linda Blömer$^{(\boxtimes)}$, Henning Brink$^{(\boxtimes)}$, and Uwe Hoppe$^{(\boxtimes)}$

Katharinenstr. 1, 49069 Osnabrück, Germany

Abstract. The digitalization increasingly determines the way knowledge is conveyed at universities. A concept resulting from this is Flipped Classroom (FC) that reverses the structure of the classical teaching concept and integrates the use of digital media. The introduction of new concepts is often challenging and therefore associated with inertia. We have examined the structure of inertia in a FC course with the aim of a better understanding of which components favor the adherence to old habits. The empirical analysis of a questionnaire carried out led to two important results. First there was no cognitively based inertia observed in the course. The tendency to status quo results purely from emotional and routine-based motivations in the course. Secondly, we were able to make conclusions about the different factors influencing affective and behavioral inertia, which among other findings showed a clearer division of the perceived value in the Flipped Classroom.

Keywords: Flipped classroom · Inertia · Digital learning · Barriers of change · Habit · Quantitative research

1 Introduction

The progress of digitalization changes the economic and private spheres of life [1]. Thus, it is also posing new opportunities and challenges for teaching [2]. An innovative approach resulting from this is the Flipped Classroom (FC) [3]. It has been modified in numerous ways and is increasingly used in schools and universities since. According to Handke and Sperl [4], the basic idea of the Flipped Classroom is to reverse the structure of the classical lessons. A FC concept consists of two major parts – the online preparation and the in-class interaction. In the flipped classroom, the students prepare the basic content at home.

Online materials like videos or digital test elements are dedicated to this purpose. The in-class time is used to deepen knowledge. It is based on the interaction between the students and the lecturer. The Flipped Classroom can be regarded as a blended learning arrangement [5]. Even though today's learners are used to use technical devices, the FC is a rather new concept, that is different from traditional teaching designs. The concept can, therefore, not be based on familiar behavioral patterns. New concepts often encounter resistance when use habits are no longer addressed, and the behavior patterns have to be changed [6]. This resistance is generally referred to as change resistance or the so-called inertia [7, 8].

© Springer Nature Switzerland AG 2019
M. Pańkowska and K. Sandkuhl (Eds.): BIR 2019, LNBIP 365, pp. 219–232, 2019.
https://doi.org/10.1007/978-3-030-31143-8_16

Even though the FC can provide benefits such as improved grades, increased communication, and greater satisfaction, there is a risk of lacking student participation, especially in the initial phase [9]. The efficiency of the FC depends considerably on the willingness of the students to accept the new concept. In the field of FC, the barriers towards this concept are only little explored. The inertia theory, which has so far been mainly used in connection with organizational changes, is now investigated in the context of Flipped Classroom. Understanding the barriers to FC is an important basis for developing appropriate countermeasures in time.

This paper aims to scrutinize the structure of change resistance regarding a FC concept and the basis on which decisions relating to digital change are made. We want to answer the underlying research question: *which decision processes of students' shape the inertia in a FC course?* Therefore, a quantitative evaluation based on a questionnaire was carried out. We used the factor analysis and Q-test to interpret the results. In the next chapter, we first give a brief overview of the basic terms used in this paper, FC and inertia. We then present the research method, including the data collection and empirical analysis. Afterward we explain and discuss our results. In the end, the limitations of the paper and an outlook to future research are given.

2 Theoretical Background

2.1 Flipped Classroom

Digital media have become an indispensable part of everyday life and are increasingly determining the way knowledge is conveyed at universities [10]. Flipped Classroom is a form of digital or blended learning [11]. In a FC, the basic content is conveyed online, while the intensification and the practical application takes place in presence phases. This concept goes back to Bergmann and Sams, who wanted to make it possible for pupils to independently rework the contents of their school lessons [3]. Learners and teachers now have completely new tasks. While the lecturer in the presence phases rather functions as a learning coach, he must at the same time also develop skills to prepare and make available online material didactically well. Learners, on the other hand, are more dependent than ever on their systematic approach in this concept.

We used an ad hoc literature review [12] with the keywords "inertia" and "Flipped Classroom" individually as well as together and then analyzed the focus of the articles. Although research in the field of FC is still quite young, some major research areas have established themselves. A large part of the research contains reports and individual case studies. Research often focuses on the impact of FC on students and their learning effort [11]. Primary analyses exist on (a) the effect of FC [13] (b) the design [14, 15] as well as in-class and out-class activities [16] and (c) the comparison of FC with traditional courses [17]. A large part of the research attests to the FC's consistently positive aspects. For example, learning outcomes are increased, and the motivation of students, in general, is promoted [11]. First approaches examine the acceptance of the FC concepts and students perceptions [9]. Only a few researchers criticize the concept and can also report negative implications [18]. However, there is a lack of long-term studies on habits and long-term changes in FC concepts in this relatively new field of research. So far, the inertia of students in the context of an Flipped Classroom has scarcely been examined at all [19]. However, identifying the attitudes of students towards an FC concept is important in order to take timely action against potential barriers.

2.2   Inertia

If new systems, information systems, or technical products are introduced, open and hidden resistances often occur [8]. Therefore, the topic of user resistance has a long tradition in research and practice [20]. The introduction of a new system often replaces an existing, established system in whole or in part. The resistance becomes clear when the changeover is not carried out by the users [21].

The remaining in old habits is generally described by the term inertia. This research area is primarily based on consumer research results, where inertia describes the phenomenon of remaining loyal to a brand instead of looking for new, different or even better brands [22]. Inertia is the result of long-trained habits [23]. This behavior can also be observed in other decision areas. There are research approaches to organizational inertia, which have close connections to the field of change management [7, 24]. Other authors transferred the phenomena of inertia to the field of IS (information systems) utilization [8, 25]. Inertia is often based on individual habits.

Inertia thus describes the (individual) insistence on form and function. If the existing form is advantageous, then inertia does not necessarily have to be perceived as negative, it can even be evaluated positively. However, if the change brings about improvements, inertia can be problematic for further development. Inertia has behavioral, cognitive and affective components [8]. Behavior-based inertia means that habitual behavior is continued simply because one has always done it that way. The individual does not even have to be aware of this habit. This results in a resistance to change. The cognitive component of inertia, on the other hand, describes that insistence despite awareness of existing alternatives. The individual may also be aware that the alternatives are more efficient and effective [24], or that the existing system is not the best. The cognitive response depends on the personally perceived profit based on costs and benefits, the fair implementation, as well as the conditions and timing of the change [26]. The affective component of the inertia describes the effort that an individual would have to make when changing [24, 27]. Here the transition costs outweigh the benefit of the new system. This component is strongly linked to convenience. Often the existing system is positively occupied so that an alternative is not considered at all. For this affective norm, the perceived benefit as well as social aspects such as communication are essential [26].

All in all, high inertia leads to refuse the change to a new system. Although, low inertia not necessarily means, that a new alternative will be chosen. If one is convinced that the existing system is better and one, therefore, remains with the old one, then this cannot be equated with inertia.

In the tradition of new teaching concepts, much is written about the obvious advantages (see chapter 2.1). Only a little research is available, that discusses the negative sides of course improvement [15] or shows the resistance to change established concepts. Although they must exist, as there is still a great number of lectures that are held traditionally. One way to understand that phenomenon is to find out, where and how resistance occurs. Therefore, it is important to understand which variables affect inertia.

Thus, we will examine the inertia of students, measuring their cognitive, behavioral and affective inertia towards the newly introduced FC course. For the examination of inertia of students in the field of FC, we orient towards the definition of inertia by Polites [8]. In the following, we will define the term inertia as the students' *attachment to, and persistence in, choosing an incumbent course design (i.e., the status quo), even if there are better alternatives or incentives to change to the new Flipped Classroom course.*

Various predictors of the inertia are investigated in the research. These are strongly dependent on the respective context. Routines, transition costs and individual prereq-uisites play an important role and influence the degree of strength and nature of the individual inertia [25]. In the following chapter, we will focus on the methodical basics of our research by describing the data collection, the selected dimensions of inertia, and the data analysis.

3   Research Method

3.1   Data Collection

The present study is based on a questionnaire. It was completed by master students, who attended a FC course the winter term 2017/2018. The total population includes 138 students who were signed up for the course "Project Management" at the time indicated. This course is created as a FC as it combines online learning units like audio-supported slides and videos with practical in-class activities such as directed reading, case study processing, and exercises. The media created for the online phase were made available to the students during the semester via the university's Learning Management System (LMS) "Stud.IP".

The data collection was carried out as a written, standardized, anonymous, and voluntary survey. A total of 40 students took part and thus form the sample of the research presented. The low response rate is due to the fact that the survey was voluntary and that not all students, who were signed up for the course, were present on the day of the survey. The questionnaire used was developed specifically for this survey based on previous research to measure the influencing factors of the individual inertia of the students. It is necessary to take a closer look at the dimensions of inertia examined by the survey to convey a common understanding of the subsequent data analysis and the following presentation of the results.

The FC setting is not just a change of learning habits, but is also strongly linked to a technology use. That is why we have designed the questionnaire in such a way that the important area of "use" and "use intention", which is central in socio technical studies, is also depicted here. In the following we combined dimensions from the socio tech-nical research with pure inertia research as proposed by Kim [28]. Our model is based on the assumption that different influences affect change resistance or inertia [28]. The value of the change, and also the effort to switch, influence the decision to change. In addition, this decision is impacted by the environment in which the change takes place. The environment is represented by the social surroundings and also by the organization [24] proves that inertia is also influenced by different decision-making processes. We combine these approaches and complement them with a socio-technical perspective [7].

We assume four dimensions as decisive for the inertia: I character, II outcome, III change process and, IV decision making. In our basic model, the first dimension character (of the participant) is described by the constructs "intention to participate" (following [29]) and "perceived benefit" [30]. The second dimension outcome displays the transition costs and is aligned to the constructs of "change resistance " [31] and the "switching costs" [32] of FC use. The third dimension, the change process, is divided into the constructs of "trust in the teacher" (as representative of the organizational trust [33]), "subjective value" (or social norms) [29] and "ease of use" [29, 34]. Finally, we ask in the fourth dimension about the decision-making norm, which is classified into affective, cognitive and behavioral constructs [25]. The last dimension is a typical representative of the inertia research stream. We measure three to five items per construct. The actual composition of the fourth dimension "decision making", which determines the target value for the following hypotheses, is presented in Fig. 1.

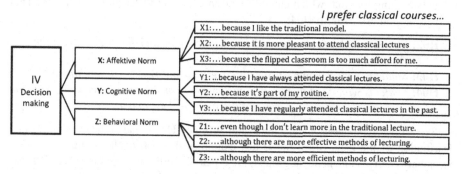

Fig. 1. Composition of the principles of decision making

For this survey, a 7-point Likert scale and a total of 37 Likert items was used, whose answers range from "I strongly agree" to "I strongly disagree". The distances between the individual scales are to be treated as equal, which is explicitly formulated at the beginning of the questionnaire and allows us to assume an interval scaling of the data.

3.2 Analysis

The empirical analysis is divided into two parts. First, we investigate the suspected model. For this purpose, the statistical quality criteria such as objectivity, reliability and validity are assessed and items are removed on the basis of their Cronbach's Alpha-values and Item-Scale-Correlations. Also, an exploratory factor analysis is used to verify the assumed model derived from the theory. About this path, the appropriateness of the factor analysis according to Kaiser-Meyer-Olkin and Barlett test is confirmed.

In the second step, we test the previous theoretical assumptions by proposing four hypotheses. The existence of affective, cognitive, and behavioral components of the inertia in the course is tested within the first hypothesis.

H01: *Affective, cognitive and behavioral inertia exists in the course.*

The further three hypotheses test the influencing factors of the different components of inertia. In theory, a fair implementation, the perceived value and the conditions of change were observed as influencing factors for the cognitive norm. Both affective and cognitive behaviors depend upon the perceived value of change. The affective norm is also related to the communication in the decision-making process. We interpret the fair implementation and the context of the change as the attitude towards the teacher and the user-friendliness and test by constructs "trust in teacher" and "ease of use". The process of change, which is determined by the temporal component of change and the possible loss of control caused by an external constraint, plays no role in the special course, since the students themselves could decide when and whether they want to participate in the new teaching concept. In theory, the behavioral norm was determined to act according to habit, which can be found in construct C "change resistance". This leads to hypothesis H02 to H04.

H02: *Students with affective inertia particularly consider the perceived value and the subjective norm.*

H03: *Students with behavioral inertia have a strong resistance to change.*

H04: *Students with cognitive inertia particularly consider the perceived value, the cost of FC, the ease of use and the trust in the teacher.*

To test the hypotheses, we use the Mann-Whitney U-test due to the missing normal distribution of the data. Since the U-test examines the statistically significant differences between two independent groups, the types of inertia must be classified. For this purpose, the following two assumptions have to be made in order to differentiate: 1. A behavior according to norm X, or an assignment of the test person to group 1, should always exist if the mean value of the items X1, X2 and X3 $\geq$ 5. The same applies to norm Y and Z with their corresponding items. 2. A test person can act according to more than one decision norm. From this, two groups can be determined compared with each other: Group 0 "There is no inertia according to affective, behavioral or cognitive norm" and group 1 "There is inertia according to corresponding norm". To verify a significant influence of the determinants of inertia on the three groups of norms, we now use the Mann-Whitney U-test under the H0 hypothesis that there are no significant differences between the distributions of rankings. In addition to the general influence, we also consider the effect strength "r" of the result.

4 Results

4.1 The Basic Model

The two indicators Cronbach's Alpha and Item-Scale-Correlation for measuring the quality of the data showed anomalies for one item from the construct "perceived value". The Cronbach's Alpha of the corresponding dimension I before deletion is 0.721 and is the smallest of all dimensions. Since the item "this learning concept prepares me better for my professional life than classical lectures" has been omitted, it has risen to a value of 0.785. The corrected item-scale correlation of this item is likewise inadmissible and also on construct level the Cronbach's Alpha of the construct "perceived value" rises through the omission of the item. Beyond that, the reliability and validity of the data were permissible. However, the factor analysis revealed some redistributions of the basic model. Figure 2 shows the new model after reliability reliability and factor analysis.

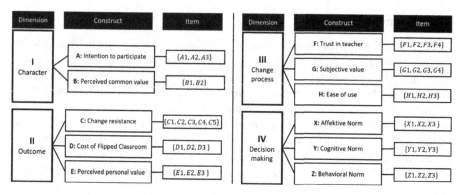

Fig. 2. New model of the composition of inertia after reliability and factor analysis

While the assumptions regarding the initial model were confirmed for dimension III and IV, some resorting was carried out in the first two dimensions. Thus, one item that was originally assigned to the cost of FC and measures the perceived stress at the thought of the new teaching concept had the highest factor load within the construct "change resistance" and was reassigned. However, the most striking reordering occurred in the construct of "perceived value". As shown in Fig. 3, this initial construct "perceived value of FC" is divided into two separate new parts. The items of the first construct of the new model after factor analysis focus on the knowledge of the general utility and the advantages of this learning concept, while the items of the second new construct look at students' learning success and the expected benefits in terms of the exam. Two items from this construct were not previously included in the construct "perceived value" and originate from the initially formulated construct "switching cost" of FC. This separation into common and personal value can be interpreted as a different view of the benefits and is relevant throughout further analysis. Two new constructs are developed: Construct B "Perceived common value" and construct E "Perceived personal value".

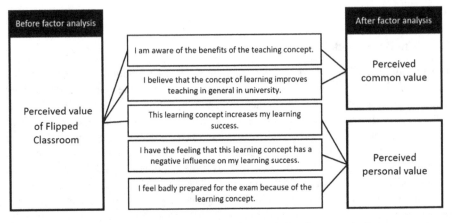

Fig. 3. Perceived value of FC before and after factor analysis

4.2 Determinants of Habit Change

We examine the four hypotheses by testing the influence of the group belonging to the items of constructs X, Y and Z on the rest of the constructs using a U-test. Table 1 shows only items for which the H0 hypothesis of the U-test can be rejected with respect to at least one decision norm, which means that there is a significant influence.

The H0 hypothesis was assumed if $p > 0.1$. Hypothesis H01 tests the existence of affective, cognitive and behavioral inertia in the course. For this purpose, we determine whether there is a significant influence of the respective groups with the construct A "intention to participate", since this provides an indicator for the inertia. Item A1 "I would reconfirm such a learning concept" shows a significant influence on the affective

Table 1. Effect strength of statistically significant results after U-test

Dimension	Item	Affective	r	Behavioral	r	Cognitive	r
I	A1	$p < 0.05$	0.41	$p < 0.05$	0.45	$p > 0.1$	–
	A3	$p > 0.1$	–	$p < 0.05$	0.41	$p > 0.1$	–
	B2	$p > 0.1$	–	$p > 0.1$	–	$p < 0.1$	0.27
II	C1	$p > 0.1$	–	$p < 0.1$	0.28	$p > 0.1$	–
	C4	$p > 0.1$	–	$p < 0.1$	0.3	$p > 0.1$	–
	D1	$p < 0.05$	0.36	$p < 0.1$	0.3	$p > 0.1$	–
	D2	$p < 0.05$	0.38	$p > 0.1$	–	$p > 0.1$	–
	D3	$p < 0.1$	0.28	$p > 0.1$	–	$p < 0.1$	0.32
	E1	$p < 0.05$	0.5	$p > 0.1$	–	$p > 0.1$	–
	E2	$p < 0.1$	0.3	$p > 0.1$	–	$p > 0.1$	–
	E3	$p > 0.1$	–	$p < 0.1$	0.32	$p > 0.1$	–
III	G3	$p < 0.05$	0.38	$p > 0.1$	–	$p > 0.1$	–
	H1	$p > 0.1$	–	$p > 0.1$	–	$p < 0.05$	0.55
	H2	$p > 0.1$	–	$P < 0.1$	0.3	$p < 0.05$	0.5
	H3	$p > 0.1$	–	$p > 0.1$	–	$p < 0.05$	0.24

and behavioral norm at a significance level of 0.05 with a medium effect strength. The behavioral inertia also has a significant influence with item A3. However, the cognitive norm has no significant influence with the construct A "intention to participate" at all. The H0- hypothesis of the U-test that there are no significant differences between the distributions of the rankings can therefore only be rejected for the affective and for the behavioral norm. Thus, there is no cognitively based inertia in the course, which means that the tendency to status quo results purely from emotional and routine-based motivations under the assumptions made above.

The remaining three hypotheses state the structure of the inertia. Hypothesis H02 regards the perceived value and the subjective norm as relevant for the affective inertia. The perceived value was divided into construct B "common value" and construct E "personal value". Significant influences of the affective norm can be observed with a large part of the items of the personal value. The construct B" common value" shows no significant influences, though. In the course, the affective inertia is thus only based on the personally perceived benefits, which refer to the personal learning success, as shown in Fig. 3. However, the benefits for teaching in general have no affective components in the course. An influence with the subjective norm, which was also predicted in hypothesis 02, can be confirmed since a significant influence with the item G3 was measured at the five percent significance level. Overall, hypothesis H02 can be confirmed with the exception of the common benefits. In addition, an influence of the cost of FC (construct D) on the affective inertia was observed. This was measured for all items of construct D with an effect strength of between 0.28 and 0.38.

The influences of the behavioral norm are tested by hypothesis H03, which assumes a high resistance to change within the behavioral inertia. This has been confirmed for two items of construct C at the ten percent significant level. Also, the cost of FC (construct D), the perceived personal value (construct E) and the ease of use (construct H) had an impact on the behavioral norm. These influences were likewise confirmed at the ten percent significance level and have an effect strength of 0.3 to 0.32. The consideration of these factors can thus also be seen as part of the habit and may subconsciously be compared with previous behavior. Again, only an influence of personal and not of common value was measured.

The last hypothesis H04 tests the influence on the cognitive inertia and suspects an impact of the perceived value, the cost of FC, the ease of use and the trust in the teacher. Since no cognitive inertia was present in the course, only findings about the influences on the cognitive process of decision making can be made here. The influence of the ease of use was clearly confirmed by a five percent significance and an effect strength of up to 0.55 of all items of these construct. Also, the influence of costs and benefits could be established at least to the tenth significance level. Here, however, only the influence of the common value was measured, but not the personal benefit. No significant influence could be observed for the trust in the teacher on the cognitive decision-making process. This trust represented the environmental conditions mentioned in the previous theories of cognitive inertia. Considering that no significant influence was measured here, it has to be questioned whether the trust in the teacher is regarded as an environmental condition in the context of the Flipped Classroom by the students.

In summary, hypothesis H01 could only be admitted for the affective and behavioral inertia. The hypotheses H02 and H03 were confirmed, but exclude the common value. Within the hypothesis H04, trust in the teacher could not be confirmed as an influencing factor on the cognitive decision-making process. In general, it is striking that the division into personal and common value through factor analysis led to the fact that only personal benefits have a significant influence on decision making regarding affective and behavioral inertia. The common benefit, on the other hand, is located in the cognitive thinking process.

5   Discussion, Limitations and Future Research

Based on the theoretical background about inertia as a tendency to continue in the status quo despite the existence of better alternatives, 4 hypotheses were derived. The results of these and our theoretical implications are summarized in Table 2. Overall, the suitability of the Flipped Classroom as a conceptual model for inertia could be confirmed, since a large part of the research results to date could also be observed in the course. One item was removed from the study in the course of the reliability analysis. In addition, the factor analysis showed a stronger distribution of the perceived benefits. Thus, a subdivision into personal benefit, which describes the increase in students' learning success and better exam preparation, and general benefit, which considers the potentials for teaching as a whole, became clear. This separation is consistent with the observations of previous research, since the cognitive decision norm was also said to consider various consequences for individuals and the organization as a whole. However, only affective and behavioral inertia was found in the course under the assumptions made, but not cognitive inertia (H01). In practice, one should influence or reduce the affective inertia by the personal perceived benefits of the students, the social components and the costs of FC (H02) in practice. Behavioral inertia, on the other hand, can be influenced not only by perceived personal value and FC costs, but also by resistance to change and the ease of use (H03).

With this article we take up a topic that has scarcely been examined so far. However, the large area of research on barriers to digitalization [10, 35] and barriers to innovation [36] shows that this research deserves more attention. With our approach, we pick up current research trends from the field of inertia research and apply them in a new environment. We are thus combining two major topics. Our results are therefore interesting for researchers from the field of barrier research and Flipped Classroom researchers. In addition, our study is also relevant for practitioners, i.e. for teachers who want to introduce an FC. Because only if you understand why students (don't) attend an event can you design the course responsibly [9, 37].

Though we carefully proceeded our research, the examination is not without limitations. We based our questionnaire on findings from inertia [25] and resistance to change [28] literature. We adapted the items to the corresponding setting of a FC including technology use [5, 11], still: the influence of all the decision norms could not be generally confirmed. Thus, no significant influence was found between the cognitive norm and the intention to participate in the event. Since the results of statistical significance depend on the assumptions made above, these should be questioned. Here,

Table 2. Results and implications of the hypothesis

Hypothesis	Results in course	Theoretical implications
H01: *Affective, cognitive and behavioral inertia exists in the course*	Confirmed for the affective and behavioral inertia	No cognitive Inertia was found in the course. The resistance to change only exists because of emotional and behavioural decision-making processes
H02: *Students with affective inertia particularly consider the perceived value and the subjective norm*	Confirmed for common value and subjective norm; Influence of affective inertia with cost of FC also confirmed	Common benefits have no influence with the affective norm. Thus, only personal benefits result from emotional components of change resistance in the course
H03: *Students with behavioral inertia have a strong resistance to change*	Confirmed; Influence of behavioral inertia with cost of FC, personal value and the ease of use also confirmed	The ease of use depends on the routine-based change resistance, but not the common part of the benefit
H04: *Students with cognitive inertia particularly consider the perceived value, the cost of FC, the ease of use and the trust in the teacher*	Not Confirmed, since no cognitive inertia exists; Influence for the cognitive decision-making norm with common value, cost of Fc and ease of use confirmed	Cognitive decision norms are important for the perceived user-friendliness. Likewise, the common part of the benefit is to be assigned to cognitive thought processes, but not the personal ones

the rate from which the decision norm is applied to the test person was defined as >4 in assumption 1. In other words: the results assumed that a decision according to the norms is made at least at the answer "I rather agree". A classification >3 would also be conceivable, which would include the answer "neither agree nor disagree, disagree". A relatively higher classification to the three forms of inertia can be observed in this case, but also the number of persons acting according to more than one norm increases. In addition, the individual behavior of each person may cause the limit for approval of the decision norm to vary from person to person. However, no information on this can be derived from the available data.

Furthermore, only non-parametric test procedures could be used due to the missing normal distribution of the data. Moreover, the sample of 40 test persons is small. We assume that further research under consideration of the indicated inertia model, carried out with more test persons, will lead to even more meaningful results. That's why the survey should be repeated within a larger sample.

In addition, there are some other interest groups in the FC context which we have not addressed in this paper, but which should be taken into account in the future. This refers to all stakeholders, with the exception of the already included group of students, that have to deal with the change if the implementation of a FC has been determined. There may be teachers who find it difficult to give up their learned teaching role and renounce the beloved habit of giving a lecture in the presence of numerous students [3]. There may be further staff from administration like FC developer with the knowledge of good, subject-specific contents but without technical skills to translate them into self-learning media, without enough time to do it well or without a perception of a personal value, when flipping the class. And there may be staff like technical support or administration, who look anxiously into the future because digital transformation already indicates how much they have to change their habits if they want to cope with upcoming administrative and technical challenges in the future [38]. In order to clarify these and other optional assumptions about inertia in the context of FC, future research should examine the inertia of all stakeholders concerned. The habits of these stakeholders should be listened to, understood and examined more closely in order to minimize resistance to change - not only on the part of the students but also on the part of teachers and staff.

References

1. Brynjolfsson, E., McAfee, A.: Race Against the Machine. Digital Frontier, Lexington (2011)
2. Pareja-Lora, A., Calle-Martínez, C., Rodríguez-Arancón, P.: New perspectives on teaching and working with languages in the digital era. Research-publishing.net (2016)
3. Bergmann, J., Sams, A.: Flip Your Classroom: Reach Every Student in Every Class Every Day. International Society for Technology in Education, Alexandria (2012)
4. Handke, J., Sperl, A. (eds.): Das Inverted Classroom Model: Begleitband zur ersten deutschen ICM-Konferenz. Oldenbourg, München (2012)
5. Vogelsang, K., Hoppe, U.: Development of an evaluation for flipped classroom courses. In: Proceeding of Multikonferenz der Wirtschaftsinformatik (mkwi), pp. 821–832 (2018)
6. Rafferty, A.E., Jimmieson, N.L.: Subjective perceptions of organizational change and employee resistance to change: direct and mediated relationships with employee well-being. Br. J. Manage. **28**, 248–264 (2017)
7. Pardo del Val, M., Martínez Fuentes, C.: Resistance to change: a literature review and empirical study. Manag. decis. **41**, 148–155 (2003)
8. Polites, G.L., Karahanna, E.: Shackled to the status quo: the inhibiting effects of incumbent system habit, switching costs, and inertia on new system acceptance. MIS Q. **36**, 21–42 (2012)
9. Baytiyeh, H., Naja, M.K.: Students' perceptions of the flipped classroom model in an engineering course: a case study. Eur. J. Eng. Educ. **42**, 1048–1061 (2017)
10. Abrahams, D.A.: Technology adoption in higher education: a framework for identifying and prioritising issues and barriers to adoption of instructional technology. J. Appl. Res. High. Educ. **2**, 34 (2010)
11. Bishop, J.L., Verleger, M.A.: The flipped classroom: a survey of the research. In: ASEE National Conference Proceedings, Atlanta, GA, pp. 1–18 (2013)
12. Schryen, G.: Writing qualitative is literature reviews—guidelines for synthesis, interpretation, and guidance of research. Commun. Assoc. Inf. Syst. **37**, 286–325 (2015)
13. Baker, E.: Flipped classroom learning outcomes in intro to is class: looking at student outcomes and professor performance evaluations. In: IAIM Conferenc Proceedings (2014)

14. Song, Y., Kapur, M.: How to flip the classroom - "productive failure or traditional flipped classroom" pedagogical design? J. Educ. Technol. Soc. **20**, 292–305 (2017)
15. Vogelsang, K., Droit, A., Liere-Netheler, K., Hoppe, U.: Designing a flipped classroom course - a process model. In: Proceedings of the Internationale Tagung Wirtschaftsinformatik (WI 2019), Siegen (2019)
16. Mahoney, E., Zappe, S., Butler Velegol, S.: The evolution of a flipped classroom: evidence-based recommendations. Adv. Eng. Educ. **4**, 1–37 (2015)
17. Mattis, K.V.: Flipped classroom versus traditional textbook instruction: assessing accuracy and mental effort at different levels of mathematical complexity. Technol. Knowl. Learn. **20**, 231–248 (2015). https://doi.org/10.1007/s10758-014-9238-0
18. Gillette, C., Rudolph, M., Kimble, C., Rockich-Winston, N., Smith, L., Broedel-Zaugg, K.: A systematic review and meta-analysis of student pharmacist outcomes comparing flipped classroom and lecture. Am. J. Pharm. Educ. https://doi.org/10.5688/ajpe6898
19. Baker, E.W., Hill, S.: Investigating student resistance and student perceptions of course quality and instructor performance in a flipped information systems classroom. Inf. Syst. Educ. J. **15**, 17–26 (2017)
20. Gibson, C.F.: IT-enabled business change: an approach to understanding and managing risk. MIS Q. Executive **2**, 6 (2008)
21. Ye, C., Seo, D., Desouza, K., Papagari, S., Jha, S.: Post-adoption switching between technology substitutes: the case of web browsers. In: ICIS 2006 Proceedings, pp. 1940–1958 (2006)
22. Murray, K.B., Häubl, G.: Explaining cognitive lock-in: the role of skill-based habits of use in consumer choice. J. Consum. Res. **34**, 77–88 (2007)
23. Wood, W., Neal, D.T.: The habitual consumer. J. Consum. Psychol. **19**, 579–592 (2009)
24. Rumelt, R.P.: Precis of inertia and transformation. In: Montgomery, C.A. (ed.) Resources in an Evolutionary Perspective: Towards a Synthesis of Evolutionary and Resource-Based Approaches to Strategy, pp. 101–132. Kluwer Academic Publishers, Norwell (1994)
25. Polites, G.L., Karahanna, E.: The embeddedness of information systems habits in organizational and individual level routines: development and disruption. MIS Q. **37**, 221–246 (2013)
26. Smollan, R.: Engaging with resistance to change. Univ. Auckland Bus. Rev. **13**, 12 (2011)
27. Barnes, W., Gartland, M., Stack, M.: Old habits die hard: path dependency and behavioral lock-in. J. Econ. Issues **38**, 371–377 (2004)
28. Kim, K.: Investigating user resistance to information systems implementation: a status quo bias perspective. MIS Q. **33**, 567 (2009). https://doi.org/10.2307/20650309
29. Venkatesh, V., Morris, M.G., Davis, G.B., Davis, F.D.: User acceptance of information technology: toward a unified view. MIS Q. **27**, 425–478 (2003)
30. Moore, G.C., Benbasat, I.: Development of an instrument to measure the perceptions of adopting an information technology innovation. Inf. Syst. Res. **2**, 192–222 (1991)
31. Bovey, W.H., Hede, A.: Resistance to organisational change: the role of defence mechanisms. J. Manag. Psychol. **16**, 534–548 (2001). https://doi.org/10.1108/EUM0000000006166
32. Jones, M.A., Reynolds, K.E., Mothersbaugh, D.L., Beatty, S.E.: The positive and negative effects of switching costs on relational outcomes. J. Serv. Res. **9**, 335–355 (2007)
33. Thompson, R.L., Higgins, C.A.: Personal computing: toward a conceptual model of utilization. MIS Q. **15**, 125–143 (1991)
34. Karahanna, E., Agarwal, R., Angst, C.M.: Reconceptualizing compatibility beliefs in technology acceptance. MIS Q. **30**, 781–804 (2006)

232   C. Voigt et al.

35. Vogelsang, K., Liere-Netheler, K., Packmohr, S., Hoppe, U.: Barriers to digital transformation in manufacturing: development of a research agenda. In: Proceedings of the 52nd Hawaii International Conference on System Sciences (2019)
36. D'Este, P., Iammarino, S., Savona, M., von Tunzelmann, N.: What hampers innovation? Revealed barriers versus deterring barriers. Res. Policy **41**, 482–488 (2012). https://doi.org/10.1016/j.respol.2011.09.008
37. Tan, E., Pearce, N.: Open education videos in the classroom: exploring the opportunities and barriers to the use of YouTube in teaching introductory sociology. Res. Learn. Technol. **19**, 7783 (2011). https://doi.org/10.3402/rlt.v19s1/7783
38. Shnai, I.: Systematic review of challenges and gaps in flipped classroom implementation: toward future model enhancement. In: Proceedings of the European Conference on e-Learning ECEL, pp. 484–490 (2017)

Patient Acceptance of Health Cards and Health Insurance Information Systems

Markus Siepermann$^{(\boxtimes)}$ ⓘ, Arbnesh Stadelhoff, and Richard Lackes

Technische Universität Dortmund, Otto-Hahn-Str. 12, 44227 Dortmund,
Germany
{markus.siepermann, arbnesh.stadelhoff,
richard.lackes}@tu-dortmund.de

Abstract. On new health cards as well as in the underlying information system highly sensitive information can be stored. While different studies analysed the acceptance of physicians and hospitals, the patients' side is somewhat neglected. Though, their personal rights are mostly affected. This paper investigates the acceptance of patients towards the new health card and IS that was recently introduced in Germany. For this, we conducted a survey among 183 patients and analysed the acceptance by structural equation modelling. The dependent variable has a coefficient of determination of 70% so that the model explains the acceptance of patients well. The results show that patients are still too badly informed about the health card. They highly fear a misuse of their data. The model suggests to better inform especially people of poor health about the benefits of the card and about the efforts that are made to protect the data.

Keywords: E-health · Electronic health card · Smart card · Patients · Acceptance

1 Introduction

The use of health insurance smart cards started about 20 years ago. The data stored on the cards comprised information concerning the health maintenance organisation, the kind of insurance, its valid time, and basic information about the insurant like name, surname, date of birth, and address. In 2004, the EU launched the action plan e-Health [9] that aimed in general for national e-health infrastructure systems concerning electronic health records. Since then, many countries in the EU introduced a new kind of smart card for the health insurance. According to the EU action plan, Germany now started to enlarge the system by storing medical records of patients in a central data base. The patient's smart card is the key to grant access to the medical records so that physicians have easy access to all relevant data for a medical treatment.

The advantages of such information systems (IS) are obvious: If for example physicians know about drug intolerances or former medical treatments, they can better medicate their patients. Or if a prescription is transmitted electronically, mistakes because of misspelling or unreadability are avoided.

For insurance companies, positive effects like avoidance of double medical treatments, quality improvements, simplification of data exchange, better communication

M. Pańkowska and K. Sandkuhl (Eds.): BIR 2019, LNBIP 365, pp. 233–246, 2019.
https://doi.org/10.1007/978-3-030-31143-8_17

and therefore cost reductions etc. predominate and seem to be advantageous [1, 41, 42]. For patients and physicians, the situation is different. As patient data are said to be not well protected and able to be misused, many physicians and patients as well as data protection officers oppose the new health IS. These objections have to be taken seriously because they can severely cumber the introduction of such comprehensive IS. If patients agree to the objections, they will not accept the entire system so that the system cannot succeed. For this, several studies have examined the physicians side (e.g. [2, 28, 33, 40]). After several years of discussion, the patient side is still missing although patient rights are most affected by these new systems. Since the beginning of the year 2014, patients should use the new smart card in Germany called eGK. However, still more than 2 million insurants do not have one of the new smart cards. The question is why? Therefore, this paper analyses the patient acceptance concerning the introduction of national health IS. For this, an empirical survey presented in the following was conducted among 183 insurants (91 woman, 89 men, 3 unknown) of Germany. The aim of this survey was to reveal the relevant factors that make patients accept the new IS, the smart cards and their functions.

The remainder of this paper is organised as follows. In the next section, we briefly describe the German smart card eGK and its mandatory and voluntary functions. In the third section, we give an overview over the research that was done in this field during the past years. Section 4 develops the research framework for the survey. Section 5 describes the data that was collected during the survey and provides the analysis. Section 6 discusses the results. The paper closes with a conclusion in Sect. 7.

2 The German Electronic Health Card

The German electronic health card ("elektronische Gesundheitskarte" or short eGK) is one of the biggest projects in the world concerning health insurance cards and IS. It is regulated in §§ 291a and 291b of the 5th book of Social Welfare Code. Since October 2011, the new smart cards are issued to insurants step by step and replace the old read-only health insurance cards, introduced in 1995. The new eGK is divided into mandatory and voluntary functions. The mandatory functions are:

- Basic information about the insurance and the insurant (insurance company, card ID, name, surname, date of birth, postal address, insurance status, the validity period, gender, state of additional contribution, association of SHI physicians that is responsible for the region the patient lives in).
- European Health Insurance Card (EHIC) (European wide insurance).
- Electronic prescriptions (max. 8, written by physicians, readable by pharmacists).

Data that is used by these mandatory functions is stored directly on the eGK. In addition, §291a of the 5th book of Social Welfare Code claims that the following voluntary functions have to be supported by the eGK:

- Emergency data (blood type, vaccinations, allergies, drugs intolerances etc.)
- Patient receipt (management of recent medical treatments and costs)
- Drugs documentation (prescribed drugs)

- Patient's compartment (medical data of patients, e.g. blood pressure)
- Medical report (Diagnoses, therapy recommendations, and medical treatment reports temporarily stored)
- Health record (complete history of a patient's medical treatments, i.e. diagnoses, reports, therapies etc.)
- Declaration of organ donation
- Certificates of authority

Except for the emergency data that can be stored directly on the eGK, all other data is stored in an external IS, encrypted with a key unique for each single patient that is also stored on the eGK. To protect the key, each card is protected by a personal PIN and a picture of the card holder. Thus, only the owner of a health card can grant access to the information that is associated with the card.

As in case of an emergency, health care employees need access to the emergency data, to the declaration of organ donation, or to the certificates of authority, each health care employee gets a health professional card (HPC). This card enables the holder to get access to the important information. Any information else that is encrypted by the key on the eGK cannot be accessed.

3 Literature Review

Even if health smart card projects have already a history of more than 10 years, the number of scientific analyses that deal with the acceptance of the smart cards is still limited. Apart from technical papers concerning the architecture [4, 6, 27], data security and protection [20, 38, 39] (see [14] for a comprehensive overview), special applications [31, 34] or the comparison of countries concerning the status quo [24], we can mainly distinguish two kinds of research fields that consider the acceptance of health smart cards and their underlying IS infrastructure. The first kind addresses the acceptance of those who have to use health cards directly: physicians and other health care employees or hospitals. The second kind of investigations focuses on the patients. Some surveys address both kinds of research, health care employees as well as patients.

Pizzi et al. [33] concentrated their study on the electronic prescription by physicians in the US. Instead of using smart cards for the prescription, they analysed the usage of an online prescription website that can be used by physicians. The acceptance of patients was not analysed. Liu et al. [28] investigated the impacts of the smart card system NHI-IC in Taiwan on hospitals. In particular, they tried to find out to what extent the workflow in hospitals was changed and if the adoption capabilities of hospitals are sufficient. The analysis of that paper uses only descriptive statistics and does not address the acceptance of patients. Pfaff and Ernstmann [32], Ernstmann and Pfaff [13] and Ernstmann [12] addressed the physicians'point of view, especially of registered doctors and not of those who are working in hospitals. They analysed the relevant factors that have to be considered when introducing the new health card eGK in Germany. The patients' point of view was not addressed in their study. Also Wirtz et al. [40] addressed physicians and conducted a similar survey. While the former concentrated on identifying the relevant factors, the latter analysed the relations between certain factors more deeply.

All the aforementioned studies have in common that they do not consider the patients' point of view. But in fact, patient rights are mostly affected by introducing health cards and IS. Because of this, different studies examined the acceptance of patients concerning the use of health cards. Aubert and Hamel [2] addressed both sides, physicians/health care employees as well as patients. The main purpose of their study was to find out what are the determinant factors that are relevant for the acceptance and the usage of the Canadian health smart card. There are two main differences between their study and the one that we present here. First of all, in the Canadian case all data is stored on the smart card itself and no additional IS is used. Secondly, the Canadian smart card was not already introduced and its use was not mandatory. Loo et al. [30] examined the acceptance of the Malaysian multi-purpose smart card MyKad NIC. The Malaysian smart card is not limited to the health sector but also comprises driving license, passport information, electronic purse, automated teller machine access, transit application public key infrastructure, and frequent traveler card. Because of this, their study is difficult to compare to studies of pure health smart cards. Amhof [1], forsa [17], Sunyaev et al. [35], and Hoerbst et al. [21] addressed German patients directly with their surveys. Amhof [1] analysed the patients' awareness of the eGK. The survey reports a high acceptance of patients concerning the eGK. 64% of the interviewees think that the introduction of the eGK is reasonable. Especially medical emergency data has a high acceptance (86%), followed by drugs documentation (66%) and the electronic doctor's letter (50%). The more data is concerned, the more skeptic the patients are because more than 70% fear that their data can be misused. The results of forsa [17] are similar. About 60% of the interviewees have already heard about the eGK. 63% of them felt themselves badly informed and wished more information about the data stored on the card and the data security. However, 70% agree to the introduction of the card but only 51% would unconditionally use the drugs documentation and 43% the health record. The reason seems to be clear: 73% doubt that the data can be misused. Sunyaev et al. [35] focused on the changes in a doctor's surgery. For this, they recorded the processes in a dental surgery and analysed what changes have to be made to the processes. In addition, 49 patients of the dental surgery were asked concerning their attitude towards the eGK. About 90% would use the eGK to save medical data. But only 35% would grant access to this data to all physicians, only 7% to their family doctor, and 58% would grant access only to chosen physicians. Hoerbst et al. [21] compared the attitude of patients in Austria and Germany towards health cards. Only 32% had already heard of the eGK. 47% collect their medical data at home. 88% of them do it paper based. More than 80% think that it is a good idea to provide medical data to their physicians via the eGK.

In sum, we can observe that there is a great acceptance among patients concerning the eGK. But the number of skeptic people of at least 20% is not negligible. However, times have also changed. Recent affairs like the NSA/Snowden affair sensitized people concerning privacy, data protection and misuse. Therefore, it is reasonable that the attitude towards storing intimate personnel data in external IS that cannot be directly controlled by patients may have changed. In addition, all survey concerning the patients' acceptance used descriptive statistics. An analysis of the relations between several factors has not been made and is therefore done in this paper.

4   Research Model

4.1   Acceptance

Acceptance is the willingness to positively approve someone or something, usually some kind of innovation like a new product or a new service [25]. It depends not only on the attributes of the innovation (System Attributes) but also on the intended users themselves (User Attributes). The system attributes determine the usefulness for the users. The higher the usefulness is, the more is a user willing to accept the innovation [10]. This is highly correlated with the educational and social background of the user. The higher the level of education is, the more easily the user spots the advantages that lead to acceptance. And the more people of the social environment accept the innovation the more likely a person will do so too [36].

For the acceptance of the eGK, mandatory functions and voluntary functions must be distinguished. Mandatory functions (A1: basic patient's data, A2: EHIC, A3: electronic prescription) are already in use. Voluntary functions (A4: patient receipt, A5: drugs documentation, A6: patient's compartment, A7: medical report, and A8: health record) cannot be used until now [1, 17, 21]. In addition to these functions, two not planned functions are used to check whether people know about the eGK: A9: a so-called patient's profile where patients have the possibility to document all diseases and symptoms so that suggestions for medication are made and presented; A10: a comprehensive health analysis where patients can document all their habits concerning their life (fast food, drinking etc.) so that additional analyses can be made for possible future diseases.

4.2   System Attributes

Commonly known system attributes like usability, response time etc. are not suitable for our survey because insurants do not work with the system directly. Instead, we have to find factors that can be noticed by insurants. The entire system works with very personal data. Therefore, the *data protection* is found to be a very relevant factor for the trust in a technical system [33]. While insurants cannot really check the data protection they have to trust reported technical descriptions and information that is given to them by government and insurance companies. On this basis, they judge the safety of the system. The eGK has a *picture of the owner* on it (DP1), is protected by a personal identification number (*PIN*) (DP2) and the health records by *data encryption* with a key stored on the eGK (DP3). These measures shall prevent fraudulent use of the card (*fraud prevention*) (DP4) and only healthcare employees should have access to these records. Hence, we hypothesise:

H1: Data protection positively influence the acceptance of the eGK.

The second factor consists in the *benefits* that insurants associate with the eGK. Beside the affordability of the medical care (B1), government as well as insurance companies refer to the following advantages: A quicker medical treatment (B2), medical treatments of higher quality (B3), an enhanced emergency situation (B4), a strengthening of patient rights (B5) and higher transparency (B6) [3, 26]. Therefore, we hypothesise:

H2: The perceived benefits positively influence the acceptance of the eGK.

4.3   User Attributes

If insurants should judge how much their data is protected, their risk adjustment plays an important role. If an insurant for example is very risk averse, the data protection will be judged more vulnerable than a risk taker would do [33]. This also impacts the acceptance of the eGK itself. We hypothesise:

H3: The more risk taking a person is, the higher the data protection is perceived.
H4: The more risk taking a person is, the higher the acceptance of the eGK is.

Closely connected to the risk adjustment is the *trust* of insurants in institutions of health and in general. The more confiding insurants are, the more they will possibly trust and accept the eGK. This may hold for insurants' confidence in general (e.g. in general institutions like government (T1), police (T2) and justice (T3)) as well as in the involved parties in the field of the eGK like physicians (T4), pharmacies (T5), or health insurance companies (T6), and the e-kiosk (T7). Hence, we hypothesise:

H5: Trust positively influences the acceptance of the eGK.
H6: Trust positively influences the perception of data protection.

Also the personal situation of insurants can influence the acceptance of the eGK. Especially an insurant's state of health can play an important role if functions of the eGK are used or not. People with poor health (general medicine experience (S1), blood pressure (S2), weight (S3), experience with back pain (S4) and stomach ache (S5), general frequency of illness (S6)) will turn more often to a doctor than people with good health. Thus, they may benefit from the advantages of the eGK and the underlying health IS. By contrast, people with good health may face fewer benefits from the eGK and may therefore use less functions. Therefore, we hypothesise:

H7: A poor state of health positively influences the acceptance of the eGK.

In addition to the state of health, the *healthy life* of insurants is of interest as it may influence the state of health and therefore the acceptance of the eGK. Insurants who live a healthy life with *healthy eating* (HL1) and comprising *fruits and vegetables* (HL3), doing *regular sports* (HL4) might be more open minded towards the eGK because they could think that they do not have anything to hide. On the other side, the eGK may be less useful to them because a healthy life is said to foster a good state of health. Vice versa with people who do not live that healthy and eat *fast food* (HL2), drink *alcohol* (HL5) and *smoke* (HL6). Also the frequency how often people turn to a doctor in order to make regular *routine checks* (HL7) may give hints if they live a healthy life. We hypothesise:

H8: A healthy life positively influences the acceptance of the eGK.

Beside these factors, the *affinity to technology* of insurants should not be neglected. The more experienced an insurant is to handle new technologies (in terms of time spent in the internet (AT1), the ability to navigate on unknown websites (AT2), the use of search engines (AT3), the affection for online shopping (AT4), and online payment (AT5)) the more s/he will also use new technologies. But on the other side, experienced people are also often more aware of threats due to data misuse. On the other hand, less experienced people could mistrust new technology because they do not exactly know how the new technology works. Therefore, they could also mistrust the data security as well. On the other side, because of their viridity, it is also conceivable that they are confiding to the new technology because they cannot foresee the consequences of its use. In sum, we hypothesise:

H9: The higher the affinity of technology is, the higher is the acceptance of the eGK.

The resulting model is depicted in Fig. 1.

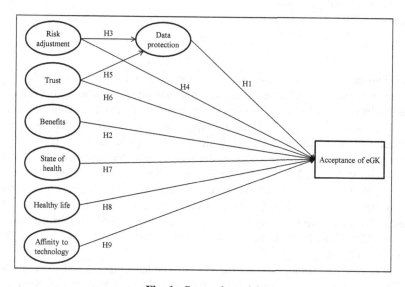

Fig. 1. Research model

5 Analysis

5.1 Sample and Data Collection

We conducted the survey with an online questionnaire. 183 people completed the questionnaire, 91 women, 89 men, 3 unknown. The structural equation model

(SEM) can be divided into the outer model named measurement model that specifies the relationship between the constructs and their indicators and the inner model referred to as structural model. Like in other studies, the effect size of the construct benefits concerning the acceptance is the strongest followed by data protection. The relation between trust and data protection has the highest effect size. Therefore, we limit the detailed description to these constructs and give only short descriptions of the other relations.

5.2   Outer Model

Within the outer model, two kinds of constructs can be distinguished: reflective and formative constructs [15]. Indicators of a reflective construct are characterisations of the construct and as such influenced by it [5]. In our model, only the construct data protection is a reflective construct. It forms the properties PIN, data encryption, fraud prevention, and picture.

Table 1. Factor analysis of the construct data protection

	Loadings	t-statistics	AVE	Composite reliability	Cronbach's alpha	1-SSE/SSO
PIN	0.7359	18.9907	0.5845	0.849	0.7664	0.5713
Data encryption	0.8012	20.4894				
Fraud prevention	0.7766	30.4067				
Picture	0.7427	15.0623				

The indicator reliability is composed of the loading and the t-statistic. It determines the share of the variance of an indicator which is explained by the construct. The value of the loading has to exceed a minimum requirement of 0.7 [7]. This constraint is fulfilled for all indicators (see Table 1). The appropriate t-statistic demonstrates the significance of the indicators [22]. All indicators are significant at the 1% level.

The convergence criterion consists of the average variance extracted (AVE) and the composite reliability [7, 22, 37]. The AVE of the reflective construct has to exceed the value 0.5 [16, 18] which is fulfilled. Simultaneously, the composite reliability exceeds the minimum requirement of 0.7 [22]. Therefore, the construct explains the indicators. Cronbach's Alpha reflects the internal consistency and exceeds the critical value of 0.65 [19]. The predictive validity is also fulfilled because the Stone-Geissers Q^2 (1-SSE/SSO Communality) exceeds zero.

The discriminant validity covers the Fornell-Larcker criterion and the cross loadings. The constraint of the first one is fulfilled if the square of the latent variable correlation is smaller than AVE [8]. In this case we receive $0.7328^2 < 0.5845$. Thus, all indicators are sufficiently different. Table 2 shows the correlation between the constructs.

Formative constructs are built by their indicators. That means a change in one indicator changes the construct and not vice versa [5, 23]. Seven of the eight constructs are formative constructs. To analyse the significance of the indicators, the weights and the t-statistics have to comply with the following constraints: For indicators that are

Table 2. Latent variable correlation

	Acceptance eGK	Affinity to technology	Data protection	Healthy life	Risk adjustment	State of health	Benefits
Acceptance eGK							
Affinity to technology	0.2259						
Data protection	0.7328	0.0365					
Healthy life	0.3380	0.1186	0.288				
Risk adjustment	0.1806	0.1424	0.1768	0.002			
State of health	0.4201	0.0420	0.3280	0.2342	0.0748		
Benefits	0.7137	0.0269	0.6581	0.2293	0.1074	0.3254	
Trust	0.5525	0.0815	0.6333	0.1227	0.1450	0.1580	0.5062

significant for a construct, the t-statistic has to exceed the limit of 1.66 and the weight has to be greater than 0.1 [8, 22]. Regarding the construct benefits, four (B1, B4, B5, B6) of six t-statistics exceed the limit of 1.66. For all of the four significant indicators, the limit of 0.1 for the weight is exceeded (see Table 3). Thus, they have a positive influence on the construct benefits [8]. The construct trust consists of seven indicators but only two indicators (T3, T7) are significant (see Table 3) with a t-statistic of greater than 1.66. Both significant indicators have a weight greater than 0.1 so that they have a positive influence on the construct [8].

Concerning the risk adjustment, three (R1, R2, R3) of five t-statistics exceed the limit of 1.66 but only two (R1, R3) of the three significant weights exceed the limit of 0.1. Thus, only R1 and R3 have a positive influence on the construct. Two (AT1, AT3) of three (AT1, AT2, AT3) significant weights of the construct affinity to technology exceed the limit of 0.1 and therefore have a positive influence on the construct. Concerning the state of health, only one (G6) of the two indicators that are significant (G3, G6) has a positive influence on the construct. Four indicators (HL2, HL4, HL5, HL6) of the construct healthy life are significant, three of them (HL4, HL5, H6L) have a positive weight.

The criterion discriminant validity is fulfilled for the formative constructs: The highest latent variable correlation that is between benefits and acceptance of eGK is 0.7173 in our model. This does not exceed the allowed maximum of 0.9.

Table 3. Indicators of constructs benefits and trust

Benefits	Weight	t-statistic	Trust	Weight	t-statistic
B1	0.1902	2.3771	T1	−0.0944	1.2145
B2	0.0553	0.8623	T2	0.1349	1.4674
B3	−0.0359	0.5634	T3	0.2546	2.2849
B4	0.2206	2.8047	T4	0.0517	0.6590
B5	0.5236	5.1064	T5	0.0749	0.9173
B6	0.3101	2.7471	T6	0.0593	0.7627
			T7	0.8855	13.2739

5.3   Inner Model

For the significance of the relationship between the constructs, it is evident that there is no multi-collinearity. The variance inflation factor VIF = $(1/(1-R^2)$ indicates whether there is multi-collinearity or not and should therefore be lower than 10 [11, 22]. The coefficient of determination R^2 is substantial if R^2 exceeds the limit of 0.67 and said to be average if R^2 exceeds the limit of 0.33 [8]. In addition the predictive validity has to be fulfilled. Therefore, the Stone-Geissers criterion has to exceed zero. Table 4 shows the values for the different criteria of our model. The Stone-Geissers criterion is greater than 0, VIF is much lower than 10, and R^2 is average for data protection and substantial for the acceptance of eGK.

Table 4. Factor analysis of the inner model

	R Square	VIF	1-SSE/SSO
Acceptance eGK	0.7017	1.96999	0.3524
Data protection	0.4084	1.20020	0.2237

The accuracy of our hypotheses is determined by the t-statistics and the path coefficients. For the t-statistics, it is essential to exceed the limit of 1.66 in order to be meaningful [37] and the path coefficients have to exceed the limit of 0.1 [29], ([7] claims a limit of 0.2). Table 5 shows the path coefficients and the t-statistics of the hypotheses. Only hypothesis H4 is not meaningful. However, as we measured a good state of health instead of a poor one, H7 has to be rejected as the influence is positive and not negative. The coefficient of determination R^2 for the acceptance of the eGK is high with 70% and average for data protection with 40%.

Table 5. Hypotheses

ALT		t-statistic	Path coefficient
H2	H1***	4.6959	0.3520
H4	H2***	4.9511	0.3589
H1	H3*	1.8536	0.0868
H3	H4	0.9828	0.0301
H8	H5***	16.9771	0.6207
H9	H6*	1.7080	0.0959
H5	H7***	2.8903	0.1425
H6	H8**	2.1443	0.0884
H7	H9***	4.0283	0.1748

6 Discussion

The general result is very satisfying. The explanatory power of the model is substantial. Seven of nine hypotheses could be confirmed, one shows the opposite sign but is still meaningful and only one hypothesis could not be confirmed.

Interestingly, a poor state of health does not lead to a higher acceptance. Instead a good state does so. Even if the influence of state of health on the acceptance is low, that means that people with poor health need to be elucidated better about the benefits of the eGK and its security. This will improve the acceptance of the eGK but also the situation of people with poor health as doctors have better access to information about the patients' state of health, prescriptions etc. so that the treatment can be improved.

Like other surveys, also this one has shown that the benefits and the perceived data protection have in comparison to other constructs the highest influence on the acceptance. The construct data protection is explained sufficiently well by risk adjustment and trust. Of the institutions, only the trustworthiness of justice plays a role for the trust. Neither physicians, nor insurance companies nor pharmacists influence the trust significantly. Therefore, their trustworthiness is not of interest for the construct data protection. Not surprisingly, the last indicator, the judgement about the e-kiosk is significant for the trust and therefore also for the perceived data protection. Its significance criteria are much higher than the ones of justice. But, as we can see, e-kiosks are not seen as trustworthy. Only about 20% say so. Nearly 40% mistrust and 40% are indecisive. That means that the opinion about the e-kiosks should be improved in order to foster the acceptance of the eGK. It has a positive influence on trust and therefore on the data protection. Even if trust has no direct influence on the acceptance, an increased belief in the trustworthiness of the e-kiosks would increase the trust, the belief in an appropriate data protection and finally the acceptance of the eGK.

Even if the trust in physicians and insurance companies is not important for the construct, it is interesting that the reputation of insurance companies is quite low with 20% of trust and 40% of mistrust. The situation is similar for physicians with 45% of trust and still 27% of mistrust. (For a comparison, police 65% to 16% and justice 65% to 11% trust to mistrust). Thus, the reputation of and the trust in insurance companies and also physicians should be heavily improved. Insurance companies issue the eGK and physicians use the data of the eGK. Therefore, even if these indicators are not significant it is conceivable that if the reputation and trust is improved they become significant and improve the acceptance of the eGK. For this, further research should be done to examine the influence of insurance companies and physicians more deeply.

Four of six indicators of the construct benefits are significant and have a positive influence on it. Therefore, they also have a positive influence on the acceptance because the effect size criterion between benefit and acceptance of eGK is fulfilled. Interestingly, more than 60% of the interviewees do not expect a quicker medical treatment and 55% deny a treatment of more quality. That means that patients do not see the postulated advantages of the eGK. Therefore, it is evident to better inform patients about the benefits of the eGK and the functions in combination with the efforts that are made for protecting the patients' data.

The affinity to technology has a light influence on the acceptance. Hence, in order to raise the acceptance of the eGK, the task is to better inform people with a lower affinity to technology.

At last, seven (A1, A3, A4, A5, A7, A8, A9) of ten indicators of the acceptance are significant whereas five of them exceed the limit of 0.1 (A1, A3, A5, A7, A9). For A6 and A8 the acceptance lies above 40%, for all other indicators above 50%. Even if this indicates a certain acceptance of the eGK, there is still much room for improvement. More than 20% of the interviewees do not want to use the electronic prescription, 25% the drugs documentation, 34% the patient's compartment, 24% the medical report. We also asked for two functions that neither exist nor are planned in the future. Interestingly, more than 36% of the interviewees want to use a patient's profile and still 22% want to use an analysis of their health data.

7 Conclusion

After several years of introducing the eGK, the information level of patients is still too low and must be improved. Only well informed patients can perceive all functions of the eGK and can judge the advantages and disadvantages. That leads to the current situation that less than 60% of all patients want to use the voluntary functions. Even the mandatory functions are only accepted by 60%. But the more patients see the benefits of the eGK the more they are willing to use its functions. The acceptance of the eGK declines, the more sensible data are affected. In contrast to other surveys [1] where people with chronic illness favour the eGK as well as others do, in our survey especially people of poorer health do not accept the eGK. Thereby this is the group that can benefit most of it. This may result from the NSA affair so that today people are much more afraid of a misuse of their data. Concerning this, further research should be done.

In sum, it is evident to better inform the patients about the functions of the eGK its advantages and all the efforts that are made to protect the data. This task does not seem to be intractable because especially those people are more critical who are of poorer health and therefore are more often to see the doctor. These visits are a good opportunity for information and also for an amelioration of the reputation of physicians and probably insurance companies. If patients are well informed and appeased concerning the protection of their data, even more continuative functions like a patient's profile or health data analysis are feasible than the ones that are currently planned.

References

1. Amhof, R.: Die elektronische Gesundheitskarte: Bekanntheit, Einstellungen und Akzeptanz. Health Policy Monit. **4**, 1–7 (2006)
2. Aubert, B.A., Hamel, G.: Adoption of smart cards in the medical sector: the Canadian experience. Soc. Sci. Med. **53**(7), 879–894 (2001)
3. Bales, S.: Die Einführung der elektronischen Gesundheitskarte in Deutschland. Bundesgesundheitsblatt Gesundheitsforschung Gesundheitsschutz **48**(7), 727–731 (2005)

4. Blobel, B., Pharow, P., Spiegel, V., Engel, K.E., Engelbrecht, R.: Securing interoperability between chip card based medical information systems and health networks. Int. J. Med. Inform. **64**, 401–415 (2001)
5. Bollen, K.A., Lennox, R.: Conventional wisdom on measurement: a structural equation perspective. Psychol. Bull. **110**(2), 305–314 (1991)
6. Caumanns, J., et al.: Die eGK-Lösungsarchitektur, Informatik Spektrum, pp. 341–348 (2006)
7. Chin, W.W.: Issues and opinion on structural equation modeling. Manage. Inf. Syst. Q. **22**, 7–16 (1998)
8. Chin, W.W.: The partial least squares approach for structural equation modeling. In: Marcoulides, G.A. (ed.) Modern Methods for Business Research, pp. 295–336. Lawerence Erlbaum Associates, London (1998)
9. Commission of the European Communities 2004. e-Health - making healthcare better for European citizens: an action plan for a European e-Health Area. http://ec.europa.eu/information_society/doc/qualif/health/COM_2004_0356_F_EN_ACTE.pdf
10. Davis, F.D.: Perceived usefulness, perceived ease of use, and user acceptance of information technology. Mange. Inf. Syst. Q. **13**(3), 319–340 (1989)
11. Diamantopolus, A., Winklhofer, H.M.: Index construction with formative indicators: an alternative to scale development. J. Mark. Res. **38**, 269–277 (2001)
12. Ernstmann, N.: Determinanten der subjektiven Nutzenbewertung der elektronischen Gesundheitskarte und des elektronischen Rezepts. Lit Verlag, Berlin (2008)
13. Ernstmann, N., Pfaff, H.: Es gibt noch Vorbehalte: Erwartungen von Ärzten in Krankenhaus und Praxis an die elektronische Gesundheitskarte. Krankenhaus Umschau **5**, 370–372 (2006)
14. Fernández-Alemán, J.L., Carrión Señor, I., Lozoya, P.A.O., Toval, A.: Security and privacy in electronic health records: a systematic literature review. J. Biomed. Inform. **46**, 541–562 (2013)
15. Fornell, C., Bookstein, F.L.: Two structural equation models: LISREL and PLS applied to consumer exit-voice theory. J. Mark. Res. **19**(4), 440–452 (1982)
16. Fornell, C., Larcker, D.F.: Evaluating structural equation models with unobservable variables and measurement error. J. Mark. Res. **18**(1), 39–50 (1981)
17. forsa 2008. Versichertenbefragung: Elektronische Gesundheitskarte (2008). http://www.deutsche-versicherungsboerse.de/download/pressrelease/id/730
18. Fuchs, A.: Das strategische Management von Corporate Entrepreneurship. Springer, Berlin (2013). https://doi.org/10.1007/978-3-658-01358-5
19. George, D., Mallery, P.: SPSS for Windows Step by Step. A Simple Guide and Reference, 11.0 update, 4th edn. Allyn and Bacon, Boston (2003)
20. Gostin, L.: Health care information and the protection of personal privacy: ethical and legal considerations. Ann. Intern. Med. **127**(8,2), 683–690 (1997)
21. Hoerbst, A., Kohl, C.D., Knaup, P., Ammenwerth, E.: Attitudes and behaviors related to the introduction of electronic health records among Austrian and German citizens. Int. J. Med. Inform. **79**(2), 81–89 (2010)
22. Huber, F., Herrmann, A., Meyer, F., Vogel, J., Vollhardt, K.: Kausalmodellierung mit Partial Least Squares. Gabler Verlag, Wiesbaden (2007)
23. Jarvis, C.B., Mackenzie, S.B., Podsakoff, P.M.: A critical review of construct indicators and measurement model misspecification in marketing and consumer research. J. Consum. Res. **30**(2), 199–218 (2003)
24. Jha, A.K., Doolan, D., Grandt, D., Scott, T., Bates, D.W.: The use of health information technology in seven nations. Int. J. Med. Inform. **77**(12), 848–854 (2008)

25. Kjellen, U., Sklet, S.: Integrating analyses of the risk of occupational accidents into the design process Part I: a review of types of acceptance criteria and risk analysis methods. Saf. Sci. **18**(3), 215–227 (1995)

26. Klein, M.: Milliardengrab Gesundheitskarte: Wir fangen wieder von vorne an! eGovernment Comput. **10**(6), 1 (2010)

27. Lambrinoudakis, C., Gritzalis, S.: Managing medical and insurance information through a smart-card-based information system. J. Med. Syst. **24**(4), 213–234 (2000)

28. Liu, C.T., Yang, P.T., Yeh, Y.T., Wang, B.L.: The impacts of smart cards on hospital information systems- an investigation of the first phase of the national health insurance smart card project in Taiwan. Int. J. Med. Inform. **75**(2), 173–181 (2006)

29. Lohmöller, J.B.: Latent Variable Path Modeling with Partial Least Squares. Springer, Heidelberg (1989). https://doi.org/10.1007/978-3-642-52512-4

30. Loo, W.H., Yeow, P.H.P., Chong, S.C.: Acceptability of multipurpose smart national identity card: an empirical study. J. Glob. Inf. Technol. Manage. **14**(1), 35–58 (2011)

31. Marschollek, M., Demirbilek, E.: Providing longitudinal health care information with the new German Health Card – a pilot system to track patient pathways. Comput. Meth. Prog. Biomed. **81**(3), 266–271 (2006)

32. Pfaff, H., Ernstmann, N.: Akzeptanz-Untersuchung zur Gesundheitskarten-Einführung (AUGE). Abschlussbericht einer Studie im Auftrag der Ärztekammer Nordrhein. Cologne: Verö ffentlichungsreihe des Zentrum fü r Versorgungsforschung Köln (ZVFK) (2005)

33. Pizzi, L.T., Suh, D.C., Barone, J., Nash, D.B.: Factors related to physicians' adoption of electronic prescribing: results from a national survey. Am. J. Med. Q. **20**(1), 22–32 (2005)

34. Sanna, A., Serafin, R., Maganetti, N.: e-Health. In: Camenisch, J., Leenes, R., Sommer, D. (eds.) Digital Privacy. LNCS, vol. 6545, pp. 697–720. Springer, Heidelberg (2011). https://doi.org/10.1007/978-3-642-19050-6_26

35. Sunyaev, A., Göttlinger, S., Mauro, C., Leimeister, J.M., Krcmar, H.: Analysis of the applications of the electronic health card in Germany. In: Hansen, H.R., Karagiannis, D., Fill, H.G. (Eds.) Business Services: Konzepte, Technologien, Anwendungen, Band II, pp. 749–758. OCG, Wien (2009)

36. Venkatesh, V., Morris, M.G., Davis, G.B., Davis, F.D.: User acceptance of information technology: toward a unified view. Manage. Inf. Syst. Q. **27**(3), 425–478 (2003)

37. Weiber, R., Mühlhaus, D.: Strukturgleichungsmodellierung. Eine anwendungsorientierte Einführung in die Kausalanalyse mit Hilfe von AMOS, SmartPLS und SPSS. Springer, Berlin (2010). https://doi.org/10.1007/978-3-642-35012-2

38. Weichert, T.: Die elektronische Gesundheitskarte. Datenschutz und Datensicherheit **28**(7), 391–403 (2004)

39. Winandy, M.: A note on the security in the card management system of the German e-health card. In: Szomszor, M., Kostkova, P. (eds.) eHealth 2010. LNICST, vol. 69, pp. 196–203. Springer, Heidelberg (2011). https://doi.org/10.1007/978-3-642-23635-8_25

40. Wirtz, B.W., Mory, L., Ullrich, S.: eHealth in the public sector: an empirical analysis of the acceptance of Germany's electronic health card. Publ. Admimistration **90**(3), 642–663 (2012)

41. Yasnoff, W.A., et al.: A consensus action agenda for achieving the national health information infrastructure. J. Am. Med. Inf. Assoc. **11**(4), 332–338 (2004)

42. Zhou, Y.Y., Garrido, T., Chin, H.L., Wiesenthal, A.M., Liang, L.L.: Patient access to an electronic health record with secure messaging: impact on primary care utilization. Am. J. Managed Care **13**(7), 418–424 (2007)

Author Index

Printed in the United States
By Bookmasters